America Enters the Cold War

America Enters the Cold War provides a succinct and insightful analysis of the foreign policy decisions which shaped America's early involvement in the Cold War. In focusing on key documents and detailing the ideological foundations of U.S. foreign policy, Kevin E. Grimm situates the events of the early Cold War in the context of postwar American history. Including the full text of primary source documents such as the Long Telegram, the Truman Doctrine, and NSC-68, this text provides an essential overview of this period for students of the Cold War, diplomatic history, and twentieth century US history and foreign policy.

Kevin E. Grimm is assistant professor of history at Regent University.

Critical Moments in American History
Edited by William Thomas Allison, Georgia Southern University

A full list of titles in this series is available at: https://www.routledge.com/ Critical-Moments-in-American-History/book-series/CRITMO.

Recently published titles:

The California Gold Rush
The Stampede that Changed the World
Mark Eifler

Bleeding Kansas
Slavery, Sectionalism, and Civil War on the Missouri–Kansas Border
Michael E. Woods

The Marshall Plan
A New Deal for Europe
Michael Holm

The Espionage and Sedition Acts
World War I and the Image of Civil Liberties
Mitchell C. Newton-Matza

McCarthyism
The Realities, Delusions and Politics Behind the 1950s Red Scare
Jonathan Michaels

Three Mile Island
The Meltdown Crisis and Nuclear Power in American Popular Culture
Grace Halden

The 1916 Preparedness Day Bombing
Anarchy and Terrorism in Progressive-Era America
Jeffrey A. Johnson

America Enters the Cold War
The Road to Global Commitment, 1945–1950
Kevin E. Grimm

America Enters the Cold War

The Road to Global Commitment, 1945–1950

Kevin E. Grimm

NEW YORK AND LONDON

First published 2018
by Routledge
711 Third Avenue, New York, NY 10017

and by Routledge
2 Park Square, Milton Park, Abingdon, Oxon, OX14 4RN

Routledge is an imprint of the Taylor & Francis Group, an informa business

© 2018 Taylor & Francis

The right of Kevin E. Grimm to be identified as author of this work
has been asserted by him in accordance with sections 77 and 78
of the Copyright, Designs, and Patents Act 1988.

All rights reserved. No part of this book may be reprinted or
reproduced or utilised in any form or by any electronic, mechanical,
or other means, now known or hereafter invented, including photocopying
and recording, or in any information storage or retrieval system,
without permission in writing from the publishers.

Trademark notice: Product or corporate names may be trademarks
or registered trademarks, and are used only for identification
and explanation without intent to infringe.

Library of Congress Cataloging-in-Publication Data
A catalog record for this book has been requested

ISBN: 978-1-138-20836-0 (hbk)
ISBN: 978-1-138-20837-7 (pbk)
ISBN: 978-1-351-45941-9 (ebk)

Typeset in Bembo & Helvetica Neue
by Florence Production Ltd, Stoodleigh, Devon, UK

Visit the Companion Website: www.routledgetextbooks.com/textbooks/_author/
criticalmoments/

To my wife Jenn, who has shared life's adventures with me, and to my son David, who came along while I was writing this book. May we all make a better world for you.

Contents

Series Introduction	viii
List of Figures	ix
Timeline	x

1	A World Changes: Europe in the Mid-1940s	1
2	Envisioning the Soviets: Kennan versus Wallace	26
3	Opening Salvos: Truman and His Doctrine	48
4	How to Fight: NSC-68 and Planning Global Strategy	69
5	The View After: Victories and Costs	89

Documents	115
Bibliography	223
Index	231

Series Introduction

Welcome to the Routledge Critical Moments in American History series. The purpose of this new series is to give students a window into the historian's craft through concise, readable books by leading scholars, who bring together the best scholarship and engaging primary sources to explore a critical moment in the American past. In discovering the principal points of the story in these books, gaining a sense of historiography, following a fresh trail of primary documents, and exploring suggested readings, students can then set out on their own journey, to debate the ideas presented, interpret primary sources, and reach their own conclusions – just like the historian. A critical moment in history can be a range of things – a pivotal year, the pinnacle of a movement or trend, or an important event such as the passage of a piece of legislation, an election, a court decision, a battle. It can be social, cultural, political, or economic. It can be heroic or tragic. Whatever they are, such moments are by definition "game changers," momentous changes in the pattern of the American fabric, paradigm shifts in the American experience. Many of the critical moments explored in this series are familiar; some less so.

There is no ultimate list of critical moments in American history – any group of students, historians, or other scholars may come up with a different catalog of topics. These differences of view, however, are what make history itself and the study of history so important and so fascinating. Therein can be found the utility of historical inquiry – to explore, to challenge, to understand, and to realize the legacy of the past through its influence of the present. It is the hope of this series to help students realize this intrinsic value of our past and of studying our past.

William Thomas Allison
Georgia Southern University

Figures

1.1	Harry S. Truman and Joseph Stalin meeting at Potsdam	14
1.2	President Harry S. Truman speaks with Secretary of State James F. Byrnes and Senator Arthur Vandenberg on an airport tarmac	18
2.1	American Diplomat George F. Kennan, the author of the famous "Long Telegram"	29
2.2	An accidental prop on the desk of former Secretary of Commerce Henry A. Wallace gave graphic significance to this photo, made in September, when Wallace signed his resignation	43
3.1	Ernest Bevin signs the North Atlantic Treaty as Harry S. Truman and Dean Acheson look on	49
3.2	C–47 airplanes used in the Berlin Airlift task force at the Wiesbaden air base being loaded with food and supplies for the people of the Russian blockaded city of Berlin	64

Timeline

August 1941	Atlantic Charter
May 1943	Stalin ends Comintern
November–December 1943	Tehran Conference
July 1944	Bretton Woods Conference (Imf/World Bank)
February 1945	Yalta Conference
May 1945	End of World War II In Europe
July 1945	Potsdam Conference/U.S. successfully explodes atomic bomb
August 1945	Atomic Bombs dropped on Japan/End of World War II
September–October 1945	London Council of Foreign Ministers meeting
December 1945	Moscow Council of Foreign Ministers meeting
December 1945–January 1947	General George Marshall in China
February 1946	Stalin's Bolshoi Theater election speech
February 1946	Kennan's Long Telegram
February 1946	Winston Churchill's Iron Curtain speech
March 1946	Iranian Crisis
April–July 1946	Paris Council of Foreign Ministers Meeting
May 1946	General Lucius Clay suspends reparations from Western zones
July 1946	Henry Wallace's letter to Truman
July–October 1946	Paris Peace Conference
August 1946	Turkish Crisis
September 1946	Truman fires Wallace
November–December 1946	New York Council of Foreign Ministers Meeting
February 1947	Paris Peace Treaties signed

TIMELINE xi

March 1947	Truman Doctrine announced
March 1947	Henry Wallace's speech against the Truman Doctrine
September 1947	National Security Act
October 1947	Cominform founded
February 1948	Communist coup in Czechoslovakia
February–June 1948	London Conference meetings (to create West Germany)
April 1948	Marshall Plan begins
June 1948	Yugoslavia kicked out of Cominform
June 1948–May 1949	Berlin Blockade/Airlift
January 1949	COMECON founded
February 1949	West Germany (Federal Republic of Germany) officially formed
April 1949	NATO formed (Senate approves in July)
August 1949	Soviets successfully test atomic weapons
October 1949	Mao Zedong declares communist People's Republic of China
October 1949	East Germany (German Democratic Republic) officially formed
January 1950	Truman orders policy review
February 1950	Kennan's letter to Truman
February 1950–June 1954	Senator Joseph McCarthy is prominent
April 1950	NSC-68 completed
June 1950	Korean War begins
September 1950	Truman officially approves NSC-68
April 1951	European Coal and Steel Community treaty signed
October 1986	Reagan-Gorbachev meeting in Reykjavik, Iceland
December 1987	Reagan-Gorbachev meeting in Washington
May 1989	Hungary takes down border fences
August 1989	Solidarity and other groups in Poland form first non-communist government in Soviet sphere
November 1989	Berlin Wall opened/taken down
November–December 1989	Communism collapses in Eastern Europe
December 1991	USSR becomes Russian Federation and fourteen other nations

CHAPTER 1

A World Changes

Europe in the Mid-1940s

SETTING THE DEBATE

In late May 1947 the State Department's brand new Policy Planning Staff (PPS) sent a report to Under Secretary of State Dean Acheson expressing their concern "that the Truman Doctrine is a blank check to give economic and military aid to any area in the world where the communists show signs of being successful."[1] President Harry Truman had announced the month before in front of both houses of Congress, without any qualifiers, "It must be the policy of the United States to support free peoples who are resisting attempted subjugation by armed minorities or by outside pressures."[2] Instead, suggested the PPS, "It must be made clear . . . that such aid will be considered only in cases where the prospective results bear a satisfactory relationship to the expenditure of American resources and effort."[3] Such caution is remarkable given the fact that the head of the PPS was diplomat George Kennan, the architect of America's Cold War containment policy. Although he had laid out that policy only fifteen months earlier in his famous Long Telegram, by the spring of 1947 he agreed with such warnings. He would later be even more opposed to the 1950 document many historians consider the "blueprint" for fighting the Cold War—National Security Council document 68 (NSC-68). Why? Essentially, Kennan feared the expansive application of his doctrine far beyond the places and circumstances where he believed it would actually benefit the United States. Although he provided the ideology for American Cold War foreign policy in his 1946 Long Telegram, the 1947 Truman Doctrine globalized that ideology and in 1950 NSC-68 militarized it[4].

Kennan's worries revealed that in the second half of the 1940s, it was not inevitable the United States was going to conduct four decades of

A WORLD CHANGES: EUROPE IN THE MID-1940s

Harry Truman

Harry Truman was born in Missouri in 1884 and fought in World War I. He joined local politics in the 1920s, became a U.S. Senator in 1935, and was then tapped to be President Franklin Roosevelt's Vice President for his fourth term. Truman held that position for less than four months because FDR died in mid-April 1945 and Truman became president, subsequently winning the 1948 presidential campaign and remaining in the White House until early 1953. He was followed in office by President Dwight D. Eisenhower and he died in 1972.

According to most historians, Truman was a man who thought in binary terms—he liked things to be black and white, right or wrong. He was also insecure about being president at first and there were stories from aides that reflected his uncertainty about governing early in his administration. Due to the immense international changes occurring as he entered the White House, Truman became America's first Cold War president and is thus at the center of most historians' accounts of why and how the Cold War developed.

militarized containment around the world. Leaders made choices to move in that direction. Moreover, at each critical moment of policy development there were alternative paths forward. The history of the Cold War might have been different had those paths been followed. President Truman eventually adopted the ideas and policies in the Long Telegram, the Truman Doctrine, and NSC-68. Yet first Secretary of Commerce Henry Wallace and then George Kennan himself expressed dissenting views, respectively arguing for a more conciliatory approach to the Soviet Union or a less expansive, less military-oriented application of containment. These are not mere "what ifs" because a number of historians have begun to argue that the original laudable goal of Kennan's doctrine of containment, to hedge in the Soviet Union in Europe, had been achieved during the early Cold War. Thus the United States could have, in large part, avoided the high price in lives, treasure, social cohesion at home, and political turmoil that it incurred in the intervening forty years until the collapse of communism in Europe. Similarly, the costs to other peoples and their societies, mostly in the Third World, would have been much reduced. Other historians acknowledge some mistakes by American Cold War presidents, but still believe the overall costs of the Cold War were justified in order to block and ultimately defeat a powerful, nuclear-armed, ideological enemy.

The Cold War was, at a high level, a deepening of tensions between two economic and military superpowers that at times risked yet another general world war. More often it led to proxy wars, forced changes in government, and deep involvement in the political, economic, and social development of other nations around the globe. Indeed, millions died not only in Korea, Vietnam, and Afghanistan, but in many other countries due to superpower support of one faction or another. Where should one place blame for such destruction outside Europe and for the decades of tension, at times bordering on war, between the most powerful countries on earth? This work will explore the ongoing debates over the extent and worth of these costs, as well as debates over the beginning, course, and end of the Cold War. Core to this analysis is the concept of contingency— decisions were made amidst real world circumstances and there were usually alternative foreign policy options available at a given moment, often voiced by Wallace or Kennan. Exploring conflicting policy views in the past can help us become more aware of the varied possibilities for policy in the present and future, and can encourage us to at least explore and compare their potential outcomes before embarking down one path. Specifically regarding the Cold War and the concept of costs, if one considers unworkable the alternative policy paths that were presented, perhaps one is less critical of the actions of American leaders. If, however, one thinks those paths were viable, the blame for unnecessary costs may be assigned more readily to U.S. policymakers. Ultimately, it is up to the reader to decide whether or not alternative options to containment and the globalization and militarization of American Cold War foreign policy between 1945 and 1950 would have worked, whether or not those alternative policies were likely to be adopted when they were presented, and whether or not the costs in not adopting them were justified. First, though, parts of these debates will be illuminated by a survey of the main schools of historical thought on why and how the Cold War came to be.

KEY QUESTIONS IN THE EARLY COLD WAR

As World War II neared its bloody end, the French politician and traveler Alexis De Tocqueville's famous prediction that the United States and Russia would eventually each control "the destinies of half the world" seemed particularly accurate as they developed military machines virtually unseen in human history.[5] The two nations also had distinct, and differing, visions on how societies should organize themselves and were led by men confident in their own systems who sought to spread their respective ideas outside their own borders. There, as we move into specifics, the similarities end, but the larger historical context of 1945 is worth remembering. It was a rare moment in world history when old power structures were largely

A WORLD CHANGES: EUROPE IN THE MID-1940s

ROMAN, MONGOLIAN, AND BRITISH EMPIRES

While the Soviet Empire in Eastern Europe and Central Asia seemed vast, in part due to the size of Russia itself, and while the United States was a continental-wide power with strong European allies, comparisons to former empires can illustrate that the size of these superpower spheres of influence were not new in human history, although their technological capabilities certainly were. The Roman Empire controlled some sixty-five million people, which was an estimated 21 percent of the world's population. The Mongolian Empire controlled 16 percent of the world's surface and around 110 million people, 25 percent of the world's population. The British Empire controlled 22 percent of the world's land surface as well as 458 million people, 20 percent of the world's population.

gone and two new superpowers emerged. This was not Rome replacing Greece or the spread of the Mongols or the expansion of the British Empire because this time there were two, not one, nations that emerged capable of imposing their wills on large swathes of the globe. In addition, their divergent ideologies and foreign policy objectives made a clash more likely than if they were simply geopolitical rivals vying over territory or resources.

Still, the Cold War was not inevitable, although some historians hold that view. Throughout the final months of the war and into the second half of 1945 the United States and the Soviet Union, joined at times by other powers, held several major conferences to determine the structure of postwar Europe. Attended either by heads of state or secretaries of state and foreign ministers, the meetings were attempts to hash out arrangements, borders, and governments across diverse countries in ways acceptable to both sides. Agreements were few and hard won if they did arrive, and tension over Germany, Eastern Europe, and financial assistance and reparations for the devastated Soviet Union consistently marred negotiations. Historians, though, debate who is to blame for these tensions, and why they emerged, because they ultimately flowered into the full Cold War. The various schools of thought on the emergence of the Cold War offer different answers to these questions. Were individuals most important? Domestic influence? Ideology? The international context in which decisions took place? Most importantly, what were the chances of some sort of broad postwar settlement in which both sides got at least most of what they wanted? Was this peaceful path forward possible in mid-1945, late 1945, or ever? These are the ways Cold War causation and contingency are tightly wound together in the months after Allied victory in Europe.

HISTORIOGRAPHY OF THE COLD WAR'S BEGINNING

Who caused the Cold War? Although this volume will primarily analyze the development of a global and militarized American policy to conduct the Cold War, the most contentious scholarly debate about the early Cold War years focuses on why the Grand Alliance of World War II fell apart. Indeed, some historians see the development of American policy as wrapped up in this question. For instance, if one believes the Cold War began in the fall of 1945, then one might blame the Soviets for their machinations in Eastern Europe, which will be covered in more detail below. If, however, one sees the onset of a true Cold War later, say mid-1947, one might reserve some (or all) of their criticism for U.S. President Harry Truman, since by then he had adopted a very hard line toward the Soviets and had issued his famous Truman Doctrine in March 1947 promising U.S. aid to anyone resisting communist infiltration or influence. There are three main schools of thought on who or what caused the Cold War—the Soviets, the Americans, and the international system as it stood in the second half of the 1940s. Perhaps not surprisingly, the first generation of American scholars in the late 1940s and throughout the 1950s blamed the Soviet Union for the deepening of international tensions. They argued that Stalin was a communist dictator and, in his desire for global domination, would always seek to impose communism and Soviet authority beyond Russian borders. His domination of Eastern Europe and parts of Central Europe were violations of international free trade and, more importantly, his installation of pro-Soviet, communist governments were certainly not in line with democratic self-determination. Stalin and the Soviet Union thus threatened not only the physical security of the West, but also Western capitalism and Western values such as individual rights and democracy. The only way to prevent Soviet advances was to deter any further Russian aggression by building up significant political, economic, and military strength and containing the Soviets, per George Kennan's ideas, at any and all points where they tried to expand. Obviously, this scholarly approach tended to reflect official American policy and rhetoric during the first fifteen years of the Cold War.

Scholarship on the early Cold War changed, however, in 1959 with the appearance of William Appleman Williams's *The Tragedy of American Diplomacy*. Williams argued that American policymakers, often in league with American business interests, pursued an "Open Door" policy toward global trade. They wanted markets around the world, including in Europe, to remain open to American products. This would keep the American economy strong and prevent a return to depression after the war, especially

A WORLD CHANGES: EUROPE IN THE MID-1940s

Joseph Stalin

Joseph Stalin was born in 1878 in what today is the independent country of Georgia, in the Caucasus region between the Black and Caspian Seas. At the time it was part of the extensive Czarist Russian Empire. He was an early participant in the Bolshevik faction of communists led by Vladimir Lenin and was in Lenin's inner circle during the Russian Revolution, the Russian Civil War, and the period of the New Economic Policy during the 1920s. When Lenin died in 1924, Stalin began his pursuit of ultimate power and by the end of the decade was fully in control. He then turned the Soviet Union away from the New Economic Policy, which had included a certain level of private market activity at the local level, and toward rapid, state-directed industrialization and agricultural collectivization throughout the 1930s.

Stalin's policies caused much hardship and he reigned through secret police and bloody political purges, but the Soviet Union did advance significantly in industrial terms during the 1930s. He was always wary of Adolf Hitler and German power, but signed the infamous Molotov-Ribbentrop Pact in 1939, and then jointly invaded Poland with Germany later that year, because he believed the Western democracies either would not or could not stand up to Hitler. Stalin thus felt Russia had to act alone. He led the Soviet Union through the immensely costly Second World War and then stood astride half of Europe afterwards, contributing to postwar tensions between the two new superpowers. He died in 1953.

as the economy at home absorbed millions of workers upon military demobilization. Beginning his analysis with the 1890s, he argued that U.S. leaders held "the firm conviction, even dogmatic belief, that America's *domestic* [emphasis his] well-being depends upon such sustained, ever-increasing overseas economic expansion."[6] The "tragedy" to Williams was that, in reality, this focus obscured the need and opportunities for change within the United States and caused Americans "to explain the lack of the good life by blaming it on foreign individuals, groups, and nations."[7] By 1945, Williams argued, "American leaders had internalized, and had come to *believe* [emphasis his], the theory, the necessity, and the morality of open-door expansion" regarding trade and American political and economic influence.[8] Williams argued they even came to believe that "those who did not recognize and accept that fact were . . . not only wrong, but incapable of thinking correctly."[9] Thus, instead of recognizing legitimate Russian concerns regarding rebuilding and physical security in the aftermath of a devastating conflict, "American policy offered the Russians no real choice on those key issues" and the United States "readily embarked upon a program to force the Soviet Union to accept America's traditional conception of itself and the world."[10] Williams thus merged the domestic

A WORLD CHANGES: EUROPE IN THE MID-1940s

and the international, placed economic motives for American actions at the center of Cold War causation, and largely blamed American leaders for the onset of the Cold War because, he believed, they sought to keep all regions of the world "open" for American goods and for the U.S.-led global capitalist trading system the Western nations had constructed after World War II.

Williams therefore played a central role in developing what came to be known as the "revisionist" school of scholarship on Cold War causation. This school lays primary blame at the feet of American policymakers and portrays them as, at best, unnecessarily stoking tensions with the Soviet Union over issues that actually mattered little to American security or economic wellbeing or, at worst, themselves bent on the type of global dominance they accused the Soviets of pursuing. Economic motivation remained central to many works in this school and was applied to many episodes of Cold War foreign policy, including Korea and Vietnam. Another historian who assigned primary causation for the onset of the Cold War to U.S. leaders was Gar Alperovitz, who in his 1965 *Atomic Diplomacy* addressed the American atomic bomb attacks on Japan. He "contended that political rather than military considerations were the key to understanding the use of the bomb . . . it was dropped primarily to impress the Soviets rather than to defeat the Japanese."[11] Alperovitz fit clearly in the revisionist school because his claim that dropping the bombs was not a military necessity implied blame for the Truman administration both for causing unnecessary death in Japan and for unnecessarily stoking tensions with the Soviets. For instance, at the May 1945 Potsdam Conference Truman hinted that the United States had a powerful new weapon, angering Stalin, and his administration later more explicitly touted American power based on the bomb. While historians have, since Alperovitz, argued at length over Truman's motivations for dropping the bomb, they do generally agree that, whatever the hoped for effect on the Soviets, the American possession of an atomic arsenal in fact stiffened Soviet resolve to show they were not intimidated by such a powerful weapon.

Overall, revisionists mostly criticize the United States for the onset of tensions that would cause the Cold War. In their view, the Soviets were largely concerned with recovery and reconstruction, not expansion. Russia remained communist, yes, but outside the Soviet sphere in Europe, communism was not much of a threat in 1945. The United States emerged from the war in a position of immense economic strength, with a homeland barely touched physically by the war, and with a new weapon that, for most of the Cold War's early years, gave the United States a monopoly on atomic power. In fact, some revisionists claim, while Stalin was a brutal dictator internally, his international moves indicated a sense of caution and

A WORLD CHANGES: EUROPE IN THE MID-1940s

an adherence to the concept of postwar spheres of influence among the great powers that he thought Roosevelt and Churchill had approved during wartime conferences. As evidence of Stalin's willingness to avoid antagonizing the West, they point to his 1943 suspension of the Comintern (Communist International), an international organization of revolutionaries committed to bringing communism to their respective countries from within. Dissolving that organization, and not restarting it until September 1947 in the guise of the Cominform (Communist Information Bureau), showed that Stalin was not actively seeking to foment communist takeovers outside his sphere of influence immediately after the end of World War II. Even within the areas he controlled, revisionists note that while Stalin did not exactly create democratic governments, he had allowed free elections in Hungary in 1945 and Czechoslovakia in 1946 and had at least publicly displayed a willingness to allow popular-front type coalitions of parties in Eastern Europe, as long as communists were included and the foreign policies of those nations were pro-Soviet. Not until late 1946 and into 1947, after a series of East–West confrontations had already occurred, did the Soviets force everyone not sufficiently pro-Soviet out of government positions in Eastern Europe. Revisionists do not see Stalin and the Soviets as moral angels by any means, but they emphasize that U.S. leaders unnecessarily increased the risk of war (and later, nuclear war) by their unwillingness to allow the Soviets an unmolested sphere of influence. While not a revisionist himself, as we'll see below, Melvyn Leffler provides a concise summary of actions that seem to show Stalin's willingness to work with the West,

> For although Stalin delayed the withdrawal of his troops from northern Iran, asked for new rights in the Turkish Straits, and installed progressively more communist governments in Poland, Romania, and Bulgaria, he also withdrew Soviet troops from Czechoslovakia and from the island of Bornholm in the Baltic; allowed free elections in the Soviet occupation zone in Austria and in parts of Hungary and Czechoslovakia; pulled Soviet troops out of Manchuria; and continued to discourage revolution or communist seizures of power in Greece, Italy, and France. In Germany, Stalin consolidated the Soviet hold over the Soviet occupation zone yet talked repeatedly, both privately and publicly, about honoring the Potsdam pledges to keep Germany unified and demilitarized [12]

Indeed, Leffler further notes that "throughout 1946 and 1947, Stalin ordered [Soviet Foreign Minister V.M.] Molotov to work with [U.S.

A WORLD CHANGES: EUROPE IN THE MID-1940s

Secretary of State James F.] Byrnes and British foreign minister Ernest Bevin to complete peace treaties."[13] As evidenced by the long quote from Leffler, the immense number of people, places, and events involved in figuring out what to do with Europe after a devastating war tends to provide both sides today with ammunition for the way they seek to portray the early Cold War.

Although revisionists remained dominant and influential throughout the 1960s, by the 1970s and into the 1980s a postrevisionist school emerged, led by John Lewis Gaddis. They focused less on blaming one side or the other and more on explaining how aspects of the postwar international environment helped produce the Cold War. The immediate memories of global depression and war convinced American leaders to build a new world in which a repeat of these threats were less probable, and this new world of international organizations, global capitalist trade, and liberal democracies was something quite at odds with Stalin's view of the world.[14] In addition, Gaddis argued, "Revisionists are correct in emphasizing the importance of internal constraints, but they have defined them too narrowly: by focusing so heavily on economics, they neglect the profound impact of the domestic political system on the conduct of American foreign policy."[15] U.S. policymakers thus faced certain limits and were less at fault for the onset of the Cold War because, although Gaddis admits Stalin took a while to "impose communist regimes" in Eastern Europe and "showed notoriously little interest in promoting the fortunes of communist parties in areas beyond his control," in the final analysis, Stalin "failed to make the limited nature of his objectives clear" to the West.[16] Viewing domestic influence as central in the making of foreign policy, Gaddis argues that since American leaders had fewer options available to them, Stalin is more to blame for the coming of the Cold War because "the very nature of the Soviet system afforded him a larger selection of alternatives than were open to leaders of the United States. The Russian dictator was immune from pressures of Congress, public opinion, or the press. Even ideology did not restrict him: Stalin was the master of communist doctrine, not a prisoner of it, and could modify or suspend Marxism–Leninism whenever it suited him to do so."[17] Gaddis is careful to say that neither side sought out the Cold War intentionally, but he argues Stalin had "greater freedom of action" and so must share a larger portion of culpability based on his choices in the early Cold War.[18] Since the postrevisionists believed structural elements, primarily the international states system and domestic politics, mattered more in producing the Cold War, they reached less strident conclusions than the extreme anti-Soviet polemics of the early Cold War scholars while still ultimately pointing a finger at the Soviet Union. Indeed, after the fall of the Soviet Union, Gaddis was more clear in his opinion of Stalin, writing in 1997, "*As long as Stalin was running the Soviet Union a cold war was unavoidable* [italics his]."[19] There have been, and continue to be, numerous refinements to various elements of each school over time—expansions, clarifications, and occasional changes in view—but these are the broad outlines of the first several decades of Cold War scholarship.

The most balanced treatment of the Cold War's beginning, which seems to take the postrevisionist arguments focused on structural elements to their complete conclusion, is Melvyn Leffler's influential 2007 work *For the Soul of Mankind*. While Leffler takes into account personal flaws of both Stalin and Truman, namely paranoia and lack of nuanced thinking respectively, he emphasizes the roles of ideology and historical experience.[20] U.S. leaders feared a return to the era of depression and war that had almost consumed Western civilization in the 1930s and 1940s. They sought to create a stable capitalist and liberal democratic world system.[21] Likewise, the Russians had been scarred immensely by the German invasion and sought to create, finally, an impenetrable security buffer to their west.[22] They also remained adherents of Marxist–Leninist ideology from which, Leffler points out, Stalin took the belief that capitalist self-contradictions would inevitably lead to another major war among capitalist powers, or one between the Soviets and the capitalists.[23] Either way, Russia had to be ready to fight or take advantage of the situation in order to spread communism further. Leffler thus combines "ideology and memory . . . structure and agency" and, fundamentally, argues that "the structure of the international system intersected with the beliefs of human agents to produce the Cold War."[24] He largely avoids attributing blame because, he claims, "In 1948, Stalin and Truman set forth the visions and ambitions that would drive their nations for the next forty years. They could not do otherwise in an international order that engendered so much fear and so much opportunity."[25] Where one places causation directly relates to where one places blame for the onset of the Cold War. For Leffler, if several structural elements produced the Cold War by conditioning American and Soviet responses to each other's actions, blaming one side more than the other is not very useful, or even fair. Of course, other schools attribute more causative influence, and thus blame, for the start of the Cold War to one side or the other, with the revisionists focusing on domestic U.S. economic needs and the postrevisionists focusing on Stalin's freedom of action as respective driving forces in helping to cause the Cold War. The debate thus continues over who bears primary responsibility for the heightened risk of nuclear war over the next several decades, the financial and social costs to societies on both sides, and the immense human and material costs counted by regions around the world caught up in the East–West standoff.

WARTIME CONFERENCES

Despite conflicting ideologies, there were opportunities before the end of World War II for the Western democratic powers and the Soviet Union to reach agreements on the structure of postwar Europe. For instance, both British Prime Minister Winston Churchill and President Franklin Roosevelt recognized that the Soviet Red Army's control of Eastern Europe essentially gave Stalin the ability to shape those nations as he wanted, although they could not state so publicly due to domestic opposition to communism. Stalin would indeed later claim confusion when Western criticisms flew regarding Soviet actions in their sphere, since he thought the Western nations had already acknowledged his control of Eastern Europe. At the same time, there were of course serious and deep differences over how postwar Europe was to be organized politically and economically. Historians can thus find evidence of both division and consensus at the three most important Allied wartime conferences, which took place in the Iranian city of Tehran in late 1943, the Black Sea resort city of Yalta in February 1945, and the Berlin suburb of Potsdam in July 1945.

The summit in the Iranian capital from November 28 to December 1, 1943 between the American, British, and Russian heads of state witnessed some tension over the opening of a second front against Germany, but ended with a mutual sense of cooperation. While Soviet victories at Stalingrad and Kursk in 1943 had begun to turn back the Nazi Wehrmacht, Russian losses continued to pile up and Stalin pressed the British and Americans to open a second front. At dinner on the evening of November 29, Stalin, upset with what he believed was unnecessary British caution in opening a serious second front in Western Europe, joked "that Mr. Churchill nursed a secret affection for Germany and desired to see a soft peace."[26] Instead, Stalin ruminated that to prevent a scenario in which "Germany would rise again within 15 or 20 years to plunge the world into another war" one of the victory "conditions" should be the execution of tens of thousands of German officers. While Churchill protested, Roosevelt "jokingly" agreed with Stalin that around 49,000 should die.[27] The president certainly did not actually believe such a course of action was humane, but it showed the relatively amiable relationship between the American and Soviet heads of state eighteen months before the war in Europe ended. The conversation also indicated the type of harsh treatment the Soviets planned to mete out to Germany, which the Western nations would come to oppose. Most importantly, the major Allied leaders sought for the first time to define the outlines of postwar Europe. While vague, the general attitude toward Germany at the time was to ensure a lack of industrial capacity so it could never again make war on such a scale.

Despite the ribbing from Stalin, the next day Churchill indicated that Britain "had now no objections to Russia's access to warm water ports," a longstanding Russian geopolitical goal.[28] When Stalin pointedly asked about access to the Dardanelles Straits held by Turkey, Churchill "saw no objections to this legitimate question" and claimed "we all hoped to see Russian fleets, both naval and merchant, on all seas of the world."[29] Remarkably, in August 1946, less than three years later, Stalin's insistence on Russian access to the same straits, and thus directly to the Mediterranean, would cause a major Cold War crisis. Yet in late 1943, the Western powers were not much bothered by the idea of such Russian access. Overall, both Stalin's desire for a punitive treatment of Germany, including altering borders, and his expansionary aims were present at Tehran, but American and British leaders seemed willing, at least in Stalin's eyes, to acquiesce to his postwar goals. As many historians have noted, Roosevelt especially believed that stable spheres of influence for the great powers would create an orderly postwar world. Thus when Western leaders later began to criticize Stalin for his geographic expansion and his treatment of Eastern Europe, he felt the sentiments of Tehran had been undermined and he believed he was justified in pursuing his goals against what appeared to be a fickle West. Truman and others felt otherwise—that it was Stalin himself who was undermining agreements regarding postwar borders, the makeup of governments, and the treatment of Eastern and Central European nations.

As victorious Allied armies closed in on Germany from both sides, the Big Three met at Yalta on the Crimean peninsula in February 1945 to discuss more specifically the postwar structure of Europe. Unlike Tehran, however, serious divisions emerged, with the most contentious issue

POLAND

During the late Middle Ages and into the early modern period, between the 1500s and 1600s, Poland was joined to Lithuania in a geographically large entity known as the Polish-Lithuanian Commonwealth. Howevere, as other nations around Poland grew stronger, they eventually took over, with Austria, Prussia, and Russia dividing Poland among themselves. Between the late 1700s and the end of World War I in 1918, no independent Poland existed. During World War II, Poland suffered horrific devastation at the hands of the Nazis and then more than four decades of communist rule under the Soviet Union, although it remained a thorn in Russia's side. In fact, Poland was an important Eastern European nation that helped spur the end of communism in Europe when Lech Walesa and his independent trade union Solidarity began protesting strict communist control in the 1980s.

A WORLD CHANGES: EUROPE IN THE MID-1940s   13

the nature of the new Polish government. Poland had been controlled by both the Germans and Russians from 1939 to mid-1941, then by the Nazis until early 1945, and then by the Red Army. Therefore, the Western Allies considered the legitimate government of Poland to be made up of certain Polish exiles in London, known as the London Poles. Shortly before the Yalta conference, however, Stalin declared a group of mostly communist Polish leaders, the Lublin Poles, as the head of a newly reconstituted Polish government.[30] It seemed Stalin was directly imposing communist rule outside Russian borders. After protesting, in the end Roosevelt and Churchill realized they could do nothing to prevent Stalin's control of Poland and so at least convinced him to issue vague assurances about making the Polish government more democratic.[31] Similarly regarding the future of Germany, the Western leaders agreed, at least on paper, to Stalin's strident demands for a harsh punishment, including reparations and, according to public State Department pronouncements after the conference, perhaps even "the complete disarmament, demilitarisation and the dismemberment of Germany as they [the Allies] deem requisite for future peace and security."[32] For their part, the Americans and British convinced Stalin to issue with them jointly a Declaration of Liberated Europe, which mentioned "democratic means," "democratic institutions," "self-government," "elections," and "broadly representative" governments and also invoked the principles of the Atlantic Charter, an announcement by Roosevelt and Churchill in 1941 that had envisioned a postwar world built along democratic lines.[33] Although the conference seemed to end on a high note, the seeds of tension had been sown. Stalin believed his allies had given him a free hand wherever the Red Army was present. When the West turned against him later, he felt they had lied to him. For their part, Churchill and Roosevelt still recognized Stalin's de facto grip on large swathes of Eastern and Central Europe, but both the language of the Declaration of Liberated Europe and their insistence on a more representative Polish government would later give Truman, his aides, members of Congress, and the American public a basis to insist that Stalin adhere to the letter of such agreements regarding postwar Europe. When Stalin did not, Truman, and others, felt justified in adopting tougher stances toward the Soviet Union. As with Tehran, Yalta was both a moment of cooperation and a glimpse of a more contentious future.

That future began to come more clearly into focus at Potsdam in July 1945. Two months after the formal surrender of German forces, but with fighting in the Pacific still raging, the major powers met again to hammer out more concretely the structure of the postwar world. There had been, however, significant changes in leadership. President Roosevelt died in mid-April and Vice President Harry Truman ascended to America's highest

Figure 1.1 Harry S. Truman and Joseph Stalin meeting at Potsdam. From left to right, first row: Joseph Stalin, Harry S. Truman, Soviet Ambassador Andrei Gromyko, Secretary of State James Byrnes, and Soviet Foreign Minister Vyacheslav Molotov. Second row: General Harry Vaughan, interpreter Charles Bohlen, interpreter V. N. Pavlov (mostly obscured by Truman), Captain James K. Vardaman, and Charles Ross (partially obscured).

office. Then, halfway through the conference, a British general election handed a victory to Clement Attlee's Labor Party and he replaced Churchill at the head of the British delegation. While the American–Soviet conversations were most significant, the British were still substantially involved, especially when it came to countries such as Greece, which Stalin had guaranteed as a British sphere of influence as long as the British allowed him a free hand in Bulgaria and Romania. Overall, Truman is central to debates over Cold War causation. Some historians portray him as coming into the presidency an insecure man who sought to compensate by acting "tough" toward the Soviets, thus unnecessarily increasing tension between the two superpowers. Others see him as wisely taking the necessary steps required to prevent any further Russian advances in Europe and around the world, given the expansionist ideology of the Soviet state. Here a note on historical contingency can be instructive. Would the Cold War have begun as it did or tensions have run as deep if Roosevelt had lived longer and held to his initial vision of spheres of influence for the great powers? Or, given Stalin's personality, which historians often describe as paranoid, and the goals of communist ideology, would Roosevelt eventually have acted as Truman did? It is impossible to know, of course, but the exercise can be helpful when thinking about historical causation and methodology. Were contingent events, specifically Roosevelt's death and Truman's ascension to the presidency, or larger forces, especially the fundamental conflict between capitalism and communism, more influential in causing the Cold War? Are personalities or structural forces more important in the making of history?

These questions become more important in light of the discussions at Potsdam. The main contentious topics were the economic treatment of Germany, the German–Polish border, and the nature of Eastern European governments, namely in Bulgaria, Romania, and Hungary. As at Yalta, Stalin demanded reparations from Germany. The Western nations balked until they agreed that everyone could extract reparations from their own areas, with the Russians only allowed to take a quarter of theirs from the more industrialized western parts of Germany. The German–Polish border was settled largely in favor of Russian desires, creating, at the expense of Germany, an enlarged Poland already under the control of Stalin's Lublin Poles. For other Eastern European nations, both sides agreed that formal peace treaties would be addressed in future sessions of the newly created Council of Foreign Ministers. The latter would meet periodically over the next two years in various attempts to solve lingering issues on borders, treaties, and the economic treatment of Germany. Overall, as historian Daniel Yergin notes, "It was an exercise in ambiguity. The real decision was a lack of common decision. . . . On each of the outstanding issues, the Great Powers had found that the best way to cooperate was to give each a freer hand in its own sphere. Because they could not agree on how to govern Europe, they would begin to divide it; this was how the Yalta system worked."[34] This allowed both sides to save face, while most knew Stalin and the Red Army would do as they wished.

As at Yalta a few months earlier, Stalin formally agreed to language about self-determination, elections, and other democratic measures in the areas he controlled, but unlike Roosevelt, Truman really hoped Stalin would follow through. If he did not, the good news for the United States was that during the conference Truman learned of the successful testing of the atomic bomb, and thus knew the United States held a trump card. While at this point Truman still thought he could strike a deal with the Russians, as long as it benefited the United States, some of his officials began to urge a harder line toward the Soviets based on their actions in Eastern Europe.[35] The president would increasingly listen to those voices as tensions increased over the next months and years, but initially he sought to work with Stalin, thus showing that events had to occur to deepen the

16   A WORLD CHANGES: EUROPE IN THE MID-1940s

divide between the two nations and to push Truman toward a more strident anti-Russian stance. What caused him to listen to those voices later? What events moved him down a less conciliatory road? Even when those events occurred, could he have chosen a less antagonistic path and sought a measure of normalized relations with Stalin? Perhaps Truman's Secretary of State who had done much of the haggling at Potsdam, James F. Byrnes, best described, in his 1947 memoir, both the president's mindset in mid-1945 and the influence of later events when remarked, "The agreements did make the conference a success but the violation of those agreements has turned success into failure."[36]

DOMESTIC INFLUENCE AND FINANCIAL TENSIONS

Some historians argue that Stalin's actions made it difficult for Truman to choose anything other than a stronger foreign policy stance, and ultimately containment. In between Yalta and Potsdam, and especially after the latter, Stalin's machinations in Eastern Europe worried Western leaders. As the eastern front moved closer to Berlin throughout the spring of 1945, the Soviets consolidated their hold both on areas of Eastern Europe "liberated" from the Germans and on countries allied to Hitler. In his memoir, Secretary of State Byrnes related the intricate details of Soviet moves in Romania in March 1945 to mold the government in their image. When Soviet Foreign Minister Molotov asked the United States months later to approve the Soviet creation, Byrnes responded they could not "because of the character of the government which had been installed by virtue of a two-and-a-half hour ultimatum given to the [Romanian] King by [Molotov's representative Andrei] Vyshinski."[37] Likewise in Poland, Stalin firmly placed the pro-Soviet Lublin Poles in power and ignored repeated calls for a more inclusive government. In Poland, Romania, Bulgaria, Hungary, and in other places the Red Army held sway, as historian Melvyn Leffler notes, "Soviet military commanders worked with local leaders to enhance communist strength and thwart non communist opponents. Stalin was willing to pay lip service to notions of free elections and self – determination, as he did at Yalta, but in practice he was determined to establish a sphere of influence that would safeguard the Soviet periphery for all time."[38] Historical Russian problems, namely foreign attacks, that stemmed from having an open western periphery are important to take into account here because some historians view Stalin's actions in Eastern Europe as undemocratic and reprehensible, to be sure, but not necessarily as existential threats to the West. Creating a security buffer around an oft-invaded nation made sense, goes the argument, given the massive losses in people and infrastructure sustained during the war. Other historians, of course, see Stalin's moves simply as precursors to what he hoped to do in the rest of Europe, and the world.

Certainly some American leaders at the time increasingly came to think so. The first meeting of the Council of Foreign Ministers, set up at Potsdam to finalize peace treaties between the major powers, occurred in London from September 11 to October 2. Present were representatives from Britain, the United States, the Soviet Union, France, and China, which was still embroiled in a civil war between communists and nationalists. Discussion hinged mainly on the nature of Eastern European governments, but neither side budged and the conference ended on the petty note of both sides seeking to insure the failed meeting would conclude on a day when their opponent sat as chairman.[39] Nothing was decided. Soviet intransigence angered American leaders while American unwillingness to recognize pro-Soviet governments in Eastern Europe upset the Russians. A second meeting of only British, American, and Soviet ministers in Moscow from December 16 to 26 promised better days ahead. Preliminary agreements were reached on issues relating to Japan, nationalist China, Korea, and even atomic energy.[40] While not much was officially decided on Eastern Europe, apart from vague Soviet promises to have more non-communists in the Bulgarian and Romanian governments, the meeting seemed to be a step toward a more cooperative future, quite apart from the results of the London conference.[41] Despite differences, maybe the two sides could work together after all. Byrnes was "far happier" than after the London conference, although he also noted that "our common problems in Iran" remained unsolved.[42] That issue, in fact, would lead to a major diplomatic crisis in less than three months, illustrating that periods of mutual goodwill during the immediate postwar period were often short-lived as U.S.–Soviet relations vacillated weekly between animosity and cooperation.

The domestic arena also increasingly began to play a role in U.S.–Soviet relations as criticism of the Soviet Union's actions in Eastern Europe mounted. Despite Roosevelt's desire for great power spheres of influence, Byrnes's relatively successful negotiating in Moscow, and Truman's indecision on the nature of the Soviet threat, by late 1945 important public figures claimed the United States had forfeited millions of people to communism. Key Republicans such as Senator Arthur Vandenberg and foreign policy expert John Foster Dulles, later to be Eisenhower's Secretary of State, were concerned with apparent American weakness in the face of Soviet intransigence. Vandenberg especially believed the Russians had taken advantage of Byrnes at Moscow.[43] As early as January 1945, even before Yalta, Vandenberg was warning of Soviet machinations, claiming in a Senate speech that "Moscow wants to assert unilateral war and peace aims which collide with ours" and criticizing Roosevelt for an "almost jocular, and even cynical, dismissal of the Atlantic Charter as a mere collection of fragmentary notes."[44] Roosevelt and Churchill had issued the Charter in August 1941 as the first expression of general postwar aims, with self-determination at the core of the Charter's principles. For his part, Dulles had in fact been present at the London Conference in the fall and had urged a firmer stance toward the Soviets because by then, according to Daniel Yergin, he "saw only malevolent purpose in Soviet behavior."[45] In fact, by the late 1940s and into the 1950s, Dulles would oppose containment because he thought it too lenient, not too harsh, toward the Russians. Under Eisenhower, Dulles would often speak of "liberation" and "roll back" regarding an active U.S. role to free the populations under Soviet control, which often increased superpower tensions.

Figure 1.2 President Harry S. Truman (right) speaks with Secretary of State James F. Byrnes (left) and Senator Arthur Vandenberg (center) on an airport tarmac.

A WORLD CHANGES: EUROPE IN THE MID-1940s   19

Truman himself began to contribute to the growing anti-Soviet domestic consensus. In a revealing foreign policy address in New York City for Navy Day on October 27, 1945, Truman laid out eleven "fundamentals" for U.S. foreign policy, with at least five relating to the need for self-determination and democratic practices around the world.[46] He claimed that the United States "shall refuse to recognize any government imposed upon any nation by the force of any foreign power."[47] While the Soviet Union was not named explicitly, it was certainly Truman's target. The president's opposition to Soviet measures was becoming more pronounced. He had initially sought to engage the Soviets in the spring, summer, and early fall of 1945—the immediate postwar period. As Stalin went on to violate his own public promises that he would allow more "democratic" governments in Eastern Europe, however, Truman became increasingly hostile toward Russia. Several of his aides also actively supported this shift. While there would still be moments during the next several years when policy development could have moved in different directions, Truman in late 1945 was increasingly willing to listen to those in his administration advocating tougher measures against Stalin— namely Admiral William D. Leahy, Secretary of the Navy James V. Forrestal and, to a lesser extent, U.S. ambassador to the Soviet Union W. Averell Harriman. To these officials, the Soviets were now the primary threat to world peace and democracy. They also cautioned Truman that the Soviets only understood strength and thus the best strategy was to give Stalin nothing.[48] Appeasing the Soviets would not work.[49]

In late 1945, therefore, Truman began to adopt a harder line with the Soviets due to his own views, the influence of key advisors, and growing Republican pressure, which blurred the line between the domestic and international arenas. Still, other Truman officials, including Secretary of State Byrnes and especially Secretary of Commerce Henry A. Wallace, continued to think agreements could be reached with the Soviets and argued that relations riddled with tension need not be the norm. Some members of Congress and some segments of public opinion felt likewise. Historian Melvyn Leffler aptly sums up the unusual, at times confusing, situation as 1945 turned to 1946,

> By the end of 1945 Stalin and Truman were eyeing each other warily. They were both angry with their foreign ministers for inclining toward compromise. They felt that their respective nations had the power and the right to forge a new international order that would enhance their security and their ideals. They were not inclined to tolerate opposition. But they also grasped that confrontation made little sense. They had more to gain from

20 A WORLD CHANGES: EUROPE IN THE MID-1940s

> sustaining the alliance than from rupturing it, though cooperation
> was logical only if it served national interests. During 1946, they
> wavered between toughness and conciliation.[50]

What, therefore, was the key causative factor in Truman's increasingly hard line toward the Soviets over the next months and years—public opinion, Congressional leaders, aides, his own belief in the importance of the American role in the world, or Stalin's actions? Relatedly, when did the Cold War begin? Did it begin when significant elements of domestic opinion turned against America's wartime ally and began to pressure the president? Did it begin only after Truman put new policies in place during 1946 and 1947? Or did it begin as soon as the Red Army left Russian borders, given that Stalin's dictatorial personality and expansionary ambitions meant the Soviets would never allow opposition in their sphere of influence and would inevitably be antagonistic toward the West? The questions of Cold War causation and chronology are intimately tied together.

Financial issues also plagued the U.S.–Soviet relationship over the course of 1945. Obviously capitalist and communist economies are not very compatible, but American companies had operated in Russia during the interwar period and the United States had been providing Lend Lease aid to the Russian war effort ever since the German invasion in mid-1941. On the very day fighting ended in Europe, however, U.S. vessels carrying Lend Lease material were told to turn around and head home, since the program was viewed as a wartime necessity.[51] Truman's defenders argue that while Truman did approve the cessation of aid, the decision was not malicious because it was subordinates who actually implemented it so quickly, some additional aid did resume until fighting in the Pacific was over, and the decision affected aid to both the Russians and the British.[52] Still, the Soviets felt as though a tie between wartime allies had been abruptly severed without concern for Russia's rebuilding needs. The Soviets also sought help for reconstruction by asking the United States for a loan. At first Roosevelt demurred and then as Truman hardened his stance toward the Soviet Union, he, according to John Lewis Gaddis, "sought to withhold economic assistance until the Kremlin made certain concessions in the political sphere."[53] Some members of Congress pushed (or aided, depending on how one views Truman) the president in this direction, especially those who visited Moscow in September 1945 and then, according to Gaddis, "demanded that, in return for an American loan, the Soviet Union reform its internal system of government and abandon the sphere of influence it had so carefully constructed in Eastern Europe."[54] Some historians thus blame Truman and some in Congress for unnecessarily stoking postwar tensions by requiring concessions that were so extensive there was no possibility the Russians would agree to them. Indeed, the demands may have been made primarily to extend America's economic influence. When the Truman administration provided a loan of almost $4 billion to the British in early 1946, the president used it as a lever to crack open the global imperial British trading network by demanding the convertibility of pounds into dollars. American businesses now had easier access to the markets of the empire, "the effect of which was to subordinate Britain to an American-dominated international economic order," in the words of Daniel Yergin.[55] In the end, the United States never provided a large postwar loan to the Soviet Union, contributing to tensions and serving to increase the division of the world into communist and capitalist camps. As noted above, however, the reason for not providing a loan continues to be debated.

> ## THE GOLD STANDARD
>
> Virtually no country actually uses the gold standard today in the sense of having their currency tied directly to a certain amount of physical gold, although most countries do try to have some sort of gold stock in reserve. The post-World War II ties between gold, the U.S. dollar, and other currencies, in that order, aided the recovery of Western Europe and Japan by providing a stable economic environment in which everyone knew the value of each other's currencies, making trade and investment easier. U.S. spending in the Vietnam War, however, led the United States to "float" the U.S. dollar in 1971, essentially ending any last official ties between major currencies and fixed amounts of gold. Now, currencies rise and fall in value in relation to each other based mostly, in theory, on global market activity.

Beyond the specific issue of a loan, the United States and its Western allies created an international capitalist trading framework after World War II that would end up not including the Soviet Union. As World War II moved toward conclusion, American and Western leaders feared a return to depression and war and believed new institutions were needed both to avoid such dangers and to create a more prosperous future. At a conference in Bretton Woods, New Hampshire in July 1944, forty four countries, mostly from Europe and the Western Hemisphere, decided on three major developments. First, the World Bank (officially titled the International Bank of Reconstruction and Development), with an initial grant of more than $7 billion, would help provide postwar recovery loans to Europe.[56] Second, the International Monetary Fund would have a similar amount for loans to shore up troubled currencies this meant that, as Walter LaFeber notes, "trade could be conducted without fear of sudden currency depreciation or wild fluctuations in exchange rates, ailments which had nearly paralyzed the international community in the 1930s."[57] When currencies became worthless, financial instability was of course a concern, but Western leaders also worried that people plagued by that sort of instability were susceptible to radical political solutions. Finally, and most beneficial to the United States, many barriers to trade were reduced or eliminated and all other currencies were tagged at certain rates to the U.S. dollar, which was itself set against a certain value in gold ounces. Thus currencies, including after early 1946 the British pound, could easily be converted into U.S. dollars and everyone knew how much all other currencies were worth in relation to each other. The idea was that this would help avoid a repeat of the financial uncertainty of the 1930s. Also in America's favor, as LaFeber points out, was that "voting in the organizations depended on money contributed. Since Americans would have to contribute the most, they would also control the World Bank and IMF."[58] Therefore, in addition to the capitalist nature of this setup, the Russians, who attended the initial conference, were wary of joining institutions in which their emerging rival for global influence would be able to exert control over elements of the Soviet economy. Given until the end of 1945 to make a decision, Russia vacillated and, ultimately at the very end of the year, Stalin refused to join the new organizations.[59] The economic division of the world deepened further as 1945 ended and 1946 dawned.

THE CONTEXT FOR CONTAINMENT

Few episodes in European history have matched the devastation of the Second World War, although the Thirty Years War and Napoleon's numerous conflicts compare in some ways. Estimates vary of course, but combined military and civilian deaths in Europe, including those murdered in the Holocaust, approached the staggering number of forty million. Of that total, more than half occurred in the Soviet Union. The infrastructure and major cities of large parts of Europe had been destroyed by massive aerial bombing and by armies as they moved across the continent. When the fighting ended, neither the suffering nor the movement of people did. Russian prisoners of war from Germany, those who had survived, returned to Russia. Between twelve and fourteen million ethnic Germans were expelled and forced westward from several nations in Eastern and Central Europe. Recovery was not simple, quick, or easy as tens of millions lay dead, tens of millions were homeless, and tens of millions went hungry. Amidst this devastation, the competing postwar visions of the United States and the Soviet Union began to clash. Both sides sought to remake Europe in their respective image. On the American side, while communism and a number of Stalin's moves were intensely disliked, there had yet to emerge either a concise and coherent explanation of why the Soviets acted as they did or a general strategy on how to assert and accomplish U.S. interests in Europe. Soon, though, George Kennan would provide the Truman administration with both.

NOTES

1   Memorandum, George Kennan to Dean Acheson, May 23, 1947, *Foreign Relations of the United States, 1947, Volume III: The British Commonwealth; Europe* (Washington, D.C.: U.S. Government Printing Office, 1972), 229. Hereafter *FRUS 1947,* Vol. III.
2   Speech, Harry Truman, "Truman Doctrine." (Lillian Goldman Law Library, 2008), (http://avalon.law.yale.edu/20th_century/trudoc.asp, accessed 3/30/17). Hereafter "Truman Doctrine."
3   Kennan to Acheson, May 23, 1947, *FRUS 1947,* Vol. III, 229.
4   As usual, historians debate a number of things about NSC-68 specifically — whether it was new or not, what was most important in causing it to be written, even whether it made much sense in its recommendations. For a short, clear window into these debates, read Luke Fletcher's article in the September 2016 edition of *Diplomatic History*. He argues that "the more immediate fear that Germany and/or other European allies were losing their desire to remain in the U.S.-led 'free world' system" was the main stimulation in the writing of NSC-68. He also claims that Secretary of State Dean Acheson, who directed the overall policy review in the administration in early 1950, had for a while wanted to make the argument for increased military spending, which Fletcher calls "the all-important primary recommendation" in the document, and so "in the general panic and excitement of the Soviet nuclear acquisition, the 'loss' of China,' and the desire by military hawks to build the H-bomb, Acheson saw an opportunity to begin the process of binding Germany and Europe more permanently to the United States." For the purposes of this book, the main point is still that NSC-68 marked a new militarization, through spending and attitude, of American Cold War foreign policy in early 1950. Luke Fletcher, "The Collapse of the Western World: Acheson, Nitze, and the NSC 68/Rearmament Decision," *Diplomatic History* 40, no. 4 (September 2016): 750–755, 767, 773–776.
5   Harvey C. Mansfield and Delba Winthrop, eds., *Alexis de Tocqueville: Democracy in America* (Chicago: The University of Chicago Press, 2000), 396.
6   William Appleman Williams, *The Tragedy of American Diplomacy* (New York: W.W. Norton & Company, 1972), 15.
7   Ibid., 15.
8   Ibid., 206.
9   Ibid., 206.
10 Ibid., 206.

24   A WORLD CHANGES: EUROPE IN THE MID-1940s

11   J. Samuel Walker, "The Decision to Use the Bomb: A Historiographical Update" in Michael J. Hogan, ed., *America in the World: The Historiography of American Foreign Relations Since 1941* (New York: Cambridge University Press, 1995), 208.

12   Melvyn P. Leffler, *For the Soul of Mankind: The United States, the Soviet Union, and the Cold War* (New York: Hill and Wang, 2007), 53.

13   Ibid., 55.

14   John Lewis Gaddis, *The United States and the Origins of the Cold War, 1941–1947* (New York: Columbia University Press, 1972), 354.

15   Ibid., 357.

16   Ibid., 355.

17   Ibid., 360.

18   Ibid., 360–361.

19   John Lewis Gaddis, *We Now Know: Rethinking Cold War History* (New York: Oxford University Press, 1997), 292.

20   Leffler, *Soul of Mankind*, 79–83.

21   Ibid., 82.

22   Ibid., 80.

23   Ibid., 81.

24   Ibid., 8, 82.

25   Ibid., 83.

26   Minutes by Charles E. Bohlen, "Tripartite Dinner Meeting, November 29, 1943, 8:30 P.M., Soviet Embassy," in *Foreign Relations of the United States: The Conferences at Cairo and Tehran, 1943*. (Washington, D.C.: U.S. Government Printing Office, 1961), 553. Hereafter *FRUS, Conferences at Cairo and Tehran*.

27   Ibid., 553–554.

28   Minutes by Charles E. Bohlen, "Roosevelt-Churchill-Stalin Luncheon Meeting, November 30, 1943, 1:30 PM, Roosevelt's Quarters, Soviet Embassy," in *FRUS, Conferences at Cairo and Tehran*, 566.

29   Ibid., 566–567.

30   Walter LaFeber, *America, Russia, and the Cold War, 1945–2002*, 9th Ed. (New York: The McGraw-Hill Companies, 2002), 15.

31   Robert J. McMahon, *The Cold War: A Very Short Introduction* (New York: Oxford University Press, 2003), 20.

32   Department of State, "Protocol of Proceedings of the Yalta Conference," March 24, 1947, in *Foreign Relations of the United States: The Conference of Berlin (The Potsdam Conference) 1945 (In Two Volumes)*, Volume II. (Washington D.C.: United States Government Printing Office, 1960), 1569.

33   Ibid., 1568–1569.

34   The details in this paragraph to this point are mostly from Daniel Yergin, *Shattered Peace: The Origins of the Cold War and the National Security State* (Boston: Houghton Mifflin Company, 1978), 114–119. Quote from 118.

35   Leffler, *Soul of Mankind*, 41–42.

36   James F. Byrnes, *Speaking Frankly* (New York: Harper & Brothers Publishers, 1947), 87; Yergin, *Shattered Peace*, 113.

37   Byrnes, *Speaking Frankly*, 50–52. Quote from 52.

38   Leffler, *Soul of Mankind*, 33. The long Russian historical memory could stretch back to the threat from Poland-Lithuania in the late Middle Ages and early modern period,

the Swedish invasion in the Great Northern War fought by Peter the Great in the early 1700s, the Napoleonic invasion of 1812, and of course the two world wars.

39 Byrnes, *Speaking Frankly*, 106. For full details see Yergin, *Shattered Peace*, 122–132.

40 Yergin, *Shattered Peace*, 147–151.

41 Ibid., 149.

42 Byrnes, *Speaking Frankly*, 121–122.

43 Yergin, *Shattered Peace*, 153.

44 Speech, Arthur H. Vandenberg, "American Foreign Policy," January 10, 1945 (United States Senate) (http://senate.gov/artandhistory/history/resources/pdf/VandenbergSpeech.pdf, accessed 3/30/2017), 600, 602; Gaddis, *Origins*, 291.

45 Yergin, *Shattered Peace*, 129.

46 Speech, Harry Truman "Address on Foreign Policy at the Navy Day Celebration in New York City," October 27, 1945 (Gerhard Peters and John T. Woolley – The American Presidency Project, 1999–2017) (http://www.presidency.ucsb.edu/ws/?pid=12304, accessed 3/30/2017). Hereafter "Navy Day Speech."; Leffler, *Soul of Mankind*, 47.

47 "Navy Day Speech."

48 Yergin, *Shattered Peace*, 153, 156.

49 Ibid., 159.

50 Leffler, *Soul of Mankind*, 48.

5` Alonzo L. Hamby, *Man of the People: A Life of Harry S. Truman* (New York: Oxford University Press, 1995), 319.

52 Ibid., 319.

53 Gaddis, *Origins*, 261.

54 Ibid., 260.

55 Yergin, *Shattered Peace*, 177.

56 LaFeber, *America, Russia*, 11.

57 Ibid., 11.

58 Ibid., 11.

59 Gaddis, *We Now Know*, 193.

CHAPTER 2

Envisioning the Soviets

Kennan versus Wallace

A CONTINGENT FUTURE

Although the euphoria of military victory had turned to confusion and frustration as the two superpowers argued over the future of Europe, four decades of steely-eyed standoffs were still not inevitable. American leaders disliked Stalin's increasingly icy grip on Eastern Europe, but they were not yet ready to abandon the Grand Alliance completely. At the same time, they could not just jettison the principles for which Western leaders claimed the war had been fought—democracy, self-determination, and an open trading environment. As Truman and his officials struggled to make sense of their new world, two policy alternatives emerged during the first half of 1946. George Kennan's famous Long Telegram, advocating a policy of containment of the Soviet Union and declaring no accommodation could be reached with Russia, arrived in Washington in February and quickly caught the attention of many in the administration. In July, however, Secretary of Commerce Henry Wallace urged American leaders to view postwar events, especially American moves and declarations, from the Soviet perspective. He argued the West could in fact reach accords with Stalin since the Soviets only sought geographic security along their perimeter. While the Truman administration ended up adopting containment, it is useful to note the different future an embrace of Wallace's ideas may have created—a future that may have held fewer wars, less economic and human loss both in the United States and abroad, and less risk of nuclear war. Historians debate why Truman ultimately went with Kennan's ideas, and such debates are helpful in exploring the role of domestic actors, ideology, personality, and international structures in the making of foreign policy. In addition, adding Wallace to the mix, reveals a moment when history might have taken a different path.

THE LONG TELEGRAM

As the U.S.–Soviet relationship remained murky and muddled during the first weeks of 1946, Stalin did something that pushed American policymakers to develop a more precise vision of the postwar world. On February 9 at the Bolshoi Theater in Moscow, Stalin gave an "election" speech, which was also broadcast by radio. The speech provided a public snapshot of Stalin's beliefs at the time, especially his views on international relations. Most of the speech covered internal Soviet industrial and agricultural development and praised Soviet sacrifices and bravery during World War II. Yet the section on diplomatic relations was telling. Instead of "a result of blunders committed by certain statesmen," the recent global conflict "broke out as the inevitable result of the development of world economic and political forces on the basis of present-day monopolistic capitalism." Stalin explicitly invoked Marxist arguments that self-contradictions within capitalism led to "crises and catastrophic wars." Due to the "uneven development of capitalist countries," the latter will vie for "raw materials and markets," usually through violent means. He noted a vague hope that conflict might end if nations could peacefully "redistribute raw materials and markets," but, Stalin claimed, "This is impossible under the present capitalist conditions of world economic development."[1] While he did not explicitly state so, according to Gaddis, "Stalin clearly implied that future wars were inevitable until the world economic system was reformed, that is, until communism supplanted capitalism as the prevailing form of economic organization."[2] It was a clear and pointed criticism of the capitalist world.

While subsequent decades would prove this prediction about intracapitalist warfare wrong, the content of the speech worried American leaders. Voicing core elements of Marxist thinking regarding international relations, Stalin seemed to remain a committed ideological communist. To U.S. policymakers, this meant he also still believed in expanding communism around the globe. Two days after the speech, the head of the Office of European Affairs in the State Department, H. Freeman Matthews, claimed,

THE BOLSHOI THEATER

The Bolshoi Theater in Moscow was one of the few large theaters in Czarist Russia, built in the 1850s, and continuing to operate throughout the Soviet period. Just as the United States State Department did during the Cold War with jazz bands, the performers of the Bolshoi Theater often toured both communist and non-communist nations to try to generate goodwill for the Soviet Union by displaying aspects of Russian culture.

"Stalin's speech of February 9 constitutes the most important and authoritative guide to post-war Soviet policy."[3] Likewise, the next day Elbridge Durbrow, who led the Division of Eastern European Affairs in the State Department, warned that based on the "new Soviet line," future Soviet actions "in all probability will be directed primarily at dividing the British and ourselves in order to give the Soviets a freer hand to attain their own aims."[4] Before his more famous Long Telegram, on February 12 George Kennan, the second highest ranking U.S. diplomat in Moscow at the time, described Stalin's speech as a "straight Marxist interpretation of World Wars one and two as products of crises inherent in monopoly capitalism." Addressing similar speeches by other Soviet leaders, Kennan noted that they also did not "place any serious reliance on [the] future of international collaboration."[5] Indeed, one high-ranking Soviet official had recently warned of "capitalist encirclement," another key Marxist idea regarding international relations, and a second official displayed "an attitude of total suspicion toward motives of [the] outside world."[6] It now seemed clear that the Soviets would pursue international goals aligned with Marxist thought and would not cooperate with capitalist nations in any way.

Stalin's Bolshoi Theater "election" speech catapulted Kennan's views into the center of American foreign policymaking for the rest of the Cold War. Kennan had been a first-hand observer of the Soviets, including Stalin's purges, in the mid-1930s and after his return to Russia in 1944 he issued a number of warnings about Stalin's intentions. Unfortunately for him, as Gaddis relates, until early 1946 he was "at odds with the prevailing policy of cooperation with the Russians" and so his views "made no impression whatsoever in Washington, if, indeed, they were ever read."[7] Things were now different, however, and, according to historian Daniel Yergin, officials such as Durbrow and Matthews now considered Kennan to have been quite prescient.[8] They asked him for, as they put it, "an interpretive analysis of what we may expect in the way of future implementation of these announced policies" by the Soviets.[9] This request came on February 13, four days after Stalin's speech, and while it would take Kennan a further nine days to respond, the impact of his views would be momentous. Many U.S. policymakers readily embraced Kennan's prescriptions for a line-in-the-sand approach to the Soviet Union. Others, however, would continue to recommend engagement and cooperation, at least for a while. Kennan himself would soon come to regret the expanded scope and methods others attached to his recommendations.

Kennan began with an analysis of the "Post War Soviet Outlook," which would have included both Stalin's recent speech as well as other pronouncements Kennan had been observing while in Moscow. The list

Figure 2.1 American Diplomat George F. Kennan, the author of the famous "Long Telegram."
Courtesy of the Library of Congress Prints and Photographs Division, LC-DIG-hec-12925.

George Kennan

Born in 1904 in Milwaukee, Kennan lived just over a century until 2005 and was one of the most influential men in American foreign policy in the twentieth century. He became involved in international politics early in his professional life, starting in the mid-1920s, and between 1933 and 1938 he was stationed in the Soviet Union. He developed both a fondness for the Russian people and traditional Russian culture and an intense dislike of the Soviet system under Stalin's repressive rule. He was in Russia again from 1944 to 1946, when his famous Long Telegram caused the Truman administration to bring him back to the United States as a key advisor. From then on, he held various positions in the State Department and remained a respected figure in the field of foreign policy for the rest of his life, even when not officially in government.

Throughout his life he wrote and spoke extensively about foreign relations, but always remained consistent in his argument that containment, as he originally envisioned it, was meant to be a political and economic solution for the state of international affairs in Europe, not a military solution to be applied around the globe. He always held an optimistic belief that the West would eventually win the Cold War and that communism would eventually implode from within. He was fortunate enough to see his predictions come true in his own lifetime when the most important and powerful communist nation, the Soviet Union, peacefully gave up both control of Eastern Europe and then communism itself between 1989 and 1991.

of Soviet views largely replicated elements of Marxist dogma on international relations, including fears of "capitalist encirclement."[10] Especially important was the idea that internal contradictions within capitalism and conflicts between capitalist nations would lead them to fight each other, and perhaps also the Soviet Union. The communist world needed to be ready, therefore, either to take part directly in one of the forthcoming conflicts or to take advantage of the chaotic situation. In fact, to the Soviets, intracapitalist feuding held "great possibilities for advancement of [the] socialist cause" because such conflicts could "be turned into revolutionary upheavals within the various capitalist countries."[11] Kennan also claimed the Russians would actively adopt actions geared "toward [the] deepening and exploiting of differences and conflicts between capitalist powers."[12] In fact, as Kennan noted when beginning this opening section of the Long Telegram, the Soviets believed that "in the long run there can be no permanent peaceful coexistence" with the capitalist world.[13] As the telegram went on Kennan continued to build his argument that the Soviets believed the two sides could not live together amiably. To Kennan, however, they were wrong because "if not provoked by forces of intolerance and subversion [the] 'capitalist' world of today is quite capable of living at peace with itself and with Russia."[14] Overall, this Soviet view of a world inevitably riven by international conflict had a direct impact on Kennan's policy prescriptions for how America was to deal with the communist superpower.

Kennan proceeded to explain why Soviet leaders held such views, and he did not find the root cause to be in Marxist thought. He believed, "At [the] bottom of [the] Kremlin's neurotic view of world affairs is [a] traditional and instinctive Russian sense of insecurity" and "Marxist dogma, rendered even more truculent and intolerant by Lenin's interpretation, became a perfect vehicle for [this] sense of insecurity with which [the] Bolsheviks, even more than previous Russian rulers, were afflicted."[15] Kennan saw all Russian history as marked by a sense of insecurity, from the era of steppe invaders to the growing technological and economic gap compared to Western and Central Europe during the eighteenth and nineteenth centuries to the new fear of capitalists undermining their communist project.[16] Kennan did believe the Russian masses were "friendly to [the] outside world" and that the Czars and communists were really the only ones "afflicted" with such paranoia about both foreign intervention and about "what would happen if Russians learned [the] truth about [the] world without."[17] Kennan thus saw the Soviets as "only the last of that long succession of cruel and wasteful Russian rulers who have relentlessly forced [the] country on to ever new heights of military power in order to guarantee external security for their internally weak regimes."[18] The last phrase is especially important. Since the Soviets realized they had poor reasons for ruling and since they knew the Russian people were not the most ardent communists, they had to portray the "outside world as evil, hostile and menacing" to the people and then argue no peaceful accord could be reached with such a world.[19] In Kennan's view then, based both on Marxist dogma and on an insecurity about the strength and validity of their own internal rule, which caused them to justify their control to their people by continually warning of external threats, the Soviets would not agree to compromises, cooperation, or coexistence.

Given both their ideology and sense of insecurity, the Soviets would, Kennan argued, seek to expand their power in multiple ways. They would continue to pressure the countries on their periphery, try to use the United Nations to their own advantage, get involved in decolonizing areas, and seek to take advantage of anti-Western or pro-communist sentiment within countries all around the world, even in the West.[20] Kennan did, however, exhibit a bit of paranoia himself by explaining the "Unofficial, or Subterranean" methods, beyond official government actions, by which the Soviets would try to expand their power.[21] These included not only actual communist parties outside Russia, but also a "wide variety of national associations or bodies," including the Eastern Orthodox Church, Pan-Slavic associations, and diverse types of "labor, youth and women's organizations."[22] To Kennan, these actions were "in line with [the] basic Soviet instinct that there can be no compromise with [a] rival power" and therefore they would pursue "insistent, unceasing pressure" to take control of other nations from within.[23] It was a frightening portrait of a powerful ideological enemy bent on expansion.

Ultimately, according to Kennan, the Soviets held "an outlook already preconceived" and were "a political force committed fanatically to the belief that with [the] US there can be no permanent modus vivendi."[24] Soviet actions were based both on Marxist ideology and on the need by Soviet leaders to justify their internal rule, warning of external enemies against whom they protected the people. How, then, should the United States respond? Perhaps surprisingly, Kennan did not think "recourse to any general military conflict" would be needed.[25] Instead, he emphasized a more general Western resolve because he found that while Stalin and the Soviets were "impervious to [the] logic of reason," they were in fact "highly sensitive to [the] logic of force" and would back down "when strong resistance is encountered at any point."[26] Kennan believed that for the Soviets, therefore, "if the adversary [i.e. the West] has sufficient force and makes clear his readiness to use it, he rarely has to do so."[27] Standing firm right away was how one dealt with the Soviet Union. It would in fact reduce the chance for armed conflict between the superpowers because the Soviets would just retreat when confronted. Kennan did provide a caveat, though, when he noted, "If situations are properly handled there need be no prestige-engaging showdowns."[28] Of course, over the subsequent course of the Cold War, such advice was not always heeded.

Overall, while Kennan did not use the word "containment" in his Long Telegram, it was the policy he advocated—firm, consistent diplomatic and political pressure on the Soviet Union's periphery to keep the Russians in place. Then, over time, since the "internal soundness" of the Soviet regime could "not yet be regarded as assured" and because the Soviets would face problems due both to changes in leadership and their attempts to expand, Kennan hoped the Marxist system in Russia would eventually soften and fall apart.[29] This was the key to U.S. strategy— remaining firm, but avoiding military confrontation until the self-contradictions and problems within the communist system caused its collapse. Kennan did not promise a short path to success, but he was reasonably confident in the West's ability to emerge victorious. He argued that since the "Soviets are still by far the weaker force . . . their success will really depend on [the] degree of cohesion, firmness and vigor which [the] Western World can muster. And this is [a] factor which it is within our power to influence."[30] Yet he also warned, "We must have courage and self-confidence to cling to our own methods and conceptions of human society. After all, the greatest danger that can befall us in coping with this problem of Soviet communism, is that we shall allow ourselves to become like those with whom we are coping."[31] Some historians, as discussed below, suggest the United States, in its international endeavors during the Cold War, at times did fall into this trap. Fundamentally for Kennan, it was up to the West to avoid becoming too marred itself while seizing the methods that would eventually, but inevitably, bring victory in the emerging Cold War.

Truman and his aides who had already advocated a harder line toward the Soviets enthusiastically embraced Kennan's ideas. Both his explanations for Soviet actions and his prescription for how to deal with them seemed to make sense in the international environment of early 1946. As historian Daniel Yergin outlines, the document spread widely among American military and diplomatic personnel both as an idea and in physical form because Secretary of the Navy James Forrestal, one of those officials pushing Truman to stand firm against the Soviets, "had hundreds of copies made, and distributed them throughout the Navy department" and elsewhere.[32] In addition to confirming existing views among many, historians note part of the reason many U.S. officials latched onto Kennan's explanation was that they simply had no other framework for understanding the new and different postwar world in which America found itself facing a powerful ideological enemy. They had been haphazardly attempting to define this new environment, but had yet to generate, before February 1946, an overarching view of the situation. Therefore, as John Lewis Gaddis writes, the Long Telegram ended up "providing American officials with the intellectual framework they would employ in thinking about communism and Soviet foreign policy for the next two decades."[33] While détente, a period of measured cooperation and lessening of tensions with the Soviet Union, would follow those first two Cold War decades, containment was substantially revived during the second half of President Jimmy Carter's term and the years of President Ronald Reagan's two terms. Ultimately, Kennan's Long Telegram was of grave importance both for generating many subsequent U.S. foreign policy actions and for the effects many of those actions would have in nations around the world. Kennan, however, would soon come to caution against the global application of his ideas.

CRISES OF 1946

While a new and distinct way of understanding the postwar world had taken shape in the minds of American leaders, subsequent international events would help drive Kennan's message home. This leads to an important question—did events occurring in real time or high-level intellectual conceptions of international relations do more to increase tensions and cause the Cold War? Perhaps the best answer is both. Such interplay is apparent in the first major Cold War crisis, which was unfolding as the Long Telegram arrived. The standoff occurred not in Europe, however, but in Central Asia, and seemed to threaten an expansion of superpower tensions beyond Europe's borders less than a year after victory against Nazi Germany. Iran, along with Afghanistan, had long been an area where Britain, seeking to create buffers for its empire in India, had vied with Russia for influence throughout the 19th and early 20th centuries. Looking to escape the traditional threats from these two powers, the leader of Iran in the 1930s turned to Germany for help in railroad construction. When the Nazis invaded the Soviet Union in June 1941, these railroads became a critical lifeline over which American Lend-Lease aid could reach reeling Russian forces. Other routes existed, but the ice-infested waters north of Russia and the German U-boats roaming the North Atlantic made the overland routes across Iran very attractive to the Allies. A Nazi sympathizer leading Iran seemed to threaten these supply lines, particularly with German divisions pouring into Russia and the United States not yet in the war, so in August 1941

THE GREAT GAME OF EMPIRE IN ASIA

During the second half of the 1800s, Russian imperial expansion into Central Asia made the British, who had taken over most of India by the early years of the 1800s, very nervous. For centuries, the traditional invasion route from Central Asia south into the heavily populated and wealthy regions of northern India could only go through Afghanistan due to deserts to the west and mountains to the east. With only Iran and Afghanistan in between the Russian and British Empires, both sides continually sought to install leaders friendly to their own interests. The British even twice sent large armies into Afghanistan, in the First and Second Anglo-Afghan Wars of 1839–1842 and 1878–1880, to prop up pro-British rulers. Neither intervention went well, often with the British Indian Army suffering heavy losses. Some scholars therefore see the Soviet threat to the Middle East and Central Asia during the Cold War as an extension of this "great game" that had been going on for almost a century before the Cold War began.

British and Russian forces jointly occupied Iran and placed a pro-Allied leader in power.

By early 1946, however, Stalin did not want to leave Iran. A staunch pro-Western ally still more than three decades from the Revolution of 1979, Iran charged the Russians with meddling in their internal affairs. Particularly, the Soviets were supporting separatists in the oil-producing northwestern region, located near the larger oilfields around Baku in the Soviet Republic of Azerbaijan and populated by the same ethnic group as Azerbaijan.[34] In fact, at one point in December 1945 Iranian forces moved north to deal with an "insurrection" in the northwestern region, according to U.S. Secretary of State Byrnes, and were blocked by some of the thirty thousand Soviet troops still in the country.[35] Despite Iranian protests, the U.N. took no action, stymied by Russian excuses and vetoes, and when British and American forces withdrew according to the original timetable, Russian forces remained past the March 2 deadline. As related by Byrnes, Stalin claimed he did not trust the Iranian government and thus Soviet troops were staying to protect the oilfields and refineries just over the border in Soviet Azerbaijan.[36] To Stalin, northern Iran was simply another region, similar to Eastern Europe, where he could ensure Russian security through buffer zones.

To the United States, however, it appeared as an unprovoked attempt to expand Russian control, fitting easily into Kennan's formulation then making the rounds of U.S. officialdom. The Soviets were threatening an ally. American resolve seemed under question. In public forums, at the United Nations, and in direct communications with Moscow, U.S. officials criticized Russian intransigence, firmly backed the Iranian government, and demanded Soviet withdrawal. On March 25, just over three weeks past the deadline, the Russians announced they would pull out in exchange for certain oil concessions from the Iranians. Once the withdrawal was complete, however, the Iranian government reasserted control over the northwestern region and refused any oil agreements for the Soviets, angering Stalin. Yet for Truman and U.S. officials who were increasingly wary of Russia, the lesson was that the United States had stood tough and won, effectively practicing containment a mere few weeks after Kennan first penned the concept. In his memoirs, Truman believed the Iranian crisis had shown that "Russian's ambitions would not be halted by friendly reminders of promises made. The Russians would press wherever weakness showed—and we would have to meet that pressure wherever it occurred, in a manner that Russia and the world would understand."[37] By the spring of 1946, the president had fully embraced the doctrine of containment through strength.

Other events in the first half of 1946 further solidified Truman's perceptions of Soviet actions and added to superpower tensions. A mere three days after the deadline for Russian soldiers to leave Iran, and thus in the middle of the Iranian crisis, former British Prime Minister Winston Churchill spoke in Fulton, Missouri at Westminster College and warned, "From Stettin in the Baltic to Trieste in the Adriatic, an iron curtain has descended across the Continent. Behind that line lie all the capitals of the ancient states of Central and Eastern Europe."[38] The phrase "iron curtain" quickly became commonplace and was a revealing image of the way U.S. leaders had come to think about the Soviet presence outside Russian borders. Yes nothing could get in or out past that curtain, but now with Kennan's advice accepted, the goal was also to keep Soviet iron enclosed behind the curtain. Despite this view of a continent divided, several high-level meetings over the next eight months finalized peace treaties with all the defeated Axis powers in Europe except Germany. The Allied foreign ministers met in Paris from April to July, the Paris Peace Conference took place from July to October, and another meeting of the top foreign ministers occurred in New York from November to December. Agreements regarding Finland, Italy, Bulgaria, Romania, and Hungary were collectively known as the Paris Peace Treaties and signed in February 1947. Despite progress on these other Axis nations, the future of the most important Axis power in Europe created an insurmountable barrier between the two superpowers.

Although FDR had appeared to agree tacitly with Soviet plans for a complete deindustrialization and generally harsh treatment of Germany, Truman and other U.S. officials increasingly moved away from that postwar vision. They came to realize that an economically revived Germany, denazified of course, would be a linchpin in the economic recovery of Europe. German economic strength could also help Western Europe contribute to the standoff with the Soviet Union that was taking shape. In early 1946, both sides still publicly supported the idea of one German nation, but neither superpower was willing to allow a unified Germany if it was under the sway of their ideological enemy. In addition, as the Soviets continued to strip reparations out of their zone in the east, the Americans, British, and French became less interested in extraction and began to focus on rebuilding their zones. The negotiations in Paris in April 1946 had in fact begun with a proposal by Secretary of State Byrnes for, as he put it, "the disarmament and demilitarization of Germany for a period of twenty-five years."[39] The Soviets, however, according to John Lewis Gaddis, "rejected Byrnes's proposed treaty on the grounds that demilitarization could not be guaranteed until all reparations deliveries had been completed."[40] A further point of contention was that shortly after the meeting in Paris began, the man in charge of the American zone in Germany, General Lucius Clay, "announced the suspension of further reparations shipments from the American zone until the four occupying powers agreed to treat Germany as an economic unit," according to Gaddis.[41] To the Soviets, this violated the agreement reached on reparations at the Potsdam Conference. Part of the American frustration with the Soviets came from the fact they were obviously doing whatever they wanted to the eastern portions of Germany, largely extracting industrial equipment and raw materials for use in the Soviet Union. Western Germany could not be treated likewise if it was to help with European recovery. No final agreements were reached on Germany during the rest of 1946 and, as Gaddis relates, already by mid-1946 Truman and Byrnes "became convinced that the Russians would never allow implementation of the Potsdam accords, and from this time on moved toward the concept of a divided Germany as the only alternative to a Russian-dominated Reich."[42] Neither side would allow a unified and economically powerful Germany to complement the strength of their adversary. Lack of agreement on Germany became a main point of Cold War tension over the next several decades, with two formal German nations appearing in 1949.

As if the crises over Iran and the future of Germany were not enough for 1 year, August of 1946 brought another—this time stemming from Russian demands on Turkey. As Daniel Yergin describes, "The Russians sought to have control of the Dardanelles [the Straits separating Europe from Asia] vested solely in the Black Sea powers, and also wanted to share joint fortifications in the Straits with Turkey. The Straits and an assured warm-water port were of course historic obsessions

RUSSIA VERSUS TURKEY

Russia and Turkey had been at odds with each other long before the post-World War II period. They were on different sides in World War I and for centuries Russian leaders had claimed to be the champions of the Slavic populations and Orthodox Christians under Ottoman rule in southeastern Europe. During the late 1800s, Russia and the Ottoman Empire either fought or almost fought several small wars as populations in Bulgaria, Romania, and elsewhere emerged from Ottoman rule. As far back as Peter the Great's reign in the late 1600s and early 1700s, the emerging Russian state fought both the Muslim Tatars of the Crimea, who were Ottoman allies, or the Ottomans themselves. The Russian advance southward into former Ottoman lands was therefore a centuries-old pattern and the Soviet desire in the early Cold War for access to the Mediterranean through Turkey was just the latest in a string of Russian–Turkish clashes.

of Czarist as well as Soviet policy."[43] After the Iranian episode, such potential Russian expansion immediately alarmed U.S. leaders. As Truman later remembered, "This was indeed an open bid to obtain control of Turkey. If Russian troops entered Turkey with the ostensible purpose of enforcing joint control of the straits, it would only be a short time before these troops would be used for the control of all of Turkey."[44] As with Iran, the Truman administration supported Turkey firmly with both public pronouncements and messages to the Russians to rescind their demands. When Stalin did so, Truman believed the encounter had again demonstrated that a tough policy toward the Soviet Union would work. In his eyes, containment had won twice in 1946.

HENRY WALLACE'S ALTERNATIVE PATH

Still, containment could be risky. At some level, the United States had to declare or imply the use of force to back up Iran and Turkey. Although compared to supporters they were fewer in number, critics of Truman's increasingly hardline approach to the Soviet Union charged that he risked war over places mattering little to American security. Others even urged a more accommodating line with the Soviets that recognized their geopolitical security requirements. Why couldn't America work with the Russians as she had during the war years? The future did not have to be a tension-filled standoff between two antagonistic superpowers. The person who came to personify these alternative approaches to containment was in fact a member of Truman's own cabinet—Secretary of Commerce Henry Wallace. In July 1946 Wallace sent a private letter to Truman, in response to the president's request for his take on global events, which stood in stark contrast to the ideas and prescriptions for action laid out in Kennan's Long Telegram. Wallace's pleas for a different view of Soviet actions and a different approach to the other superpower on the planet could have led the Cold War down an alternative path with less tension and fewer war scares. Both Kennan's Long Telegram and Wallace's letter, generated only five months apart, appeared at a time when global events were pressing American leaders to develop new foreign policy agendas and methods. Although the Truman administration, and most subsequent Cold War presidents, would choose Kennan's containment theory, the presence of a clearly articulated alternative very early in the development of the Cold War shows the contingent nature of policymaking. It was not inevitable that Truman would treat the Soviet Union as an enemy or that he would subsequently adopt the Truman Doctrine and NSC-68, which would enhance the American ability to fight a globalized, militarized

Henry Wallace

Henry Wallace was born in 1888 in Iowa and served as the Secretary of Agriculture between 1933 and 1940. He was then President Franklin Roosevelt's Vice President during his third term in office. Ironically, given that Wallace would become a vocal critic of President Harry Truman's foreign policy, he was replaced as Vice President by Truman shortly before FDR died, thus narrowly missing becoming president. He was, instead, Truman's Secretary of Commerce until 1946 when, after a speech in which he seemed to portray the administration's foreign policy toward Russia as more in line with his own desire for a conciliatory approach than it actually was, his opponents in the administration pressured Truman to fire him.

After leaving the administration, Wallace continued to advocate an alternative vision for the nation's foreign policy and largely received support from those on the left of the Democratic Party. He ran for president in 1948 as a candidate on the Progressive Party ticket and while he received no electoral votes, more than a million Americans cast a ballot for him. After 1948, with the Cold War deepening and the McCarthy era on the horizon, Wallace's version of a more progressive politics fell out of mainstream American life for the next two decades. He remained largely out of the public eye until his death in 1965.

Cold War. A different path marked by more cooperation with the Soviet Union was open in mid-1946.

In his letter, one of Wallace's main themes centered on the new nature of international security in the atomic age. He argued that "all of past history indicates that an armaments race does not lead to peace but to war" and, as more countries acquired nuclear weapons, ever-larger arsenals still would not guarantee security.[45] Or at least, victory worth much of anything. To support the latter point he cited Senate testimony that in an atomic war perhaps forty million American civilians would die.[46] He lamented, "That is the best that 'security' on the basis of armaments has to offer us. It is not the kind of security that our people and the people of the other United Nations are striving for."[47] He further questioned how a number of American military developments—new long-range bombers, more atomic testing, increased military funding—"appear[ed] to other nations . . . these actions must make it look to the rest of the world as if we are only paying lip service to peace at the conference table."[48] He described the danger of how the relatively low cost of atomic weapons, "compared with the cost of large armies and the manufacture of old-fashioned weapons," made them attractive security options, but, to him "most important," was how widespread ownership of nuclear weapons would create "a neurotic, fear-ridden, itching-trigger psychology in all the peoples of the world."[49] Overall, atomic bombs might seem "cheap and easy," but nobody would ever win.[50] Instead, for Wallace, true security came in the form of cooperation with other nations, especially powerful ones such as the Soviet Union.

Therefore, claimed Wallace, the United States needed to consider how its actions appeared to others. He noted that the United States was far ahead of Russia in economic productivity and global influence and thus "any talk on our part about the need for strengthening our defenses further is bound to appear hypocritical to other nations."[51] More specifically, Wallace remarked, "It follows that to the Russians all of the defense and security measures of the Western powers seem to have an aggressive intent."[52] He was asking Truman to consider the way the world looked from the Soviet viewpoint. He even included an example whereby "if the United States were the only capitalistic country in the world, and the principal socialistic countries were creating a level of armed strength far exceeding anything in their previous history," U.S. leaders would no doubt find the world very menacing.[53] Seen from this vantage point, "Our interest in establishing democracy in Eastern Europe [Poland, Hungary, Bulgaria, Romania, the Baltic states], where democracy by and large has never existed, seems to her an attempt to reestablish the encirclement of unfriendly neighbors which was created after the last war and which might serve as a springboard of still another effort to destroy her."[54] Likewise, Wallace noted, "From the Russian point of view . . . the granting of a loan to Britain and the lack of tangible results on their request to borrow for rehabilitation purposes may be regarded as another evidence of strengthening of an anti-Soviet bloc."[55] Finally, he claimed, America's "actions to expand our military security system . . . appear to them as going far beyond the requirements of defense" and it looked as though the United States was "preparing . . . to win the war which we regard as inevitable."[56] Given such Western moves of course the Russians were scared. That they were responding with similar measures should not be surprising.

In fact, argued Wallace, the Russians were just acting as expected given their history. He discussed the numerous past foreign invasions of Russia, a country particularly vulnerable to such incursions due to its location in a relatively flat region without easily defensible natural borders.[57] Specifically for the Soviets, the experiences of World War I, Western interference in the Russian civil war, and World War II all heightened their suspicion of other nations and caused them to seek enhanced geopolitical security.[58] The Soviets "see themselves as fighting for their existence in a hostile world," an attitude that generated the Russian "attempts to obtain warmwater [sic] ports [i.e. in Turkey] and her own security system in the form of 'friendly' neighboring states."[59] For Wallace, it made perfect sense that a nation attacked so consistently throughout history would seek geographic security. Here was a fundamental point of difference between Kennan and Wallace. Kennan believed the Soviet Union was something new, due to its Marxist ideology, and would seek to spread its influence and control wherever it could. Thus the need for containment. On the contrary, although he did not explicitly state so, Wallace's language indicated he thought the Soviet Union would achieve a satisfactory level of security on its geographic periphery and then advance no further. As usual, the view one holds regarding these probabilities depends on the view one has of the nature of Stalin and the Soviet system. Were they simply heirs of the Russian Czars seeking only the age-old Russian imperial goal of control over immediately adjacent territory? Or were they bent on world ideological conquest?

What to do with the Soviet Union then? For Wallace, acknowledging their grievances and then seeking a path of cooperation was best. He concisely laid out two distinct policy choices when he noted the contrast between the idea "that it is not possible to get along with the Russians and therefore war is inevitable" and the alternative belief "that war with Russia would bring catastrophe to all mankind, and therefore we must find a way of living in peace."[60] Wallace obviously embraced the second. He called any sort of "preventive war" against the Soviets "stupid" and said it would lead to Red Army control of Europe, leaving the Truman administration with the choice of acquiescing in that control or devastating Europe's cities.[61] Instead, Wallace called for "an atmosphere of mutual trust and confidence" between the two superpowers, in part by trying "to counteract the irrational fear of Russia" among the American public.[62] More specifically, the United States needed to listen to Russian ideas about what was "essential to her own security" because that security, to Wallace, was most important to the Soviets.[63] Furthermore, the West needed "to agree to reasonable Russian guarantees of security," which was a far cry from Kennan's ideas of containment and even more strident calls by other Truman officials to "roll back" Soviet control of Eastern Europe.[64] Instead, for Wallace, mutual understandings that guaranteed the Russians the security they sought marked the path to international peace. Finally, he called for a moment of serious introspection when he labeled as "defeatists" those who wanted military victory over the Soviets.[65] To Wallace, the desire to attack the Russians stemmed from a fear that the Soviet model for society was a "successful rival" to the democratic, capitalist world.[66] Alternatively, Wallace was "convinced that we can meet that challenge as we have in the past by demonstrating that economic abundance can be achieved without sacrificing personal, political and religious liberties."[67]

His very confidence in Western values led him to be sure the West could engage the Soviets without risking its own ruin. Overall, compared to Kennan, Wallace presented a strikingly different vision regarding dealing with the Soviet Union. Engagement, recognition of legitimate Russian security concerns, and mutual understanding were key to world peace.

Given the increasingly anti–Soviet direction of Truman's foreign policy, the administration did not embrace Wallace's ideas. The president read the letter and responded briefly and noncommittally, obviously not much caring for Wallace's views.[68] In fact, Truman had become frustrated with Wallace due to his public criticisms of American and Western foreign policy in the first half of 1946.[69] George Kennan, three months before Wallace's private letter, told the State Department of the "concern and alarm" he felt when reading "a number of statements" by Wallace and others "reflecting the view that Soviet 'suspicions' could be assuaged if we on our part would make greater effort, by means of direct contact, persuasion or assurances, to convince Russians of [the] good faith of our aims and policies."[70] Wallace represented the segment of the Democratic Party still at least open to friendship with the Soviet Union. Such views, however, were becoming anathema to a president determined to stand tough against Stalin. Soviet refusals to budge on Eastern Europe and Germany, Kennan's ideas, and the Iranian and Turkish crises were convincing Truman that no accommodation with Russia was possible. Still, Truman did not finally get rid of Wallace until after a public relations nightmare two months later. On September 12 the Secretary of Commerce spoke at Madison Square Garden and criticized both Soviet and American actions. According to Gaddis, "Wallace's address was an uncharacteristically realistic plea for recognition that the world was now divided into political spheres of influence."[71] He also declared Truman had approved his views on the topic. Secretary of State Byrnes remembered his negotiations in Paris were hampered because of "newspaper reports quoting President Truman as saying at a press conference that he approved the Wallace speech in its entirety."[72] Historians have shown not only did Truman give a green light to the speech, but the two actually met and discussed the material beforehand.[73] Truman later privately noted, however, that he had been "behind in my timetable" of meetings on the day Wallace showed him the speech and implied he approved the speech mainly because he thought the essence was that the United States "wanted to be friendly with all [countries] alike."[74] Wallace, however, went into far more detail in his criticisms of American foreign policy than Truman seems to have expected. When negative reactions flooded in from both the public sector and from a number of Truman's officials, the president eventually forced Wallace out of the administration on September 20.[75]

Figure 2.2 An accidental prop on the desk of former Secretary of Commerce Henry A. Wallace gave graphic significance to this photo, made in September, when Wallace signed his resignation.
Courtesy of Bettmann/Getty Images.

44 ENVISIONING THE SOVIETS: KENNAN VERSUS WALLACE

Although Wallace's views were obviously at odds with the direction of the administration's foreign policy by September 1946, the most significant factor in Truman's decision to fire Wallace was most likely domestic. With congressional elections just two months away, in November 1946, if Wallace had stayed it may have appeared as though Truman really did approve his views. This, as Gaddis relates, "would have given Republicans a magnificent opportunity to base their fall campaign on the charge that Democrats were 'soft' on communism."[76] Divergent foreign policy views combined with domestic political considerations to produce conflict between Truman and Wallace. It is worth remembering that Truman did not simply fire Wallace two months earlier when the Secretary of Commerce sent his July letter. The break did not occur until public scrutiny of their different approaches to the Soviet Union became inescapable. Could Wallace's alternative approach to the Soviet Union have been fully adopted in 1946? The chances were increasingly slim, although not impossible. Could he have prodded Truman in a different direction if he had remained in the administration? Maybe. Perhaps it was never possible, given both Truman's own views that he needed to be tough with the Soviets and his embrace of Kennan's ideas. Still, Truman had moments in 1946 when he continued to entertain the thought of more accommodation with the Russians. Similar to issues involving Cold War causation, how one understands Truman's views of, and reactions to, rapidly occurring domestic and international events in 1946 influences how one views the likelihood that Truman would have embraced Wallace's ideas.

KEY QUESTIONS

Why did Truman and his officials embrace containment by the fall of 1946? Historians differ on the causation. Truman's tendency to view the world in stark black and white terms, the lessons U.S. leaders thought they had learned from the 1930s and World War II, the structure of the international system, and the Soviet Union as an ideological threat bent on world domination are all factors commonly put forward. The reason one finds for why Truman embraced containment also relates to what one thinks of the possibility of policy alternatives in the early Cold War. If Truman's personality was central, it seems unlikely he would have chosen Wallace's more nuanced approach of attempting to view events from the Soviet side. If Russia was always going to be seen as a force vying for global supremacy, again containment is a much more likely choice. If, however, one adopts the view that the international system was structured in certain ways that led to conflict, by presenting both opportunities and challenges as Melvyn Leffler has argued, perhaps the administration could have led the nation, both through foreign policy initiatives and by shaping public opinion, toward a less contentious relationship with the Soviet Union. By choosing to interpret events differently or by choosing to see the Russian side of things, as Wallace urged, the strident containment that would spread over the world might have been avoided. Moments as diverse as tank standoffs in Berlin to the Cuban Missile Crisis to the Vietnam War could have been different. This does depend, as well, on how one views the nature of the Soviet threat—as seeking worldwide domination or as only looking to secure its geopolitical periphery based on past experience. In the end, Truman chose the path of ardent containment. In fact, just over a year after Kennan wrote his Long Telegram, the president would expand that doctrine far beyond what Kennan had intended.

NOTES

1   Joseph Stalin, *Speeches Delivered at Meetings of Voters of the Stalin Electoral District, Moscow: December 11, 1937 and February 9, 1946* (Moscow: Foreign Languages Publishing House, 1954 (http://collections.mun.ca/PDFs/radical/JStalinSpeeches DeliveredAtMeetingsOf Voters.pdf, accessed 3/30/2017), all from 21–22.
2   Gaddis, *Origins*, 299.
3   Note 39 in Telegram, George Kennan to Secretary of State, February 12, 1946, in *Foreign Relations of the United States 1946, Volume VI: Eastern Europe: The Soviet Union* (Washington, D.C.: U.S. Government Printing Office, 1969), 695 (hereafter *FRUS 1946*, Vol. VI); Yergin, *Shattered Peace*, 167.
4   Note 39 in Telegram, George Kennan to Secretary of State, February 12, 1946 in *FRUS 1946*, Vol. VI, 695; Yergin, *Shattered Peace*, 167.
5   Telegram, George Kennan to Secretary of State, February 12, 1946 in *FRUS 1946*, Vol. VI, 695–696.
6   Ibid., 696. The "capitalist encirclement" official was Lazar Moiseyevich Kaganovich, a "member of Politburo of the Central Committee of the Communist Party and Deputy Chairman of the Council of People's Commissars." The "suspicion" official was Georgy Maximilianovich Malenkov, another member of the Politburo. The titles are from p. 696.
7   Gaddis, *Origins*, 302.
8   Yergin, *Shattered Peace*, 167.
9   Quoted Ibid., 167.
10 Telegram, George Kennan to Secretary of State, February 22 1946 in *FRUS 1946*, Vol. VI, 697.
11 Ibid., 697, 698.
12 Ibid., 698.
13 Ibid., 697.
14 Ibid., 699.

15 Ibid., 699–700.
16 Ibid., 699–700.
17 Ibid., 698–700.
18 Ibid., 700.
19 Ibid., 700.
20 Ibid., 701–703.
21 Ibid., 703.
22 Ibid., 703–704.
23 Ibid., 706.
24 Ibid., 706–707.
25 Ibid., 707.
26 Ibid., 707.
27 Ibid., 707.
28 Ibid., 707.
29 Ibid., 707.
30 Ibid., 707.
31 Ibid., 709.
32 Yergin, *Shattered Peace*, 171.
33 Gaddis, *Origins*, 304.
34 Byrnes, *Speaking Frankly*, 119.
35 Ibid., 118–119.
36 Ibid., 119.
37 Harry S. Truman, *Memoirs: Years of Trial and Hope, 1946–1952* (Garden City, NY: Doubleday & Company, 1956), 96.
38 Westminster College, "Churchill's Iron Curtain Speech" (Westminster College, 2014) (http://westminster-mo.edu/explore/history-traditions/IronCurtainSpeech.html, accessed 3/30/2017).
39 Byrnes, *Speaking Frankly*, 125.
40 Gaddis, *Origins*, 330.
41 Ibid., 329.
42 Ibid., 330.
43 Yergin, *Shattered Peace*, 233.
44 Truman, *Memoirs*, 97.
45 Letter, Henry A. Wallace to Harry S. Truman, July 23, 1946 in John Morton Blum, ed., *The Price of Vision: The Diary of Henry A. Wallace* (Boston: Houghton Mifflin Company, 1973), 589–590.
46 Ibid., 601.
47 Ibid., 601.
48 Ibid., 591.
49 Ibid., 592.
50 Ibid., 591.
51 Ibid., 598.
52 Ibid., 596–597.
53 Ibid., 597.
54 Ibid., 597.
55 Ibid., 597.
56 Ibid., 591, 597.

ENVISIONING THE SOVIETS: KENNAN VERSUS WALLACE   47

57 Ibid., 596.
58 Ibid., 596.
59 Ibid., 596–597.
60 Ibid., 595.
61 Ibid., 592.
62 Ibid., 598, 601.
63 Ibid., 597.
64 Ibid., 598.
65 Ibid., 596.
66 Ibid., 596.
67 Ibid., 596.
68 Yergin, *Shattered Peace*, 250–251.
69 Gaddis, *Origins*, 338.
70 Telegram, George Kennan to Secretary of State, March 20, 1946, *FRUS 1946*, Vol. VI, 721.
71 Gaddis, *Origins*, 339.
72 Byrnes, *Speaking Frankly*, 239. Both Gaddis (*Origins*, 340) and Yergin (*Shattered Peace*, 251) note Truman's initial public approval of the speech's content at a press conference.
73 Yergin, *Shattered Peace*, 251; Gaddis, *Origins*, 340.
74 Harry Truman, "Typed Note of Harry S. Truman, September 16, 1946. Truman Papers—President's Secretary's Files" (Harry S. Truman Library and Museum), (https://trumanlibrary.org/whistlestop/study_collections/trumanpapers/psf/longhand/index.php?documentVersion=original&documentid=hst-psf_naid735240-02&pagenumber=1, accessed 3/30/2017), 1–2.
75 Yergin, *Shattered Peace*, 252–254; Gaddis, *Origins*, 340.
76 Gaddis, *Origins*, 341.

CHAPTER 3

Opening Salvos

Truman and His Doctrine

GLOBALIZATION?

Despite processing a new ideological framework through which to interpret Soviet moves in Europe and the Middle East since the end of World War II, the Truman administration had done little to put containment into action beyond reacting to individual events. Then, from early 1947 until mid-1949, significant developments occurred that would help the United States fight the Cold War, namely the Truman Doctrine, the National Security Act, the Marshall Plan, NATO, and the formation of West Germany. Yet these moves stimulated questions both at the time and among historians since. Was the United States simply responding to the Soviet threat? Or did American moves scare the Soviets into believing their own worst fears about Western intentions, leading them to respond by deepening their hold over Eastern Europe and supporting a communist coup in Czechoslovakia? What was the best way to pursue and preserve American and Western interests in Europe and around the world? In addition, how did the creation of a national security apparatus in the United States affect policymakers and their actions abroad? Was domestic influence on foreign policy a net positive or net negative for America and the world? Henry Wallace again best represented the opposition that existed in 1947 to a growing anti-Soviet consensus and while the way this history played out is known, examining those who put forth alternative visions helps expose potentially different ways the Cold War could have proceeded.

Figure 3.1 Ernest Bevin signs the North Atlantic Treaty as Harry S. Truman and Dean Acheson look on.

THE TRUMAN DOCTRINE

Greece had suffered terribly during both World War II and the two years following its end. After initially blocking and pushing back an Italian invasion in late 1940, German forces in the spring of 1941 overwhelmed the Greek army and a British force sent to help. Anti-Axis partisan activity then erupted and lasted the rest of the war, with communists becoming some of the most effective and well-known guerillas. By the time the Germans left in the fall of 1944, in order to concentrate their forces against the Russians, an estimated half a million people had died in Greece, the majority of them civilian and mostly due to a famine caused by the Nazis. Unfortunately, the fighting did not end there. The British occupied the country and allowed the Greek king to return from exile to rule, but he faced armed opposition from communists in the mountainous north of the country.[1] As violence escalated and as communist guerillas made some advances, the British continued to provide military and financial support to the Greek government. Yet the British themselves were struggling financially, even requiring a large loan from the United States as discussed earlier. In late February 1947, therefore, the British told the Truman administration they would end their support of the Greek government and withdraw their forces within just a few weeks, by April 1.[2]

Truman and most of his officials reacted with alarm. As the president remembered in his memoirs, if Greece fell to communist control, it would mean "the extension of the iron curtain across the eastern Mediterranean. If Greece was lost, Turkey would become an untenable outpost in a sea of Communism."[3] In addition to envisioning a failure of the containment strategy should Greece fall, Truman displayed an early form of what would become known as the "domino theory." American leaders would use that concept starting in the 1950s to warn that if one nation fell to

---

GREECE IN WORLD WAR II

Although the Greek army at the beginning of World War II had been able to stop an Italian invasion, a second one by German forces overwhelmed them. The British sent forces to help, but both groups were pushed back and the British eventually had to leave, with the Greek army surrendering in April 1941. In May, a German invasion of the island of Crete, to the southeast of mainland Greece, was also successful and the Germans again defeated British forces sent there to help the Greeks. These events were only the latest in a string of German victories that lasted almost two years from the summer of 1939 to the summer of 1941, even before the initially successful German invasion of the Soviet Union.

communism, its neighbors would soon suffer a similar fate. Most famously this analogy was applied, incorrectly as it turned out, to South Vietnam. Furthermore, beyond just a potential extension of Soviet control, Truman felt American credibility was at stake. He worried about the "implications in the Middle East and in Italy, Germany, and France" if the United States failed to help countries who were still outside the Soviet orbit.[4] If the United States did not aid an anti-communist government in Greece, why should other nations trust American promises of help? The substantial and clear ties between the United States and Europe provided by the Marshall Plan and the development of NATO were still in the future. In early 1947, U.S. engagement with the world remained tenuous.

In fact, the heightened level of American involvement in Europe and around the world after World War II was not inevitable. Many Americans had of course come to consider wrong the isolationism of the 1930s, but Truman knew there were still strands of such sentiment in the American public and among some politicians. Truman, however, was a true Wilsonian. During and immediately after World War I, President Woodrow Wilson envisioned a new international order based on his Fourteen Points and a new organization, the League of Nations. Wilson advocated a much deeper American involvement in the world than in the past because he believed American security depended on events outside American borders. Arguing that other democracies would be U.S. allies, he claimed it was to America's benefit to ensure other nations were, or could become, democratic, thus enhancing American security while simultaneously spreading American ideals. The internal makeup of other governments around the world thus mattered for American security. They mattered even more in the late 1940s because a powerful enemy with an alternative ideology threatened to take over most, if not all, of the resources and populations of Europe and Asia. Should one nation control that much power in an age of massive air power, large navies, and, soon, atomic weapons, America's two-moat defense would mean virtually nothing. The United States could best defend itself by keeping the front lines of conflict far away from American shores, which meant support-ing both current and potential allies around the world. As Truman put it, "Inaction, withdrawal, 'Fortress America' notions could only result in handing to the Russians vast areas of the globe now denied to them."[5] With the Red Army appearing to loom threateningly on the horizon, Truman felt he needed to act.

Still, Truman had to prepare the ground carefully for the policy that would become the Truman Doctrine. He was correct in his assessment that isolationist streaks still existed in the public and in Congress. While Americans supported the goals of helping out a devastated Europe and

OPENING SALVOS: TRUMAN AND HIS DOCTRINE

Woodrow Wilson

Woodrow Wilson was the last president of the Progressive Era and was in office between 1913 and 1921. He was born in 1856 in Virginia, achieved high levels of education, and was even a professor before becoming governor of New Jersey. He then won the contentious 1912 election, which showcased candidates espousing various strands of the progressivism of the era. Although he kept the United States out of World War I for the first three years of the conflict, he intervened often in Latin America, twice sending troops into Mexico during that country's revolutionary period.

After the United States entered the European conflict, Wilson's rhetoric of making the world "safe for democracy" and his Fourteen Points for a peaceful postwar international system gained him worldwide fame. Unfortunately, at the Versailles Peace Conference in 1919, he was unable to convince France and Britain to adopt a less punitive approach to Germany, an approach that ultimately contributed to German resentment and the rise of Hitler. His League of Nations was created, although isolationist sentiment in the United States prevented America from joining it. While campaigning in support of the League, he suffered a stroke in October 1919 and another stroke caused his death a few years later in 1924. He did not achieve all he wanted at the time, but in the long run he was able to drastically expand America's presence overseas and its engagement with the world. While the 1920s and 1930s witnessed a resurgence of isolationist sentiment to a degree, after Wilson virtually every American president believed the United States could simultaneously pursue both its ideals and its strategic interests around the world by being globally engaged and promoting the formation of democratic nations.

opposing Soviet communism, the methods to pursue those goals were still vague and under debate. On February 27 and again on March 10 Truman met with key members of Congress to discuss his upcoming announcement of financial support for Greece and Turkey.[6] Truman felt he had some convincing to do because "some in the group were men who would have preferred to avoid spending funds on any aid program abroad. Some had, not so long ago, been outspoken isolationists."[7] For instance, Senator Robert Taft of Ohio, a major advocate of an isolationist foreign policy in the 1930s, was present at the second meeting. Historian Alonzo Hamby notes that after Truman's speech introducing his Doctrine, "Taft attacked the Greek–Turkish aid bill from virtually every angle and then wound up voting for it" because while some conservative leaders "were old isolationists and instinctive critics of any new spending program . . . they also were visceral anti-Communists who would find it difficult to vote against containment measures."[8] With key Congressional figures on board, on March 12, 1947 Truman delivered in front of Congress perhaps his most memorable speech. He laid out a globalized expansion of the containment concept, and thus the Cold War, in what would become known as the Truman Doctrine.

Of course, Truman had to focus on Greece specifically, but the way he discussed the situation in Greece helped him make the case for a larger U.S. role in the world. He admitted the Greek government was not perfect and intimated that the United States was pressuring it to make positive changes, but most of his material on Greece emphasized its poverty and resulting instability.[9] Similar to later justifications for Marshall Plan aid to Western Europe, Truman warned that people beset by deprivation tended to find radical alternatives, including communism, increasingly acceptable. As he intoned toward the end, "The seeds of totalitarian regimes are nurtured by misery and want. They spread and grow in the evil soil of poverty and strife. They reach their full growth when the hope of a people for a better life has died."[10] Only with substantial outside aid would the Greek people be enticed away from communism and be able to "restore internal order and security, so essential for economic and political recovery."[11] With American help, Greece would once again become stable and productive. Truman also saw a similar threat, and a similar opportunity for America to act, regarding Turkey. He argued that Turkish "integrity

Robert Taft

Robert Taft was born in Ohio in 1889 and was the son of President William Taft (in office 1909–1913 between Theodore Roosevelt and Woodrow Wilson). Rising up through Ohio politics, he was then one of the most important U.S. Senators during his time in Washington between 1939 and 1953. Although a visceral anti-communist, he was also one of the last proponents of American noninvolvement in world affairs. This attitude was prominent especially in the 1930s, with various groups in the United States, including key government and public figures, advocating nonintervention in Europe's problems and an overall neutralism in foreign policy. Thus the United States stayed out of the Spanish Civil War between 1936 and 1939 and did nothing to back up the Western democracies as Hitler's power grew. Taft was one of the most prominent Republicans who thought in this vein and he continued to do so immediately after World War II. Even though he came around to the idea that containing the Soviets was a good idea, he remained wary of the United States overcommitting itself abroad. He died while still in office as a U.S. Senator in 1953.

54   OPENING SALVOS: TRUMAN AND HIS DOCTRINE

is essential to the preservation of order in the Middle East" and warned, "If Greece should fall under the control of an armed minority, the effect upon its neighbor, Turkey, would be immediate and serious. Confusion and disorder might well spread throughout the entire Middle East."[12] Here again was an early form of the domino theory that the "fall" of one nation to communism would severely impact its neighbors, likely, in Truman's mind, increasing the threat of additional communist takeovers. Globalizing this idea, Truman claimed the "collapse of free institutions and loss of independence would be disastrous not only for them but for the world. Discouragement and possibly failure would quickly be the lot of neighboring peoples striving to maintain their freedom and independence."[13] An increasingly interconnected world held interconnected threats.

Those threats could be both internal and external to a given nation and, promised Truman, the United States would help any country facing them. In Greece, Truman specified the danger presented by "the terrorist activities of several thousand armed men, led by Communists" in the north.[14] Later in the speech, the president placed a general promise of American aid at the core of his Doctrine when he claimed, "It must be the policy of the United States to support free peoples who are resisting attempted subjugation by armed minorities or by outside pressures."[15] There were no caveats in this statement. While the specific context involved Greece and Turkey, Truman knew he was committing the United States to a global policy of assisting countries deemed to be under threat by communists. This statement definitively took American Cold War foreign policy beyond the boundaries of Europe (and Japan) and told the world the United States would block communism anywhere, whether the communist threat came from an internal insurrection, as in Greece, or the Red Army. Indeed, in the speech, Truman noted that the United Nations, ostensibly in efforts led by the United States, needed to be "willing to help free peoples to maintain their free institutions and their national integrity against aggressive movements that seek to impose upon them totalitarian regimes."[16] While he did not mention the Soviet Union by name, he did note "violation[s] of the Yalta agreement" in specific Eastern European countries, and thus was clearly pointing a finger at Russia.[17] Truman also focused on the stark choice between democratic capitalism and communism. The United States represented freedom in all areas of life, society, and government and the other side, personified by the Soviets, was marked by "terror and oppression, a controlled press and radio; fixed elections, and the suppression of personal freedoms."[18] Ultimately, in Truman's dichotomous thinking, a unique "moment in world history" presented itself in which "every nation must choose between alternative ways of life."[19] In sum, after March 12, 1947, countries would have to pick a side and the United States would aid any who chose the side of right.

Truman also showcased his Wilsonian vein as he combined American ideals with American interests. He spoke of democracy for Greece and of how "the United Nations is designed to make possible lasting freedom and independence for all its members."[20] He used the words "free" or "freedom" more than twenty times. In addition, Truman explicitly invoked American security. He was trying to persuade the American public to support a globally expansive policy and, lest any doubts lingered, he argued this new approach would make the nation safer. Clearly invoking the Soviet threat, Truman argued, "Totalitarian regimes imposed on free peoples, by direct or indirect aggression, undermine the foundations of international peace and hence the security of the United States."[21] No longer could America hide behind its two moats. Peace and democracy overseas mattered for American safety at home. As noted above, it is worth remembering that in March 1947 the Marshall Plan and NATO, which were explicit American commitments to Europe, were still in the future. The United States had not yet issued any ironclad, lasting guarantees that it would continue aiding the remaining non-communist nations in Europe, let alone elsewhere. Truman therefore had to tie American security deeply to places abroad, and he did so most clearly when he claimed, "If we falter in our leadership, we may endanger the peace of the world—and we shall surely endanger the welfare of our own nation."[22] In its promises to support those threatened by communism and in its call for sustained American involvement in the world, the Truman Doctrine laid the ideological and rhetorical groundwork for a number of later American policies and actions. The latter included both successful aid and security programs in Europe as well as a troubling legacy in Vietnam born of the belief that communist success there would cause a domino effect in Southeast Asia. Although there was some debate, the funding Truman requested for Greece and Turkey easily passed Congress a few weeks later. It took an additional two years, but by mid-1949 the communists in Greece were defeated, with tens of thousands dead.

The motivations for issuing the Truman Doctrine have been widely debated by historians. Truman's supporters claim his view of the communist, and especially Soviet, threat was accurate and timely. For instance, Alonzo Hamby argues that in the speech Truman "almost instinctively had grasped what was perhaps the central issue of the twentieth century," which was "the eventual triumph of a universal world order based on liberal values." [23] Furthermore, "Truman believed, on the whole rightly, that he had stated larger truths."[24] These historians largely declare the speech a triumph. Others, however, claim the international situation at the time did not truly necessitate such a drastic expansion of American foreign policy. Walter LaFeber argues, "The Soviet Union had been less aggressive in the months before the President's pronouncement than at any time in the postwar period."[25] For instance, although the Yugoslav communist leader Josip Broz Tito was supplying the Greek communists from next door, we now know Stalin had urged restraint on Tito and did not want to anger the Americans unnecessarily over Greece.[26] Therefore, American security may not have been as threatened by the Greek situation as Truman believed. If Greece had fallen to communism, it may have been allied more closely to Tito's Yugoslavia, who was on such increasingly bad terms with Stalin that in June 1948 Stalin kicked Yugoslavia out of the Cominform. Still, other historians believe the conditions in Europe in early 1947 were structured in such a way that it was likely Truman would adopt such a policy. Melvyn Leffler claims, "Truman acted in the international arena because he feared Stalin would exploit conditions to aggrandize Soviet power."[27] In essence, for Leffler, Truman could not afford the risk that Stalin would gain from a Greek communist takeover.

While historians agree the Truman Doctrine was a radically new policy committing the United States to a global presence, they hotly debate the effect of the speech. Truman's defenders usually claim the Soviet threat was imminent, omnipresent, and had to be opposed firmly, thus the effect was a correct demonstration of resolve in the face of Russian intransigence. His critics, however, argue that a policy condensing the entire world into a strict bilateral contest created blinders to any problems in America's approach to the world or to any deficiencies in anti-communist allies abroad. LaFeber notes, for instance, "The doctrine became an ideological shield behind which the United States marched to rebuild the Western political-economic system and counter the radical left. From 1947 on, therefore, any threats to that Western system could be easily explained as communist-inspired, not as problems that arose from difficulties with the system itself. That was a lasting and tragic result of the Truman Doctrine."[28] Was Truman right that communists lurked around many corners and had to be met with strength? Or did his Doctrine narrow the available policy choices for himself and for future American leaders, increasing the likelihood of conflict and preventing them from seeing the world in a more nuanced way where not every change in government significantly affected U.S. foreign policy goals or national security? While not yet a full-fledged opposition to Truman's foreign policy, two months after the speech Kennan and his Policy Planning Staff in the State Department urged the administration to "remove in particular two damaging impressions," one of which was "that the Truman Doctrine is a blank check to give economic and military aid to any area in the world where the communists show signs of being successful."[29] Fifteen months after penning the Long Telegram, Kennan was worried about what he deemed an unnecessary global commitment of American resources.

HENRY WALLACE'S WARNINGS

Although much of the public and most Congressional leaders supported Truman's position, debate did occur and the primary critic of the president's new foreign policy vision was again Henry Wallace. As Hamby relates, after Wallace's forced resignation he became editor of the left-leaning *New Republic* and "had a strong appeal to those on the left who continued to think of the Soviet Union as a wartime ally rather than a hostile power."[30] He gave a number of speeches against the Truman Doctrine shortly after its announcement and on March 27 he articulated his views most clearly. Wallace condemned Truman's ideas as militaristic and argued for spending on "an all-out worldwide reconstruction program for peace" because "the world is hungry and insecure."[31] He also warned of the open-ended nature of the Doctrine, claiming that in the new policy "there is no country too remote to serve as the scene of a contest which may widen until it becomes a world war."[32] Relatedly, American prestige would suffer because, under the Doctrine, "there is no regime too reactionary for us provided it stands in Russia's expansionist path."[33] Wallace worried that "America will become the most-hated nation in the world" if it came to support dictators and oppose democratic movements simply based on perceived Soviet threats.[34] Indeed, many historians have adopted this exact criticism. They charge that viewing the world in strictly bilateral terms led to American involvement with a number of unsavory leaders, sometimes at the expense of genuine democratic movements.

Instead of creating a more peaceful world, Wallace argued, the Truman Doctrine would in fact make it more dangerous. As he did in his private letter to Truman in July 1946, Wallace urged consideration of the way Russia would view American moves. Seeing the United States as antagonistic, the Soviet "reply" would be to "increase the pressure against us" and thus, Wallace believed, "Truman's policy will spread communism in Europe and Asia."[35] Fundamentally, "When President Truman proclaims world-wide conflict between East and West, he is telling the Soviet leaders that we are preparing for eventual war."[36] In Wallace's estimation, the Truman Doctrine would be self-defeating, ironically increasing the presence of communism around the world. It would also risk an armed conflict by essentially telling the Russians there could never be compromise between the two sides. There would be severe domestic costs too. The policy adopted ostensibly to defend the American way of life would end up destroying it because, warned Wallace, "civil liberties will be restricted; standards of living will be forced downward; families will be divided against each other; none of the values that we hold worth fighting for will be secure."[37] Ultimately in the spring of 1947, Truman's views won out with most U.S. leaders and the public. Wallace would go on to run for the presidency the next year as the Progressive Party candidate, but his ability to alter the course of American foreign policy steadily decreased, especially because he no longer held a government position. Still, he continued to represent an alternative voice to the administration's hardening line in the Cold War. In fact, his final intonations against the threat to American liberties and values at home were taken seriously by a number of American leaders, even if Wallace was not the acknowledged source. How was America to fight a global Cold War against a powerful ideological enemy without coming, in the end, to mirror that enemy?

DEBATES ON THE INFLUENCE OF "NATIONAL SECURITY"

The National Security Act of 1947 crystalized concerns over how to avoid suppressing American liberties at home. The ominous sounding title indicated U.S. policymakers were thinking in broad, encompassing ways about how to protect the country from a long term threat. Yet in the pursuit of national security, how was America to avoid becoming the very thing it opposed? The Act, along with some minor modifications later, replaced the former cabinet-level position of Secretary of War with a new Secretary of Defense, again indicating the administration's desire to enhance national security on a permanent basis. The Joint Chiefs of Staff, a council of the top military brass created during World War II, became permanent. The Act also created the National Security Council (NSC), a group of high-level aides who advised the president on national security matters. Accompanying this council was another position that by the 1950s would grow into the cabinet-level National Security Advisor. Numerous boards and departments were also created or reorganized, but the other important part of the Act was the creation of the Central Intelligence Agency (CIA), which would go on to play a prominent role in many American Cold War encounters. Essentially, Truman believed "the antiquated defense setup of the United States had to be reorganized quickly as a step toward insuring our future safety and preserving world peace."[38] By early 1947, Truman considered the prime threat to American safety and world peace

OPENING SALVOS: TRUMAN AND HIS DOCTRINE   59

to be the Soviet Union. The aspects of the National Security Act that went beyond mere military reorganization, such as the NSC and CIA, indicated the president and his aides were constructing a national security apparatus to conduct a lengthy struggle against global communism.

Yet, as excellent historical scholarship has shown, such enhanced government power did not turn the United States into a version of the Soviet Union. As much as the American state grew during the Cold War, civil liberties, capitalism, and federalism remained robust in the United States. Historian Aaron Friedberg has produced some of the best work on this subject and he argues the national security state took the specific form it did during the Truman and Eisenhower presidencies, between 1945 and 1961, due to a combination of the need to combat the Soviet Union globally and the presence of domestic forces restraining the size and growth of the state. This allowed the United States to increase its power while keeping core ideals in place, argues Friedberg. In fact, these domestic forces played a role in producing victory in the Cold War because "the ideological and institutional limits on liberal democratic states appear to have contributed to the technological and overall economic dynamism of their societies," factors that helped the United States prevail in its contest with the Soviet Union.[39] In sum, Friedberg claims,

> The fragmented character of the American political system, and in particular the separation of powers between the executive and legislative branches, tended to place considerable obstacles in the way of those who wanted to build stronger, more highly centralized power creating mechanisms. Ideas also acted to shape the struggle over policy among self-interested groups, increasing the influence of those adopting an 'anti-statist' stance, while weakening the hand of those whose views could be characterized, fairly or not, as 'statist.' [40]

Certain beliefs and domestic structures produced checks on how large the national security state would grow and shaped a number of its characteristics so that it ended up increasing American power abroad without destroying liberties at home. The line between the domestic and international spheres blurred as forces within America influenced the specific structures created to fight the Cold War overseas.)

There are others, both in the public and in the historical profession, who think the Cold War national security state grew too large and too invasive. This has been a critique since at least the 1960s and recently Campbell Craig and Fredrik Logevall have especially represented this view, arguing domestic pressures did lasting damage by perpetuating the Cold

War. Friedberg does note the influence of public opinion, but focuses largely on debates within U.S. policymaking circles. Alternatively, Craig and Logevall explore the blurring of the public–private divide and the ways the "military–industrial complex" and "party politics," in which the Soviets were always demonized, consistently influenced politicians to avoid any attempts to engage Russia.[41] Acceptable foreign policy choices thus became quite narrow for various presidents. In stark contrast to Friedberg, therefore, Craig and Logevall believe domestic influences led to enormous costs for the United States, including the lives lost in Korea and Vietnam, the "trillions of dollars [spent] on Cold War interventions of dubious worth and on weapons systems that had little or no obvious utility in an era of Mutual Assured Destruction," and, perhaps most alarming to them, "the militarization of American politics."[42] Did American institutions and ideology positively restrain "statist" growth during the Cold War or did American domestic constituencies, including arms manufacturers and party politicians, enhance the growth of the state and militarize American Cold War foreign policy for their own ends? The debate will continue.

THE MARSHALL PLAN

Truman, however, had to make decisions in real time and his advocacy of deeper U.S. engagement in the world soon expanded beyond Greece and Turkey. Despite America's willingness to defend Western Europe from the Red Army and despite America's monopoly, until 1949, on the nuclear bomb, communism could still sprout organically within Western European nations. As Europe struggled to recover from wartime devastation, millions of people remained without adequate living arrangements. The winter of 1946–1947 was also one of the harshest on record. Crops and livestock withered, fuel for heating was in short supply, and, as historian Daniel Yergin relates, as late as May 1947 some in Austria and Germany were living on as little as 900 calories a day.[43] In France, elections in late 1946 and early 1947 brought to power a government with some socialists and communists in high-level positions. While occurring before the harsh winter, Italy's election in the summer of 1946 produced a legislature that was around 40 percent socialist or communist. While the leaders and parties in power in these two countries were still only center-left, the increasing votes for candidates farther to the left worried American leaders. Truman deeply believed, as he noted in his Truman Doctrine speech, that harsh times made radical political options more attractive. He remembered that in the early months of 1947

> detailed reports came to my office daily from our government agencies about conditions abroad. A steady stream of appeals poured in from representative leaders of many foreign nations, virtually all of whom expressed the gravest concern over the economic situation and over the gains which Communism might score if there were no improvement.[44]

Truman decided to act more quickly once George Marshall, who became Secretary of State in January 1947, came back from Moscow three months later "in a pessimistic mood" after another round of talks with the Soviets had failed.[45] Instead, Truman wrote, "The Russians . . . were coldly determined to exploit the helpless condition of Europe to further Communism."[46] Truman finally felt "there was no time to lose in finding a method for the revival of Europe" because the United States could not lose Western Europe to the Soviet sphere.[47] America had to do something to speed up European recovery.

The campaign for what would become the Marshall Plan, officially the European Recovery Program, contained multiple stages and facets. In the spring and early summer of 1947 U.S. officials began introducing to the American public the idea of massive spending to reconstruct Europe. Negotiations also began with officials from several Western European nations because Truman wanted Europeans to take the lead in implementing American aid. The Russians were also invited to the negotiations and were officially offered Marshall Plan dollars, but, as American leaders predicted, they eventually refused any American money due to the conditions attached. Those conditions, with which Western European nations complied, included the removal of communists from governing coalitions and the adoption of general free market principles. There were many other parts to the program covering specific dollar amounts to be provided, credits for European nations, the reduction or elimination of tariffs, and various other agreements. In the end, the plan helped Western Europe complete its postwar recovery and oriented the region even more toward the United States. Between 1948 and 1951, around $13 billion arrived in Europe from America. Some historians, however, see the implementation of the Marshall Plan as evidence the Soviet Union was not quite the aggressor the Truman administration, and its defenders, made it out to be. They point out that the Soviet foreign minister participated in the early negotiations over the plan. They note it was only after the United States demanded certain concessions from participants in the plan, mainly to move economies toward more capitalist measures, that the Soviets quit the negotiations and began forming their own regional trading arrangements. The latter began with the mid-1947

COMECON

In response to the Marshall Plan, the Soviet Union created first the Molotov Plan between 1947 and 1949 and then COMECON between 1949 and 1991. The Molotov Plan was like the Marshall Plan in that it provided direct economic aid to Eastern European nations, but COMECON was a larger system of economic and trade treaties and arrangements designed largely to link Eastern European economies to that of the Soviet Union.

Molotov Plan and became fully formed with the early 1949 Council for Mutual Economic Assistance (COMECON).[48] Thus, goes the argument, the Soviets did not heavily consolidate or fully orient the economies of Eastern Europe toward Russia until the Americans had already started their own economic consolidation of Western Europe. The Soviets were simply reacting to American moves.

One move that clearly worked in the other direction, with Americans reacting to Soviet activity, was the February 1948 communist coup in Czechoslovakia. Although planning for the European Recovery Program began in the summer of 1947 and aid was officially requested by European nations in the fall, Congress wrangled over the amount in late 1947 and early 1948. Once again Truman faced stubborn domestic resistance to his vision of a more globally engaged United States. Events in central Europe, however, moved Congress to act. Czechoslovakia had emerged from World War II in a murky relationship with the Soviet Union. Communists in Czechoslovakia were the largest party and the country followed a generally pro–Soviet foreign policy, but after the war some leaders began to push for more internal democracy. When Marshall Plan discussions began and some top officials in Czechoslovakia indicated they were attracted to the possibility of U.S. aid, communists in the country launched a coup, backed by the threat of a Red Army invasion.[49] While the takeover was bloodless, it convinced Congress the Soviets were on the march in Europe and they rapidly issued final approvals for Marshall Plan funding in March 1948.[50] The economic and political division of Europe thus increased throughout the second half of 1947 and into early 1948.

GERMANY AND NATO

A divided Germany best personified that deepening division. Historian Vladislav Zubok has shown that until 1947 Stalin and the Soviets continued to advocate "a centralized, reunified, and neutral Germany" in the heart of Europe.[51] The United States likewise voiced support for one German nation, although Western leaders had come to see a reconstructed, reunified, capitalist Germany as key to European recovery. Given the recent past and the fact Germany still contained a large, educated population with much industrial potential and many raw materials, neither side in the dawning Cold War could allow a unified Germany to join their opponent's camp. Therefore, despite pronouncements by both sides that they desired one nation, that reality appeared increasingly unlikely. Zubok finds the point of no return to be the Marshall Plan since "Stalin's reading of the Marshall Plan left no room for German neutrality."[52] More broadly, in a balanced appraisal, Zubok points out that in Germany "every Soviet step toward creating units of military and secret police inside the zone was taken after the Western powers took their own decisive steps toward the separation of West Germany," but he also says Stalin was fine with this pattern because then he could blame the German split on the West.[53] Likewise, Gaddis believes that as late as March 1952 Stalin may have considered "the East Germans as expendable" when he proposed "free elections throughout Germany, which would in turn establish an independent, reunified, rearmed, but neutral state."[54] Western leaders, however, seriously doubted whether "a unified Germany would always remain neutral" and it also appears Stalin approved the delivery of the offer "only when assured" that "it [was] *certain* [emphasis Gaddis's] the Americans would turn the note down."[55] In the end, according to Gaddis, "Stalin seems to have become convinced that his offer had failed *before* [emphasis his] the West had formally rejected it."[56] Zubok and Gaddis thus reflect another debate among Cold War historians. Critics of American foreign policy have argued Soviet moves in East Germany were simply reactions to Western moves in their own zones, but other historians note this was simply because a devious Stalin waited until the West acted first in order to avoid appearing the aggressor.

The specific nature of Western consolidation of West Germany took both economic and political forms. After two additional conferences of foreign ministers in Moscow and London in 1947 fell apart over German issues, Western nations moved toward the development of a separate German nation made up of their zones of control. During what became called the London Conference meetings, which occurred without the Soviets between February and June 1948, the United States, Britain, France, and the Benelux nations (Belgium, Netherlands, and Luxembourg) planned the creation of West Germany.[57] Its economy would be tied closely to the economies of other Western European nations and the three occu-pation zones would be combined in a federalized political framework.[58] A further stipulation, as historian Walter LaFeber notes, was that "the Ruhr's great resources [especially coal] were to be brought under joint control of the Western powers."[59] The western part of Germany, with more people, industry, and resources than the east, was to play a central role both in the recovery of Europe and in holding the containment line against Russia. At this point, reconstituting and rearming German military forces remained out of the question. Only after years of wrangling among the Western allies, with Britain and the United States in support and the French usually in opposition, would West Germany in 1955 establish a new army within the NATO command structure.

Even though a new German army did not yet exist in 1948, Western moves in central Europe alarmed Stalin. A specific trigger came in June 1948 when the Western powers developed a new currency for West Germany and West Berlin. Stalin felt he had to act and decided to target the Western presence in Berlin, which lay completely within Soviet-controlled East Germany. On June 24, 1948 Stalin ordered Soviet forces to block the roads across East Germany that Western powers had been using to supply West Berlin. Since no treaties had been signed regarding

Figure 3.2 C-47 airplanes used in the Berlin Airlift task force at the Wiesbaden air base being loaded with food and supplies for the people of the Russian blockaded city of Berlin.
Courtesy of Byers, Joint Export Import Agency and Harry S. Truman Library & Museum.

OPENING SALVOS: TRUMAN AND HIS DOCTRINE   65

Germany, no formal agreements relating to transit rights existed and, according to LaFeber, "the Soviets now rejected arguments that occupation rights in Berlin and the use of the routes during the previous three years had given the West legal claim to unrestricted use of the highways and railroads."[60] Girded by the lessons of Iran and Turkey and seeking to fulfill the commitments he had voiced in his Doctrine, Truman felt compelled to act in defense of West Berlin. Actually fighting through East Germany to Berlin would be almost impossible and would risk a third world war. Over the next year, therefore, the Western allies conducted the Berlin Air Lift to supply West Berlin's citizens and military forces. Only in May 1949 did Stalin finally give in, with the two sides then developing formal arrangements on the Western presence in Berlin.[61]

In the midst of the Berlin Blockade and Airlift, Western nations further increased their ability to resist potential Soviet advances. In March 1948 Great Britain, France, and the Benelux countries had adopted a mutual defense agreement known as the Brussels Pact.[62] Discussions to include the United States became more urgent when the Berlin crisis began three months later and in April 1949 the North Atlantic Treaty Organization came into existence, with the U.S. Senate approving the measure in July.[63] Part of the wrangling among Western countries over NATO included the formation of an official West German nation and its integration into the new Western alliance system. France's wariness over a resurgent Germany was addressed in part by NATO since it meant America was now committed to Western Europe's defense and would ensure German power was used only for Western benefit. A constitution for a new West Germany followed in February 1949 and the new Federal Republic of Germany (FRG) appeared three months later.[64] Stalin responded in October 1949 with the creation of a formal new East German nation, the German Democratic Republic (GDR). In addition to military

NATO MEMBERSHIP

The founding members of NATO in 1949 were the United States, Canada, Britain, France, Italy, Denmark, Norway, the Netherlands, Belgium, Luxembourg, Portugal, and Iceland. Throughout the Cold War, Turkey and Greece joined in 1952, West Germany in 1955, and Spain in 1982. After the Cold War ended, the Czech Republic, Poland, and Hungary joined in 1999, Slovenia, Slovakia, Romania, Bulgaria, Lithuania, Latvia, and Estonia in 2004, and Croatia and Albania in 2009. Only a few European nations currently remain outside NATO—they include Russia, Ukraine, Belarus, Moldova, Sweden, Finland, Ireland, Austria, Switzerland, and several countries that made up the former Yugoslavia.

integration, the French-led Schuman Plan of 1950 began to link the heavy industries of West Germany, France, Italy, and the Benelux nations. The European Coal and Steel Community followed in 1952 (the treaty was signed in 1951). These were the first steps in the process of European integration that would culminate four decades later in the European Union of 1993. With a firm American military commitment in place and Marshall Plan aid flowing, Western Europe adopted new forms of economic integration to recover from war, present a firm front to the Soviet Union, and chart a new path forward that would hopefully eliminate old animosities, especially the centuries-old feud between France and Germany.

SHIFTING GROUND

As the mid-1940s turned to the late 1940s, the Truman administration adopted both new rhetoric and new methods to combat what it was coming to see as a global Soviet menace. Announcing a commitment to help anyone facing communist threats, putting the Marshall Plan and NATO into place, and helping to create a new West German nation all illustrated an expansive and long-term engagement beyond America's borders. While Henry Wallace continued to warn against unnecessary U.S. antagonism of the Soviet Union, voices such as his were becoming less common and, therefore, policy choices were becoming more limited. In 1947 and 1948 fighting the Cold War also had a profound effect on the size of the U.S. government, with new positions and new organizations created to match new overseas commitments. Historians, however, debate whether the domestic sphere had a positive or negative effect on American foreign policy. Did domestic influences prevent the new national security state from eliminating liberties at home or did those influences actively perpetuate the Cold War, increasing the human and social costs for both the United States and a number of other nations? By the beginning of 1950 George Kennan, the architect of containment in Europe, would become more vocal in his opposition to Truman's global vision of combating communists wherever they existed. While he did not blame the domestic sphere specifically for the things he found wrong in Truman's approach, Kennan feared the United States might become distracted from the real problem, the Soviet military and political threat in Europe, and warned against wasting American resources in places where American security was not truly at stake. Could his words have been heeded and a less interventionist American foreign policy been pursued over the next four decades? As with most Cold War moments of choice and transition, that possibility is still up for debate.

NOTES

1 Truman, *Memoirs*, 98–99.
2 Ibid., 99–100.
3 Ibid., 100.
4 Ibid., 101.
5 Ibid., 102.
6 Ibid., 103, 105.
7 Ibid., 103.
8 Hamby, *A Life*, 393.
9 "Truman Doctrine."
10 Ibid.
11 Ibid.
12 Ibid.
13 Ibid.
14 Ibid.
15 Ibid.
16 Ibid.
17 Ibid.
18 Ibid.
19 Ibid.
20 Ibid.
21 Ibid.
22 Ibid.
23 Hamby, *A Life*, 392.
24 Ibid., 392.
25 LaFeber, *America, Russia*, 55.
26 Leffler, *Souls*, 77.
27 Ibid., 70.
28 LaFeber, *America, Russia*, 63–64.
29 Kennan to Secretary of State, May 27, 1947 in *Foreign Relations of the United States 1947*, Volume III: *The British Commonwealth; Europe* (Washington, D.C., U.S. Government Printing Office, 1972), 229.
30 Hamby, *A Life*, 393.
31 Henry A. Wallace, "Speech on the Truman Doctrine," March 27, 1947 (Ashland University: Ashbrook Center, 2006–2017) (http://teachingamericanhistory.org/library/document/speech-on-the-truman-doctrine/, accessed 3/30/17).
32 Ibid.
33 Ibid.
34 Ibid.
35 Ibid.
36 Ibid.
37 Ibid.
38 Truman, *Memoirs*, 46.
39 Aaron L. Friedberg, *In the Shadow of the Garrison State: America's Anti-Statism and Its Cold War Grand Strategy* (Princeton, NJ: Princeton University Press, 2000), 348–349.

40 Ibid., 6.
41 Campbell Craig and Fredrik Logevall, *America's Cold War: The Politics of Insecurity* (Cambridge, MA: The Belknap Press of Harvard University Press, 2009), 7–10.
42 Ibid., 360–364.
43 Yergin, *Shattered Peace*, 310.
44 Truman, *Memoirs*, 112.
45 Ibid., 112.
46 Ibid., 112.
47 Ibid., 112.
48 LaFeber, *America, Russia*, 75.
49 Ibid., 76–77.
50 Ibid., 77.
51 Vladislav M. Zubok, *A Failed Empire: The Soviet Union in the Cold War from Stalin to Gorbachev* (Chapel Hill, NC: The University of North Carolina Press, 2007), 71.
52 Ibid., 73.
53 Ibid., 71–72.
54 Gaddis, *We Now Know*, 126–127.
55 Ibid., 126–127.
56 Ibid., 128.
57 LaFeber, *America, Russia*, 82.
58 Ibid., 82.
59 Ibid., 82.
60 Ibid., 83.
61 Zubok, *Failed Empire*, 77.
62 Yergin, *Shattered Peace*, 363.
63 LaFeber, *America, Russia*, 91.
64 Yergin, *Shattered Peace*, 395.

CHAPTER 4

How to Fight

NSC-68 and Planning Global Strategy

NEW THREATS AND NEW IDEAS

By the summer of 1949 the United States and the West had developed new methods to fight the Cold War. Marshall Plan aid was flowing to Western Europe, NATO had formed, Western European economic integration had begun, and Truman had shown he would not abandon West Berlin, facing down the Soviets until they relented and reopened supply routes across East Germany. Throughout a series of crises between 1946 and 1948, containment seemed to be working. Yet the Soviet Union remained astride half of Europe and communist ideas expanded elsewhere. In the late summer and early fall of 1949, new dangers appeared and seemed to threaten the West. The successful explosion of a Soviet nuclear weapon and the final victory of communism in China dealt serious blows to any Western sense of security that had developed. In addition, spectacular revelations of Soviet spy activity and the beginning of Senator Joseph McCarthy's communist witch hunts showed how anxiety over international events could affect the domestic realm. Responding to what they considered an increasingly dangerous world, U.S. national security officials, at the request of President Truman, conducted a broad, high-level analysis of U.S. policy as it stood in early 1950. They found it lacking and advised the president to take a series of new actions that would expand both the American military establishment and American activities around the globe. George Kennan had come, by this point, to oppose what he considered the twisting of his containment policy beyond its original purposes, but even his protests could not halt the expansion and militarization of American Cold War foreign policy after the Korean War began in June 1950. Still, Kennan's ideas are worth considering in order to examine what path an alternative foreign policy may have taken.

SOVIET NUKES

In the second half of 1949, the danger the emerging Cold War posed to world peace seemed to increase markedly. The first event that surprised some U.S. officials, and certainly the American public, was the successful Soviet testing of a nuclear weapon. U.S. leaders knew the Soviets were working on such a project, but did not expect them to achieve their goals for at least a few more years. Whatever its usefulness may have been as a deterrent against Red Army divisions poised to invade Western Europe, the American monopoly on the destructive power of nuclear bombs was no more. In addition, the manner in which the West learned of the test seemed ominous. The Soviets did not initially publicly announce what had happened. As Truman relates in his memoirs, only after an initial discovery and three weeks of examining high-level atmospheric winds for increased radiation levels did the United States confirm the Soviets must have successfully tested a bomb.[1] We now know the actual date of the test was August 29 at a remote location in what is today the Central Asian nation of Kazakhstan. The president was "surprised, of course, that the Russians had made progress at a more rapid rate than was anticipated" and admitted, "It was my belief that, as long as we had the lead in atomic developments, that great force would help us keep the peace."[2] Despite this, Truman also remembered that he thought "there was no [need for] panic, and there was no need for emergency decisions. This was a situation that we had been expecting to happen sooner or later. To be sure, it came sooner than the experts had estimated, but it did not require us to alter the direction of our program."[3] While the "direction" of policy may not have changed, historians largely agree the pace of the American atomic program increased and the United States began to develop more powerful hydrogen-based nuclear weapons.[4] Truman confirmed as much in his memoirs when he wrote, "One of the positive effects of this development was to spur our laboratories and our great scientists to make haste on hydrogen bomb research."[5] He left out what historians later proved through internal documents—that the president actively ordered and encouraged progress toward the H-bomb.[6] On September 22 Truman told the public about the Soviet test and Walter LaFeber notes how the initial funding for NATO, which had been held up in Congress, was quickly approved.[7] The pattern of events reflected how money for the Marshall Plan had been stalled until the early 1948 communist coup in Czechoslovakia convinced Congress to act.

Ironically, while Western leaders in 1949 feared Soviet machinations against them, research since the end of the Cold War has shown that, based on America's nuclear monopoly between July 1945 and August 1949, many Soviet leaders felt similarly about the West. One of the best analyses is by Vladislav Zubok, who examines internal debates among what he calls the "political class" of top Soviet officials. Zubok claims that at the end of World War II,

> Whether intended or not, the bomb had a powerful impact on the Soviets. All the previous alarm signals [about the West] now matched a new and dangerous pattern. The United States still remained an ally, but could it become an enemy again? The abrupt dawn of the atomic age in the midst of Soviet triumph deepened the uncertainty that reigned in the Soviet Union. This uncertainty forced Soviet elites to rally around their leader. . . . After Hiroshima, Soviet elites united in an effort to conceal their renewed sense of weakness behind the façade of bravado.[8]

Likewise, after U.S. nuclear tests in the Pacific in 1946, "Few in the Soviet political class had any doubt that the American atomic monopoly had become the tool of U.S. postwar diplomacy and that it threatened Soviet security."[9] What emerges is a portrait of the Soviet Union as an empire made cautious in the 1940s by Western nuclear power. Zubok does not explicitly link any specific Soviet actions during this period to their specific fear of American atomic weapons. Yet he argues such anxiety added to the general postwar insecurity Soviet leaders felt as they pursued measures designed to enhance Russian strategic security, such as controlling Eastern Europe. Of course, as noted earlier, other historians still see the Soviets as confident purveyors of Marxist doctrine who were actively seeking to expand their geopolitical influence and control. Either way, after September 1949, American leaders began to feel similar anxieties about an enemy wielding such immense power.

THE FALL OF CHINA

The final triumph of communist forces on mainland China under Mao Zedong at almost exactly the same time added to that American anxiety. The country had been in turmoil since 1911 when Nationalists led by Sun Yat-sen overthrew the centuries-old Qing Dynasty. The new Chinese government could not, however, control the whole nation and both regional warlords and communist parties sprang up by the 1920s. Mao Zedong was able to consolidate the latter groups under his leadership and fighting between Nationalists and communists erupted. While both groups fought the Japanese after they invaded Manchuria in 1931 and the rest of

Mao Zedong

Mao Zedong was born in 1893 and was the most influential person in Chinese history in the twentieth century. During the tumultuous times after the 1911 Chinese Revolution by Nationalists against the Qing Dynasty, Mao consolidated various Chinese communist groups under his control and emerged as the most prominent communist leader in China. He and his forces fought the Nationalists in the 1920s and early 1930s, the Japanese between 1937 and 1945, and the Nationalists again in the late 1940s until finally achieving victory in 1949, forcing Nationalist leader Chiang Kai-shek and the remaining nationalists to flee to Taiwan.

Mao's specific Marxist doctrine emphasized a mass movement among peasants, as opposed to Lenin's Marxism focused more on workers and a vanguard political party. Mao ruled completely, overseeing some of the most devastating periods of twentieth Century Chinese history in the Great Leap Forward, a failed rapid industrialization program, and the Cultural Revolution, a program to rid China of non-communist ideas. The two endeavors led to tens of millions of deaths and tens of millions more imprisoned or losing their jobs. Eventually, Mao became slightly more open to the United States and met with President Richard Nixon in 1972, signing some trade deals and starting the Chinese opening to the West shortly before his death in 1976.

China in 1937, most historians agree the communists gained both strength and the respect of much of the Chinese population during World War II. The Nationalist forces were often repressive, corrupt, and unwilling to fight the Japanese directly. When the global war ended, civil war continued in China. Despite initial advantages in men, material, and the control of many cities, the Nationalists did not reform their practices and eventually communist offensives forced them into permanent retreat. By the late summer of 1949, it was clear the communists were going to win, but the declaration by Mao Zedong of the communist People's Republic of China on October 1, 1949, less than two weeks after the U.S. public learned of the Soviet atomic test, still took many Americans outside of government by surprise. The nationalist leader Chiang Kai-shek and some two million followers escaped to the island of Taiwan, which today remains non-communist.

While the U.S. public was surprised, observers within the Truman administration were not. They had done all they could to aid the Nationalist cause short of committing American combat troops. In fact, the United States had been trying to prevent a communist victory since late 1945. Truman remembered in his memoirs, "The fall of 1945 had brought the

United States face to face with the serious complications which had been building up in China over the years. Few realized the depth of the split within China, the tenuous hold of the National Government over outlying areas, and the lack of popular participation in the country's government."[10] To help, the United States ordered the large Japanese force remaining in China "to hold their places and maintain order" until Nationalist soldiers could replace them, provided fifty thousand U.S. marines to guard ports to free up Nationalist troops for operations elsewhere, and the U.S. Air Force "ferried" Nationalist forces to northern parts of China to take over from the Japanese.[11] The United States was trying to prevent the communists, who already controlled significant portions of the north, from taking more ground as regional power vacuums appeared at war's end. Truman felt increasingly trapped by the situation in China because while he did not want a communist victory there,

THE QING DYNASTY

The final dynasty in China's long history, the Qing were ethnically different than the majority Han Chinese population. The Qing originated in the northeastern region of Manchuria, originally from the Jurchen people, and by 1644 had conquered northern China. They would go on to conquer both southern China and western areas to largely give China the shape it has today. While strong at first, starting in the mid-1800s the Qing were weakened by the increasing intrusion of Western powers who divided large parts of China into their own spheres of influence for trading. Between the 1840s and 1860s the Qing also lost the First and Second Opium Wars to Britain and dealt with a massive internal rebellion, the Taiping Rebellion, that killed an estimated twenty million people. By the early twentieth century the Qing had few defenders left and in 1911 a revolution overthrew them, although fighting between Nationalists and communists then followed.

> The other alternative was equally impracticable. That would have been to throw into China unlimited resources and large armies of American soldiers to defeat the Communists, remove the Japanese from the mainland, and compel Russian withdrawal from Manchuria by force. The American people would never stand for such an undertaking. We decided, therefore, that the only course of action open to us was to assist in every way in the preservation of peace in China, to support the Generalissimo [Chiang] politically, economically, and, within limits, militarily. But we could not become involved in a fratricidal war in China.[12]

HOW TO FIGHT: NSC-68 AND PLANNING GLOBAL STRATEGY

TAIWAN

When communist forces triumphed militarily on the Chinese mainland in 1949, Nationalist leader Chiang Kai-shek and around two million followers escaped to the island of Taiwan and created a non-communist Chinese government. Since the Nationalist Chinese government had been a founding member of the United Nations and since the United States would not formally recognize the communist mainland government until 1979, the Taiwanese government initially held the Chinese seat at the United Nations. This changed in 1971 during the era of détente, when superpower tensions had eased, and the United States agreed to accept the seating of communist Chinese representatives at the United Nations. Since then, though, Taiwan has remained non-communist and has developed an advanced economy and democratic political system. Although the communists on the mainland officially claim Taiwan as part of their nation, Western, especially American, economic and military support for Taiwan continues, creating an uneasy status quo between the two sides.

Truman believed domestic realities limited his policy options to methods short of renewed armed combat for American forces.

Therefore, the main goal of U.S. engagement in China was to convince the communists and Nationalists to form some sort of coalition government. Yet neither side ever agreed to cede any of their power. Although General George Marshall, sent to China by Truman in December 1945 to oversee negotiations, came close to achieving ceasefires or peace agreements at several points, he was never successful.[13] He returned permanently to Washington in January 1947 frustrated with both sides, especially the Nationalists. Truman also largely blamed Chiang Kai-shek, noting his unwillingness to listen to Marshall's military advice and criticizing the "walled-city complex" of Chiang's generals, which meant they simply abandoned the countryside to the communists and stayed in the more easily defensible cities.[14] Ultimately, Truman admitted, the Nationalists lost China "because the government of Chiang Kai-shek did not command the respect and support of the Chinese people. The Generalissimo's attitude and actions were those of an old-fashioned warlord, and, as with the warlords, there was no love for him among the people. There is no doubt in my mind that if Chiang Kai-shek had been only a little more conciliatory an understanding could have been reached."[15] On this topic, historians tend to agree with the president. Neither initial Nationalist numerical superiority nor vast amounts of U.S. aid between 1945 and 1949 translated into victory, largely due to the incompetence of Chiang and his top politicians and generals.

The communist triumph in China was not only important in a geostrategic sense, but also in terms of American politics. Truman, and the Democratic Party, would have to weather the charge of "losing" China. By the late 1940s an influential "China Lobby" had developed in the United States, composed mainly by, as Walter LaFeber puts it, "wealthy, conservative Americans [and Congressmen] who believed Truman was selling out China and the free enterprise system to communists."[16] While Truman, Secretary of State Dean Acheson, and others in the administration understood the precarious situation on the ground in China and resisted increasingly angry calls to help Chiang Kai-shek and the Nationalists at all costs, the existence of this domestic pressure group still presented problems for the conduct of Truman's policies in China.[17] Truman remembered that Congress often put forth bills to provide money or material to "Chiang Kai-shek without laying down a condition that he work with General Marshall" and therefore, the president believed, "The Chinese government [the Nationalists] sought to gain advantages from our government by applying pressures from other directions."[18] Truman felt the American China Lobby severely undermined any chances for successful negotiations in China because "every time someone in Washington or elsewhere in this country made a speech calling for 'all-out aid' to Chiang, the 'die-hards' in China gained new confidence and sabotaged Marshall's efforts to bring about peace. In turn, the Communists, of course, would point to reports of such statements as evidence of American duplicity."[19] Thus "Marshall's delicate task was made infinitely more difficult."[20]

Even as Nationalist success in China became increasingly unlikely, domestic influence on this international issue made it harder

THE SINO–SOVIET SPLIT

Although the threat of two large nations going communist by 1949 caused much concern in the West, by 1960 a Sino–Soviet split had developed. First, their interpretations of Marxist thought differed, with the Soviet Union's Marxism–Leninism focusing on workers and especially on a vanguard party to lead revolutions, while Chinese Maoism focused on a mass movement among peasants, whom Leninists usually considered backwards and not ripe for revolution. Second, the Soviets were usually more open to the idea of a stable status quo with the West, while the Chinese tended to think no such coexistence was possible. Third, the Soviets and the Chinese competed for influence in Third World countries during the Cold War as those countries, especially in Africa, emerged from European colonialism. The contentious attitude between the two nations lasted until almost the very end of the Cold War.

HOW TO FIGHT: NSC-68 AND PLANNING GLOBAL STRATEGY

for Marshall to create a coalition government that included Mao's communists. In addition, American support for the Nationalists from outside the Truman administration ironically contributed to Chiang's defeat later because it played a role in convincing the Nationalist leader he was strong enough to reject participation in any coalition government. Of course, without compromising, he was eventually defeated militarily and forced out of the country. Walter LaFeber relates that even shortly after the communist triumph in China, the China Lobby would not approve more money for South Korea, facing simmering civil unrest although not yet fully at war, unless dollars also flowed to Taiwan and the Chinese Nationalists.[21] Despite this domestic interference in foreign affairs by the China Lobby and despite the administration's awareness of the low probability of Nationalist success, Mao's declaration of a new communist government in China on October 1, 1949 came as a surprise to much of the American public, who to that point had paid little attention to, or had little access to information on, the situation in China. The new Soviet possession of atomic weapons, the movement of the most populous nation on the planet into the communist sphere, and a February 1950 Sino–Soviet Treaty all made the world a much more dangerous place in the eyes of many Americans by the beginning of 1950.

MCCARTHYISM

In this context, foreign affairs could also influence domestic politics. No one took advantage of that connection more infamously than Senator Joseph McCarthy of Wisconsin. Prior to 1950, he was not well-known outside his home state, but he launched himself onto the national stage using a foreign policy issue when on February 9 he announced in Wheeling, West Virginia that there were 205 communists in the State Department. In addition to international communist advances in 1949, the American public had also just witnessed the conviction of Alger Hiss in January 1950 for perjury while he was under investigation as an alleged Soviet spy and, according to Daniel Yergin, "on February 3, Klaus Fuchs, a physicist, confessed in London to spying on the Manhattan Project for the Soviet Union."[22] The American public was thus in no mood to be lenient to suspected Soviet agents. In a similar vein, the House Un-American Activities Committee, formed in 1937, began in 1947 to investigate alleged communist influences in Hollywood. Even those who simply refused to cooperate were often fired or blacklisted. Truman had already felt such domestic pressure on the issue that in March 1947 his Executive Order 9835 ordered federal employees to undergo loyalty

Joseph McCarthy

Born in Wisconsin in 1908, Joseph McCarthy was a relatively unknown U.S. Senator until he began his wild accusations in February 1950 that the State Department was full of communists. While he never allowed anyone to see his "proof," he became a man who could ruin reputations with just his words and for the next four years he, and those who agreed with him, riled up the American political atmosphere with fears that communists were everywhere, including in the government. While there were other domestic anti-communist trends beginning earlier, McCarthy's name is attached to both the era and the methods he used because he became so symbolic of the anti-communist hysteria during the period. Neither President Truman nor President Eisenhower were willing to take the political risk of openly confronting him in order to end his influence, since they believed the American public would electorally punish a party that seemed too friendly to communists. McCarthy's downfall was of his own doing, however, because when the army accused him of seeking special treatment for one of his aides, he began claiming the army, too, was full of communist sympathizers. At the subsequent Army-McCarthy hearings from April to June 1954 McCarthy was exposed, on live television and in a packed courtroom, as a bully to witnesses and a man without any proof. Afterwards, his influence was gone, the Senate censured him, and he died soon after in 1957.

investigations, resulting in several thousand people being fired or resigning. By early 1950, the Cold War influenced the American domestic arena to an immense degree and McCarthy was actually just the most visible manifestation of this Second Red Scare.[23]

While McCarthy's downfall would not come until the spring of 1954 during the Army-McCarthy Hearings, for the rest of his presidency Truman intensely disliked him. In his memoirs, the president railed against how McCarthy caused the public to doubt almost every government official. There might have been a few bad apples, Truman admitted, "But we should not, and we did not, want to treat the remaining 99.9 per cent [sic] of government employees, who are decent and honorable, in a way that would ruin their reputations."[24] In perhaps one of the most candid moments in his memoirs, Truman vented his disgust with the red-baiting of the time when he condemned the way "frequently hearsay evidence is accepted as the truth and is used to smear a government employee in such a way that he cannot defend himself. That is what the Communists do, what McCarthy did, what the so-called Un-American Activities Committee in the House did. It simply cannot be squared with

78 HOW TO FIGHT: NSC-68 AND PLANNING GLOBAL STRATEGY

the Bill of Rights."[25] Still, Truman wrote, "Everyone has the right to express what he thinks. That, of course, lets the crackpots in. But if you cannot tell a crackpot when you see one, then you ought to be taken in."[26] The point here is to show how easily international issues could become domestic ones, as they did with China and alleged (or sometimes real) Soviet espionage. Such was the heightened anti-communism in which the "blueprint" for the Cold War, NSC-68, came into being.

NSC-68

Both the international and domestic arenas in late 1949 and early 1950 appeared to be, fraught with danger and full of communists. It seemed something needed to be done. McCarthy's answer constituted only allegations and investigations and would fizzle out by mid-1954. The Truman administration's answer, on the other hand, was a wide-ranging explanation, justification, and expansion of America's international Cold War mission that would influence U.S. actions abroad for decades. In late January 1950, Truman ordered a comprehensive review of the nation's foreign policy. Paul Nitze, who led the State Department's Policy Planning Staff, chaired the project, which also involved ideas from State and Defense officials who staffed the National Security Council.[27] The actual document would only become publicly available in the 1970s, but the outlines of its ideas and policy implications were visible by contemporaries both at the time and in the years in between its creation and declassification. This was because it was so broad in scope, affecting virtually all aspects of American foreign policy. As Daniel Yergin writes, it was "as important as Kennan's Long Telegram and the Truman Doctrine in postwar history. It was the first formal statement of American policy. It expressed the fully formed Cold War world set of American leaders, and provided the rationalization not only for the hydrogen bomb but also for a much expanded military establishment."[28] Historian George Herring, in his survey of the entire history of America's foreign relations, calls NSC-68 "a sweeping restatement of U.S. national security policy and one of the most significant Cold War documents."[29] When the ideas, claims, and prescriptions of NSC-68 are analyzed, it becomes easy to understand why most Cold War historians echo these sentiments.

The portrait of the world situation NSC-68 put forth in early 1950 was a dire one. In the opening section the authors claimed, "The Soviet Union, unlike previous aspirants to hegemony, is animated by a new fanatic faith, antithetical to our own, and seeks to impose its absolute authority over the rest of the world."[30] In a section titled, "Fundamental Design of the Kremlin," the authors likewise warned that in the areas they already controlled, the Soviets were pursuing "the complete subversion or forcible destruction of the machinery of government and structure of society in the countries of the non-Soviet world and their replacement by an apparatus and structure subservient to and controlled from the Kremlin."[31] The danger was thus very real because "the United States, as the principal center of power in the non-Soviet world and the bulwark of opposition to Soviet expansion, is the principal enemy whose integrity and vitality must be subverted or destroyed by one means or another if the Kremlin is to achieve its fundamental design."[32] Ultimately, therefore, "This Republic and its citizens in the ascendancy of their strength stand in their deepest peril."[33] In addition to the United States being under threat, "the issues that face us are momentous, involving the fulfillment or destruction not only of this Republic but of civilization itself."[34] Similar phrases echoed throughout the document, claiming the Soviets were bent on complete global control and warning that the United States and its allies occupied a precarious position.

The theme of a slave world pitted against a free world also animated much of the document. The future lay either with Soviet victory and human slavery or the triumph of free nations. Between such drastically different ideological systems there could be no middle ground. The authors of NSC-68 assumed the Soviets would act all around the world to further their evil objectives. While specific events and places outside Europe were seldom mentioned, the times they did appear were revealing. The authors warned, "In local incidents it [the Kremlin] threatens and encroaches both for the sake of local gains and to increase anxiety and defeatism in all the free world."[35] Since western nations at the time possessed inadequate military strength to counter Soviet moves, other than nuclear weapons that would risk a third world war, the authors believed the "continuation of present trends is likely to lead, therefore, to a gradual withdrawal under the direct or indirect pressure of the Soviet Union, until we discover one day that we have sacrificed positions of vital interest."[36] Eventually the United States would be the last country standing and would inevitably fall to the Soviets. This assumption that any "local" or "indirect" Soviet advance constituted part of a larger pattern that, if not checked, would lead to ultimate Soviet victory came to figure prominently in the thinking of most Cold War presidents after Truman. As will be seen in the next chapter, picturing the world in such stark, black-and-white terms led many American policymakers to view communist advances anywhere as part of the larger Soviet desire to dominate the world.

While George Kennan would come to oppose significant aspects of the worldview presented in NSC-68, in several places the document reflected two of his key arguments from the Long Telegram. First, the Soviets always operated in crisis mode and needed external enemies to point to in order to justify their repressive rule. Second, if met with outside pressure, the Soviet system would start to collapse internally from its own contradictions. The document's authors claimed, "The Kremlin cannot relax the condition of crisis and mobilization, for to do so would be to lose its dynamism, whereas the seeds of decay within the Soviet system would begin to flourish and fructify."[37] The United States, therefore, could "frustrate the Kremlin design and hasten the decay of the Soviet system" because "if in its forward thrusts it encounters a superior force which halts the expansion and exerts a superior counterpressure," the communist framework in Russia would begin to wobble.[38] In sum, "The only sure victory lies in the frustration of the Kremlin design by the steady development of the moral and material strength of the free world and its projection into the Soviet world in such a way as to bring about an internal change in the Soviet system."[39] Overall, the authors of NSC-68 echoed Kennan's belief that the United States could not achieve victory through a military attack on the Soviet Union, but through the "superior counter-pressure" found in Kennan's idea of containment. In time, this approach would expose the fatal weaknesses and contradictions within the Soviet Union and lead to its transformation away from communism.

Doubting the efficacy of defeating the Soviet Union militarily did not, however, mean the authors of NSC-68 believed military power was useless. Indeed, their recommendations for drastically expanding the size and presence of U.S. and Western forces troubled Kennan and, according to some historians, played at least a part in the American willingness to intervene militarily around the globe in subsequent decades. The authors of the document often discussed at length the need for a stronger military footing for the free world. They worried that postwar demobilization of Western forces had left the United States with only two bad options should the Soviets present a military threat in any given location—immediately escalate to global war, likely with nuclear weapons, or retreat from "positions of vital interest" and, as noted above, eventually lose the battle against Soviet slavery. A turnaround in military strength would also bolster flagging allies who the officials worried might be unwilling to confront the Soviets if the United States did not provide a more credible sense that it could offer military support. In one of the most famous phrases of the document the authors argued, "A more rapid build-up of political, economic, and military strength and thereby of confidence in the free world than is now contemplated is the only course which is consistent with progress toward achieving our fundamental purpose. . . . These, in turn, require an adequate military shield under which they can develop."[40]

Elsewhere they claimed, "It is clear that a substantial and rapid building up of strength in the free world is necessary to support a firm policy intended to check and to roll back the Kremlin's drive for world domination."[41] They further argued "that within the next four or five years the Soviet Union will possess the military capability of delivering a surprise atomic attack of such weight that the United States must have substantially increased general air, ground, and sea strength, atomic capabilities, and air and civilian defenses to deter war and to provide reasonable assurance, in the event of war, that it could survive the initial blow and go on to the eventual attainment of its objectives."[42] Again, the theme of growing the West's military strength was so prominent because the only options in early 1950, according to these U.S. officials, were either global war or retreat in the face of any Soviet pressure. Ultimately, then, an enhanced military presence was "the only means short of war which eventually may force the Kremlin to abandon its present course of action and to negotiate acceptable agreements on issues of major importance."[43] For the authors of NSC-68 the key to protecting the freedom of the free world and to supporting every other Western political and economic objective was the "rapid build-up" of the military capability of the West, and particularly that of the United States.

To that end, the authors laid out a series of general recommendations. The United States had to defend the Western Hemisphere and allies in East Asia and Western Europe. More specifically, the officials recommended an eleven point program that included increased military spending, more military and economic aid to allies, "psychological warfare," expanded intelligence-gathering capabilities, and corresponding plans to pay for all of these items, involving both "increased taxes" and solutions to "the problem of the United States balance of payments" in international trade."[44] Also beneficial would be "covert means in the fields of economic warfare and political and psychological warfare with a view to fomenting and supporting unrest and revolt in selected strategic satellite countries."[45] While this constituted a massive expansion in military spending, foreign aid, and all sorts of other activities overseas, the authors of NSC-68 believed the economy of the United States could easily handle such efforts. Throughout the document they claimed that while the Soviets were currently putting more men in uniform and producing more military hardware than the West, the actual military potential of the West, and especially the United States, had only to be tapped, as in World War II. Then the free world would easily match the Soviets in military preparedness. The authors did warn, "In contrast to us, the Soviet world can do more with less—it has a lower standard of living, its economy requires less to keep it functioning, and its military machine operates effectively with less elaborate equipment and organization."[46] Despite these Soviet advantages, however, the authors remained convinced that if the United States decided to mobilize its strength, it could easily surpass the conventional military capabilities of the Soviet Union. The key was that this would take at least a period of months, if not a couple of years, so the United States needed to start immediately. A final recommendation was to conduct information campaigns to ensure public opinion would support all the recommended expansions of both military strength and other activities to fight the Cold War.

In sum, NSC-68 combined Kennan's concept of containment with the global vision of the Truman Doctrine and added a vastly expanded military establishment. Regarding the scope of their assessment, the authors of the document argued, "The assault on free institutions is world-wide now, and in the context of the present polarization of power a defeat of free institutions anywhere is a defeat everywhere."[47] This attitude would animate many American Cold War actions around the world. It also feeds into the debate among historians over the costs of the Cold War. Did the Soviet Union inspire every event that brought some sort of left-leaning leader or movement to power? Even if they did, were all locations around the world equally important for American and Western security? Either way those questions are answered, the costs of U.S. actions, both for the countries where interventions occurred and for the United States, must also be taken into account. The costs escalated, in part, due to the key component of NSC-68—the militarization of Cold War foreign policy beyond Kennan's original formulation of consistent economic and political pressure against the Soviet Union. In one of the most revealing passages the authors claimed, "In the concept of 'containment,' the maintenance of a strong military posture is deemed to be essential for two reasons: (1) as an ultimate guarantee of our national security and (2) as an indispensable backdrop to the conduct of the policy of 'containment'. Without superior aggregate military strength, in being and readily mobilizable, a policy of 'containment'—which is in effect a policy of calculated and gradual coercion—is no more than a policy of bluff."[48] For the authors of NSC-68, all other American objectives in the Cold War, even including the very concept of containment, depended on a vastly expanded military capability that was to be used to check communist advances anywhere they occurred around the globe. Failure to do so would lead to inevitable retreat, defeat, and the disappearance of freedom and the American way of life.

As NSC-68 made the rounds of U.S. officialdom in April 1950, it received much praise. Although Truman, on April 12, asked "that the NSC provide him with further information on the implications of its

Conclusions" and "that the NSC give a clear indication of the programs envisaged in the Report, including estimates of their probable cost," most other high-level members of the administration immediately approved the document.[49] As Daniel Yergin relates, "For the most part, the acceptance of the premises of NSC-68 was as instantaneous and complete as had been the case with the Long Telegram four years earlier."[50] Charles Bohlen, who was at the time the U.S. ambassador to France but had spent considerable time in the Soviet Union between 1934 and 1946, expressed concern over some vague parts of the document and argued that some of its recommendations and conclusions required better supporting evidence.[51] Still, he believed that "the purpose and the general conclusions" of NSC-68 were "unchallengeable."[52] William Schaub, Deputy Chief of the Division of Estimates in the Bureau of the Budget, found more at fault. He worried about the excessive discussion of military strength in the document.[53] He believed the concept of a "free world" was not helpful, in that the United States had already aligned itself with unrepresentative governments in places such as Indochina and the Philippines.[54] He warned that "many peoples are attracted to Communism because their governments are despotic or corrupt or both" and feared the United States, by supporting such leaders, might "guarantee the eventual loss of the cold war through the proliferation and subsidization of unstable little tyrants."[55] Schaub was not a very influential member of the administration and therefore the most pointed, direct, and potentially impactful criticisms of NSC-68 came from George Kennan. Daniel Yergin reveals the dilemma the author of containment found himself in by the spring of 1950. Yergin claims, "In 1946, he had discounted the utility of diplomacy. By 1950, he was on the other side, afraid that NSC-68 would sanctify the rejection of diplomatic opportunities. He also feared a vast growth in the military establishment and the militarization of foreign policy, for both of which NSC-68 provided the rationalization. And Kennan simply did not believe that the Soviet Union posed a military threat to Western Europe."[56] Instead, Kennan "thought that caution guided Kremlin calculations and that the Soviets were sometimes only responding to Western actions," as some historians, noted above, have argued since.[57] Therefore, as the creation of NSC-68 progressed, Kennan voiced his own views on the world situation in early 1950.

KENNAN AFFIRMS ORIGINAL CONTAINMENT

In mid-February 1950, Kennan issued a hard-hitting memorandum challenging many views of the Cold War U.S. that officials had adopted by that time. The Executive Secretary of the Policy Planning Staff, the group responsible for generating NSC-68, provided a copy of Kennan's ideas to the other members, noting, "It is being circulated for the information of the staff and such assistance as it may represent in the current policy review."[58] The latter phrase referred to the development of NSC-68. While Kennan had not yet seen NSC-68 in its final form, his opening statement challenged one of the central premises of the later document. He claimed, "There is little justification for the impression that the 'cold war', by virtue of events outside of our control, has suddenly taken some drastic turn to our disadvantage."[59] He argued that the final victory of Mao's communists on mainland China was "the culmination of processes which have long been apparent" and "reasonably accurately predicted, long ago by our advisors in this field."[60] More importantly, he noted what he saw as difficulties in the Sino–Soviet relationship and claimed there were "impediments" to the Soviet Union simply exerting "political power" over China.[61] In fact, he warned that divisions between the two large communist nations "would actually be apt to be weakened by any attempts on our part to intervene directly."[62] Therefore he found the "situation" in China "neither unexpected nor necessarily catastrophic," which was a far cry from the alarming language of NSC-68.[63]

Likewise, while the potential Soviet acquisition of a hydrogen bomb at some point in the future was something to be wary of, Kennan thought the Soviet testing of an atomic weapon did not change the balance of world power. He claimed it "adds no new fundamental element to the picture" and argued, "The fact that this state of affairs became a reality [a] year or two before it was generally expected is of no fundamental significance."[64] Even regarding a potential Soviet hydrogen bomb, Kennan believed, "It is we ourselves who have started the discussion about this weapon and announced the intention to develop it. The Russians have remained generally silent of [sic] the subject. . . . The idea of their threatening people with the H-bomb and bidding them 'sign on the dotted line or else' is thus far solely of our own manufacture."[65] Summing up his overall view of the "international situation" in 1950, he claimed the "basic elements are ones which were established largely by the final outcome of hostilities in 1945. Nothing that recently occurred has altered these essential elements; and in so far as we feel ourselves in any heightened trouble at the present moment, that feeling is largely of our own making."[66] Essentially, Kennan was telling fellow officials to calm down, that the twin shocks of 1949 did not actually pose an increased threat to American security.

Kennan then launched into a defense of the value of his original containment doctrine. He argued that in 1945 the "best hope" of the West was "in concentrating on the strengthening of the resistance of other countries to Soviet political aggression" and claimed that since "war was no acceptable alternative" due to Western demobilization after World War II, "a patient and wary policy of reinforcing resistance to Soviet political pressures . . . was the only thing that held out any real possibility of working."[67] The Soviet Union still presented a challenge in the realm of ideas, but the way to combat that type of threat, for Kennan, was "to prove the validity of liberal institutions, to confound the predictions of their failure, to prove that a society not beholden to Russian communism could still 'work'."[68] While Kennan admitted there was obviously a military aspect to the standoff with the Soviets, he thought it unfortunate that some programs the United States had pursued, such as NATO, "were not part of a policy of *military* [emphasis his] containment; but they looked like it. They served their purpose in Europe; but they misled many people there and here into a false concept of what it was we were doing: into a tendency to view the Russian threat as just a military problem rather than as a part of a broad political offensive."[69] In a parenthetical insertion just after the latter statement, he clearly indicated he was talking about the discussions occurring at the time that would produce NSC-68 when he said, "This error has had a great part in producing the present restlessness with our policy; for through these distorted lenses the atomic energy problems, and many other things, take on quite misleading aspects."[70] Kennan therefore demonstrated his fundamental disagreement with what would become the basis of NSC-68, namely a vastly expanded military basis to fight the Cold War. For Kennan, the conflict with the Soviet Union had to remain a primarily political issue and "any serious deviation from it [current policy] could easily lead to [the] most appalling consequences."[71] The rest of the document included Kennan's recommendations to avoid dependence on nuclear weapons, to reconsider certain economic and foreign aid issues, and to conduct a better public information campaign. Overall, however, Kennan was warning fellow policymakers against fully militarizing the Cold War.

EXPANSION PROCEEDS

By the spring of 1950, however, Kennan was out of touch with the main strands of thinking in Washington. Truman initially considered the costs of NSC-68's recommendations to be quite high and, as Daniel Yergin notes, "Truman and his advisers continued to fear that Congress would not approve the money required for the substantial military buildup outlined in NSC-68."[72] Yet when North Korean forces crossed into South

HOW TO FIGHT: NSC-68 AND PLANNING GLOBAL STRATEGY

Korea on June 25, 1950, the administration's requests for more money for the military, and other related programs, no longer faced obstacles. As with funding for both the Marshall Plan and NATO, a new communist move prodded Congress to provide the requested budget amounts. NSC-68 itself would not be declassified for more than two decades, but the programs it outlined were fleshed out and funded. Yergin notes how, although the totals also included the fighting on the Korean peninsula, "expenditures for major national security programs" more than doubled between 1951 and 1953.[73] Regarding NSC-68 specifically, on September 30, 1950 the Executive Secretary of the NSC informed other top officials, "The President has this date approved the Conclusions of NSC 68 as a statement of policy to be followed over the next four or five years, and directed their implementation by all appropriate executive departments and agencies of the U.S. Government."[74] The document thus became the "blueprint" for the Cold War. In the view of most U.S. officials, the second half of 1949 and the first half of 1950 had gone badly for the West. The "loss" of mainland China, the Soviet acquisition of nuclear weapons, and a general fear in the American public of Soviet spies among them all contributed to a sense of crisis that provided the context for the creation of NSC-68. The outlook and prescriptions of the document were therefore rooted in a particular time and place and reflected the fears, as well as the hopes, of most American policymakers almost five years into the Cold War. The view adopted was that the United States needed to expand drastically its military capabilities, and many other types of activities, in order to combat the Soviets globally. While Kennan disagreed and provided a less militaristic vision for American Cold War foreign policy, the administration did not heed his warnings. Some historians today thus wonder if an alternative path, outlined by Kennan and a few other officials, might have achieved Western victory in the Cold War at a far lower cost in lives and money than actually occurred over the course of the next forty years.

NOTES

1   Truman, *Memoirs*, 306–307.
2   Ibid., 306–307.
3   Ibid., 307.
4   Gaddis, *We Now Know*, 100.
5   Truman, *Memoirs*, 308.
6   Gaddis, *We Now Know*, 100–101. The United States successfully tested the hydrogen bomb in November 1952 and the Soviets matched the task in August 1953.
7   LaFeber, *America, Russia*, 91.
8   Zubok, *Failed Empire*, 27–28.

HOW TO FIGHT: NSC-68 AND PLANNING GLOBAL STRATEGY 87

9 Ibid., 60.
10 Truman, *Memoirs*, 61.
11 Ibid., 62, 65.
12 Ibid., 63.
13 Ibid., 66–92.
14 Ibid., 89.
15 Ibid., 90.
16 LaFeber, *America, Russia*, 93–94.
17 Ibid., 94.
18 Truman, *Memoirs*, 81.
19 Ibid., 81.
20 Ibid., 81.
21 LaFeber, *America, Russia*, 96.
22 Yergin, *Shattered Peace*, 407.
23 The First Red Scare occurred just after World War I.
24 Truman, *Memoirs*, 270.
25 Ibid., 270.
26 Ibid., 271.
27 Craig and Logevall, *America's Cold War*, 108.
28 Yergin, *Shattered Peace*, 401.
29 George C. Herring, *From Colony to Superpower: U.S. Foreign Relations Since 1776* (New York: Oxford University Press, 2008), 638.
30 "A Report to the President Pursuant to the President's Directive of January 31, 1950," April 7, 1950 in *Foreign Relations of the United States 1950* Volume 1: *National Security Affairs; Foreign Economic Policy* (Washington, D.C.: U.S. Government Printing Office, 1977), 237. Hereafter *FRUS 1950*, Vol. 1. Hereafter *NSC-68*.
31 Ibid., 238.
32 Ibid., 238.
33 Ibid., 238.
34 Ibid., 238.
35 Ibid., 264.
36 Ibid., 278.
37 Ibid., 248.
38 Ibid., 244, 248.
39 Ibid., 282.
40 Ibid., 282.
41 Ibid., 283–284.
42 Ibid., 287–288.
43 Ibid., 291–292.
44 Ibid., 285.
45 Ibid., 285.
46 Ibid., 246.
47 Ibid., 240.
48 Ibid., 253.
49 "Memorandum by the Executive Secretary of the National Security Council (Lay) to the Ad Hoc Committee on NSC 68," April 28, 1950 in *FRUS 1950*, Vol. 1, 293–294.

HOW TO FIGHT: NSC-68 AND PLANNING GLOBAL STRATEGY

50 Yergin, *Shattered Peace*, 403.
51 "Memorandum by Mr. Charles E. Bohlen to the Director of the Policy Planning Staff (Nitze)," April 5, 1950 in *FRUS 1950*, Vol. 1, 221–222.
52 Ibid., 221–222.
53 "Memorandum by the Deputy Chief of the Division of Estimates, Bureau of the Budget (Schaub) to the Executive Secretary of the National Security Council (Lay)," May 8, 1950 in *FRUS 1950*, Vol. 1, 300.
54 Ibid., 300.
55 Ibid., 300–302.
56 Yergin, *Shattered Peace*, 402–403.
57 Yergin, *Shattered Peace*, 402.
58 "Draft Memorandum by the Counselor (Kennan) to the Secretary of State," February 17, 1950, in *FRUS 1950*, Vol. 1, 160. Quote from Note 1.
59 Ibid., 160.
60 Ibid., 160.
61 Ibid., 161.
62 Ibid., 161.
63 Ibid., 161.
64 Ibid., 161.
65 Ibid., 161.
66 Ibid., 162.
67 Ibid., 162–163.
68 Ibid., 163.
69 Ibid., 164.
70 Ibid., 164.
71 Ibid., 164.
72 Yergin, *Shattered Peace*, 407.
73 Ibid., 408.
74 "Report to the National Security Council by the Executive Secretary (Lay)," September 30, 1950 in *FRUS 1950*, Vol. 1, 400.

CHAPTER 5

The View After

Victories and Costs

COMMUNISTS EVERYWHERE?

In his 1951 book *American Diplomacy*, in a concluding section titled "America and the Russian Future," George Kennan warned against "the American bad habit of assuming that there is something final and positive about a military decision—that it is the ending of something, and the happy ending, rather than a beginning."[1] He hoped "we will be less inclined to view military operations as ends in themselves, and should find it easier to conduct them in a manner harmonious with our political purposes."[2] He encouraged Americans to avoid seeking military solutions to foreign policy problems, because, ultimately, "no great end [sic] enduring change in the spirit and practice of government in Russia will ever come about primarily through foreign inspiration or advice. To be genuine, to be enduring and to be worth the hopeful welcome of other peoples such a change would have to flow from the initiatives and efforts of the Russians themselves."[3] Therefore, he concluded, "The most important influence that the United States can bring to bear upon internal developments in Russia will continue to be the influence of example."[4] For Kennan, containment would only work as originally envisioned—as political and economic pressure against the Soviet Union to buy time until communism collapsed internally in Russia and Eastern Europe. A global military presence by the United States would only prolong the standoff with the Soviet Union and perhaps undermine U.S. foreign policy objectives in the long run.

Before 1950 the Cold War reached few places outside North America, Europe, East Asia, and individual countries such as Iran during tense moments. Yet as the Cold War deepened and as vast swaths of Asia and Africa emerged from colonialism, American leaders encountered new questions. Were leftists always communist? What happened if the United

90 THE VIEW AFTER: VICTORIES AND COSTS

States did not support a strong ruler? Could political "losses," such as the removal from power of a pro-Western ally, be reversed? What places mattered for U.S. security? Presidents from Truman to Reagan answered these questions in different ways, but the overall record was a relatively consistent pattern of American interventions around the world—from Korea to Iran to Cuba to Vietnam to Chile to Angola and many more. Direct involvement tended to be more common in Latin America and East and Southeast Asia, but CIA actions or U.S. troops, at times both, appeared in every region of the globe over the next four decades. This chapter covers a number of these American interventions, including the major wars in Korea and Vietnam. It is not, however, a detailed narrative of the rest of the Cold War. That would require an extensive volume and the historians noted throughout this work have already provided many excellent such treatments of the topic. This chapter will center on the concept of costs, for both the United States and for the countries where it intervened during the Cold War. Of course, the United States ended up prevailing in the Cold War and between 1989 and 1991 many millions of people shed communist rule in Europe. The main question, though, is could this have been achieved without many, or all, of the numerous American actions around the world between 1950 and 1991. The debate among historians will be more fully addressed in the conclusion, but it is useful to note here the starting point for that debate, which is the claim by Campbell Craig and Fredrik Logevall that "the weight of the evidence, together with Kennan's clear geopolitical reasoning, suggests strongly that the mission of containment as originally conceived was largely accomplished by about 1950. . . . The optimal American strategy, according to the logic of containment, should have been to restrain itself from foreign adventures and avoid superpower showdowns. But what the United States did was quite the opposite."[5] Some historians agree and some disagree. The latter include those who argue the Soviet Union was a new type of nation dangerous both for its expansionist desires and its ideology that was antithetical to Western capitalism and democracy. Others believe the Soviets were contained successfully in Europe, largely satisfied with the geographic periphery they had constructed, and only a minimal threat after 1950. The debate, of course, continues over how we should assess the Cold War, especially its course outside Europe.

THE KOREAN WAR

Even the defense of South Korea does not escape at least some debate about whether or not excessive costs were incurred, namely by the decision

THE VIEW AFTER: VICTORIES AND COSTS 91

to try to unify Korea under a non-communist government and by the extended wrangling over armistice terms. Stalin himself approved the North Korean invasion of South Korea in late June 1950, which was clearly an act of international aggression. Yet while historians are generally united about the need to defend South Korea, they are divided over the efficacy of the strategies used to do so. In fact, Walter LaFeber notes how Truman withdrew remaining American soldiers (there to take over from surrendering Japanese troops) from South Korea in 1948 due to being "embarrassed" by "its authoritarian methods," which contributed to the more than 100,000 Korean deaths between 1946 and 1950 in a simmering civil war.[6] Likewise, Craig and Logevall claims that General Douglas MacArthur's famous Inchon Landing in September 1950 and the subsequent offensive that almost reached the Yalu River, North Korea's northern border with China, "was . . . consistent with the new thinking of NSC-68" since "NSC-68 advocated a more aggressive strategy against communism anywhere, and it was this mentality that now drove the Truman administration after the start of the war."[7] They argue that instead, U.S. forces should have just stopped when they had rid South Korea of North Korean forces, which had been accomplished by the late summer and early fall of 1950.[8] In the end, U.S. and U.N. forces pushed north toward the Chinese border, Mao poured in hundreds of thousands of Chinese troops, and allied forces retreated back down the peninsula, with the front line finally stabilizing by early 1951 near the original border between the two Koreas. Two years of bloody, stalemated fighting followed. In essence, the question here revolves around what may have happened had the Truman administration not recently adopted the new, more militarized and aggressive foreign policy of NSC-68. Might U.S. forces have halted after pushing the North Koreans out of South Korea a mere two months into the conflict, thereby minimizing casualties and avoiding the entry of China? The resulting human cost included roughly 37,000 American deaths, hundreds of thousands of Korean and Chinese military deaths, hundreds of thousands of civilian Korean deaths, and even more wounded on all sides. Financial costs for the United States and for the economy of South Korea were also enormous. Lengthy wars are never cheap.

EISENHOWER'S COUPS

After Truman left office, President Dwight D. Eisenhower fought no major wars, but some of his other international activities in pursuit of Cold War objectives incurred costs both at the time within the countries affected and later for the United States. While most historians give Eisenhower

92 THE VIEW AFTER: VICTORIES AND COSTS

credit for avoiding war in Europe as well as avoiding a major escalation over communist artillery shelling of Nationalist-held islands just off the shore of mainland China, his activities in what came in the 1950s to be called the Third World have received far less praise. Although he and his officials usually distinguished nationalism from communism, they did tend to consider any loss of position for pro-Western leaders, of any political stripe, to be a calculable reduction in Western strength. In this sense, his actions reflected the zero-sum attitude of NSC-68 that "a defeat of free institutions anywhere is a defeat everywhere," even though his administration, as would subsequent administrations, defined "free institutions" loosely.[9] Therefore, when Mohammad Mossadegh, a nationalist promoting international nonalignment, rose to power in Iran in early 1951, it alarmed Western leaders. The pro-Western Shah Mohammad Reza Pahlavi was forced to make Mossadegh prime minister in April 1951 due to the latter's popularity, but when Mossadegh nationalized the Anglo-Iranian Oil Company (AIOC) in May, Eisenhower felt he had to act. Iran had long been a nation the West considered a strategic bulwark against Russian, and then Soviet, expansion into the Middle East and Central Asia. Losing Western influence there, as well as the loss of British control over Iran's oil due to the nationalization of the AIOC, seemed to undermine Western goals in the region. While Eisenhower knew Mossadegh was not a communist, in the world of NSC-68 the loss of a strategic partner would only aid the Soviets, especially because Iranian nonalignment weakened the Western alliance system ringing Soviet territory from Western Europe to Pakistan. Subsequently, American CIA operatives and British intelligence agents fomented unrest and sponsored and supported anti-Mossadegh newspapers and protests, which provided the Shah an excuse to dismiss Mossadegh from his position and arrest him in August 1953, amounting to a political coup. The AIOC returned to British hands and all seemed well. Yet when the Iranian Revolution of 1979 occurred a quarter century later, many Iranians remembered U.S. meddling in the mid-1950s, adding to the event's extreme anti-Americanism.

The Eisenhower administration conducted a similar operation in Guatemala only a year after the Iranian coup. In 1950 a reformer named Jacobo Arbenz Guzmán became president and in 1953, to promote land reform, he nationalized 200,000 acres of unused land held by the U.S.-based United Fruit Company. He paid them for the land, but only at the artificially low value they had been claiming the land was worth when they paid taxes. Alarmed by another nationalization of Western property and by the fact Guzmán would not purge alleged or actual communists from government positions, Eisenhower authorized the overthrow of the Guatemalan leader. For a year the CIA trained and armed a small number

Mohammad Mossadegh

Born in 1882, Mohammad Mossadegh gained prominence in Iranian politics as a nationalist seeking to combat British and American influence in Iran. Both nations supported the Shah at the time, Mohammad Reza Pahlavi, because he was pro-Western and allowed the large Anglo-Iranian Oil Company to extract oil from the country. Mossadegh rode an anti-Western, neutralist, populist wave to power and was Prime Minister of Iran between 1951 and 1953. Mossadegh also nationalized the AIOC in 1951, which convinced British and American leaders that he had to be removed. They then successfully executed Operation Ajax, a concerted effort by the CIA and British intelligence to cause unrest and eventually a coup in August 1953 to remove Mossadegh from office and restore the Shah's power. Mossadegh spent the rest of his life in prison or on house arrest and died in 1967. He was one of the first prominent non-European nationalists promoting nonalignment in the Cold War, which presented the West with a problem. His views and actions seemed to undermine Western goals in the region because the United States considered Iran a staunch Western ally just to the south of the Soviet Union that could aid the goal of containment. Although the Shah was reinstalled in 1953, when the Iranian revolution of 1979 overthrew him, many Iranians remembered the 1953 coup and held very anti-Western and anti-American views.

of Guatemalan exiles under the command of Colonel Castillo Armas and they then invaded Guatemala in June 1954. Although the invasion force was small and many in the civilian population wanted to fight, the Guatemalan army refused to stop Armas and U.S. plane runs overhead made the force appear bigger than it was. Guzmán resigned and Armas became president, restoring land to United Fruit and instituting a conservative government that crushed dissent and arrested opponents, often executing them. Leftist groups in the countryside then launched a civil war that lasted for more than three decades, during which more than 200,000 people died. By the time fighting ended in the mid-1990s, the cost to Guatemala due to U.S. intervention had become enormous. The intervention also garnered much ill-will toward the United States in other parts of Latin America during the Cold War.

Near the end of his presidency, Eisenhower was involved in two other interventions—in Cuba and in the former Belgian Congo. In the latter, the Belgians provided only a six month notice that they were leaving the colony after almost eight decades of control. They had done little to prepare the colony for freedom and when independence came in June 1960 chaos among political parties and rival groups erupted, including

1960—YEAR OF AFRICA

While much of North Africa was already decolonized and while Ghana and Guinea became free before 1960, that year became known as the Year of Africa when sixteen former colonies achieved independence. Mostly former French possessions, they included Madagascar, Mauritania, Mali, Niger, Chad, Senegal, Ivory Coast, Upper Volta, Togo, Benin, Cameroon, Gabon, Nigeria, the Central African Republic, and both the smaller former French Republic of the Congo and the much larger former Belgian Democratic Republic of the Congo (known as Zaire between 1971 and 1997). In early 1960, British Prime Minister Harold Macmillan gave a speech in Cape Town, South Africa centering on the inevitability of decolonization. This speech, which came to be known as the "Winds of Change" speech, further encouraged African nationalists to push for freedom.

both the rebellion of black soldiers against white Belgian officers and the secession of a mineral-rich province, Katanga, from the new country. The prime minister, Patrice Lumumba, tried to maneuver among different factions to keep the new nation stable, but when he received support from the Soviet Union, Eisenhower began to oppose him. In late 1960, Lumumba had to flee the capital, the CIA helped capture him, and his political enemies then executed him. More chaos followed and in the mid-1960s the administration of President Lyndon Johnson helped the repressive central government put down a rebellion, even providing the use of American troop transports. Mobutu Sese Seko then ruled as a dictator between 1965 and 1997. The early promise of a more democratic system ended in part due to U.S. opposition to Lumumba and that opposition was based largely on his acceptance of Soviet aid. In Cuba, Fidel Castro led a successful rebellion to overthrow the U.S.-supported dictator Fulgencio Batista and took power on January 1, 1959. While they did not like Castro's nationalization of land and other leftist moves, members of the Eisenhower administration, such as Vice President Richard Nixon and Secretary of State Christian Herter, met with him when he visited the United States in April 1959. Yet, as with Lumumba, when Castro began accepting Soviet aid the Eisenhower administration began planning what would become the Bay of Pigs invasion. Modeled on the successful operation in Guatemala, the plan called for the CIA to train and equip exiles who opposed the new Cuban government and then insert them to overthrow Castro. President John F. Kennedy took office as the plans were finalized and he gave the green light in April 1961. The operation failed, however, and most of the exiles were immediately surrounded on the beaches, surrendering after a short firefight. More ill-will toward the United States followed in many Latin American countries.

KENNEDY, JOHNSON, AND LATIN AMERICA

In addition, tensions between Cuba and the United States continued to escalate and led directly to the placement of Soviet nuclear missiles in Cuba, causing the Cuban Missile Crisis in October 1962. The crisis was also tied to the issue of Germany, where the Soviets had continued to make threats about the status of West Berlin. They argued that no formal postwar treaty actually gave the West access to the city. At moments during both the Eisenhower and early Kennedy years, both sides would ratchet up their rhetoric over Berlin and war would seem to become more likely, although eventually cooler heads would prevail. The construction of the Berlin wall between the Western and Soviet zones, starting in August 1961, actually relieved some tension as it eliminated the growing number of people fleeing Soviet-held territory into West Berlin for flights to the free world, one of the primary sources of superpower tension regarding the city. Still, the wall then became one of the most well-known Cold War symbols of a divided Europe. Most historians believe Nikita Khrushchev, who became the Soviet leader after Stalin died in 1953, placed missiles in Cuba in part to gain leverage in negotiations over the status of West Berlin and other German issues. Of course, the Cuban Missile Crisis erupted instead. There is no space here to go into the details of the thirteen-day superpower standoff and the eventual removal of the missiles from Cuba, but the crisis stemmed at least in part from Castro's fear of another American attempt to overthrow him. Thus he accepted Soviet nuclear weapons on his soil as a deterrent. Such fears were not unfounded because the United States still sought to get rid of Castro, most notably in a series of usually ill-considered ideas known as Operation Mongoose. A communist nation in the Western Hemisphere, increasingly tied to the Soviet Union, was not acceptable according to the logic of NSC-68. American attempts to end communist control of Cuba thus played a role in producing the Cuban Missile Crisis, undermined America's reputation in Latin America, and ultimately were unsuccessful during the Cold War.

> ### OPERATION MONGOOSE
>
> After the failed Bay of Pigs invasion in April 1961 by U.S.-trained Cuban exiles, designed to overthrow Fidel Castro, the United States continued a program of trying to assassinate Castro in order to end communist rule in Cuba. While much of the information is not well documented, some of the ideas may have included exploding cigars, mafia hit men, various types of poisoning including a poisonous fountain pen, and a number of other methods. The program was obviously unsuccessful and petered out before the end of the Kennedy administration.

THE VIEW AFTER: VICTORIES AND COSTS

Many of Kennedy's other Cold War actions outside Europe often receive criticism from historians or were ineffective. For instance, the motivations and effects of Kennedy's Peace Corps and Alliance for Progress programs, which respectively sent American volunteers into the Third World and American development money to Latin America, are sometimes debated. Craig and Logevall claim the two programs were both "born of genuine humanitarianism" and "were Cold War weapons by which Kennedy sought to counter anti-Americanism and defeat communism in the developing world."[10] While the Peace Corps was usually left alone by foreign leaders, episodes such as Guinea's expulsion of all Peace Corps volunteers in 1966 revealed that Third World nationalists still sometimes distrusted American intentions. The Alliance for Progress had bigger problems in that, according to Craig and Logevall, in Latin America "economic growth rates continued to lag and class divisions widened, furthering political turmoil. . . . Many in the developing world resented meddling by outsiders and refused to be passive recipients of modernizing policies, even as they gladly accepted America's economic aid and craved its material culture. The self-interested elites through whom the assistance was usually funneled often failed to get it to the indigent population that was its target."[11] Furthermore, after Kennedy's assassination in November 1963, President Lyndon Johnson continued the pattern of U.S. intervention in Latin America. His administration adopted the Mann Doctrine, named for one of his assistant secretaries of state, which, according to historian George Herring, "was widely interpreted to mean that the administration would not look unfavorably on military governments."[12] Such governments, Johnson and other U.S. officials believed, would best prevent communist inroads until nonwhites could be adequately instructed in the creation of liberal, capitalist nations. The Johnson administration therefore helped facilitate a military ouster of João Goulart in Brazil in 1964 that led to a decade of military control and in 1965 U.S. troops went into the Dominican Republic to block a previous leader, Juan Bosch, from assuming power again, with the result that "the authoritarian Joaquin Balaguer would dominate the country for the next twenty-five years."[13] Any leader appearing unacceptably leftist, even without clear evidence of Soviet involvement, could become a U.S. target. Similarly in Africa, as will be discussed below, most U.S. administrations during the Cold War considered black populations ill-prepared upon independence to resist communism. Thus U.S. leaders tended to think that after decolonization some sort of strongman rule was best until a nation learned how to combine democracy with an effective defense against communist infiltration.

VIETNAM

The American debacle in Vietnam between mid-1965 and early 1973 was a prime example of how NSC-68's recommendations could lead U.S. officials astray. Although the communist leader Ho Chi Minh declared Vietnamese independence immediately after the end of World War II, by 1946 French troops returned to reoccupy what had been part of French Indochina and war commenced against the Viet Minh, a communist guerilla movement.

After French military defeat at Dien Bien Phu, the 1954 Geneva Conference created a North and South Vietnam, with elections that would unify the country scheduled for 1956. In the intervening two years, however, the leader of South Vietnam, Ngo Dinh Diem, consolidated his power and seemed able to provide a non-communist alternative to Ho Chi Minh's government in the north. The Eisenhower administration thus supported Diem when he refused to hold the elections stipulated by the agreement at Geneva. By 1960, however, Diem faced a growing communist insurgency in the countryside of South Vietnam, increasingly aided by North Vietnam, and the United States began providing substantial financial and military support. By the time of Kennedy's death in November 1963 there were 16,000 U.S. military "advisors" in Vietnam and Diem had been assassinated. A series of ineffective military leaders then led South Vietnam for the rest of its existence. President Lyndon Johnson used alleged attacks on U.S. destroyers in the Gulf of Tonkin off the coast of Vietnam

> ### DIEN BIEN PHU
>
> After fighting against the Viet Minh communist insurgency in French Indochina for eight years, between 1946 and 1954, the French decided to try to lure the communists into a large, final battle. They moved significant forces into rural, mountainous terrain near the border between Vietnam and Laos and took up positions in a fortified city known as Dien Bien Phu. The city was located in a valley and the French did not think the communist forces had the capability of positioning artillery on the surrounding hills. They did, however, and the two sides fought from March to May 1954 before the French surrendered and pulled out. The 1954 Geneva Conference followed, which created a North and South Vietnam with elections to be held in two years to unify the country. The elections never occurred, however, because the United States knew the communists would win. The French defeat at Dien Bien Phu ended their seven decades of rule in Indochina, but it also marked the start of a more direct U.S. role in Vietnam that would culminate in the bloody conflict of the late 1960s and early 1970s.

in August 1964 to justify an expanded American military role. Starting in February 1965, he continuously bombed the North . Then he sent Marine units to guard air bases in South Vietnam. Next, he authorized the Marines to move up to fifty miles away from those bases to seek out enemy forces. Finally, in July 1965, Johnson announced he was sending an additional 100,000 soldiers and the war became fully Americanized, with more than half a million U.S. troops fighting in South Vietnam by 1969. By the time President Richard Nixon, who prolonged the war in an effort to achieve his vague claim of "peace with honor," removed the final U.S. forces in early 1973, some 58,000 Americans were dead. Hundreds of thousands of Cambodians, tens of thousands of Laotians, and at least a million and a half Vietnamese also perished between 1954 and 1975, when communist forces captured the capital of South Vietnam and large-scale conflict ended.[14]

Historians have long debated why the United States went to war in Southeast Asia at such tremendous cost in blood, treasure, and political stability at home, where numerous anti-war demonstrations and a growing distrust of the nation's leaders undermined social cohesion. One of the most consistent explanations among historians is known as the "liberal-realist critique".[15] These historians argue that successive U.S. administrations mistook a genuinely nationalist movement as yet another chess move in the global advance of communism and claim the United States then fought a bloody, stalemated war in a place with virtually no impact on U.S. security.[16] NSC-68 had, of course, warned that a win for communism anywhere was a blow to the free world everywhere and the extension of militarized containment to Southeast Asia by the Eisenhower, Kennedy, Johnson, and Nixon administrations all stemmed at least in part from a fear that if they did not stop communism in Vietnam, it might spread throughout the region. Whatever the ultimate motivation for fighting, little was gained and much was lost in the Vietnam War. In addition to the dead, wounded, and deepening distrust of government by wide swaths of the American public at home, according to Craig and Logevall the $170 billion "spent on the war weakened investments in domestic programs, and heavy borrowing by both Johnson and Nixon, to avoid raising taxes, triggered inflation and led the nation in 1971 to give up the gold standard as the basis of its monetary system."[17] The gold standard had been one of the linchpins in the post-World War II international capitalist system that had benefited the United States immensely. Furthermore, they argue, "The war also solidified power in the White House, unbalancing the three branches of government on matters of foreign policy in ways that the authors of the Constitution had sought to prevent."[18] While a small minority of historians claim that

THE VIEW AFTER: VICTORIES AND COSTS   99

involvement in Vietnam, and the attendant costs, were needed to stop communism, most hold some version of the above critiques. Would the United States have fought in Vietnam without the existence of NSC-68? Perhaps, but NSC-68's worldview, and its acceptance among the vast majority of U.S. officials at the time, made it much more likely.

DETENTE

Regarding the various types of costs in American foreign policy, the subsequent period of détente, which meant a "lessening of tensions," initially seemed to promise better days. Some historians trace the origins of détente as far back as the immediate months after the Cuban Missile Crisis. They point to Kennedy and Khrushchev signing the first treaty on nuclear weapons between the two superpowers, the 1963 Nuclear Test Ban Treaty prohibiting testing above ground. The White House and the Kremlin also installed a telephone hotline to provide immediate communication in the event of future crises. Most historians, however, see détente as starting in the late 1960s and lasting until the late 1970s. It fully flowered during Nixon's "linkage" maneuvers in the early 1970s when he extracted concessions from both the Chinese and the Soviets by playing them against each other. In February 1972, he was the first American president to visit communist China, which came as a surprise to many in the United States since Nixon was so ardently anti-communist. When he came away with a new trade deal, the Soviets became anxious and the door opened for Nixon to travel to Moscow just three months later. He and Soviet leader Leonid Brezhnev, in charge from 1964 until his death in 1982, then signed the first Strategic Arms Limitation Treaty (SALT 1), which placed limits on the number of intercontinental ballistic missiles (ICBMs) as well as defensive missiles that could shoot ICBMs down. While the agreement did not technically limit the number of nuclear warheads each side could have, only the actual missiles on which the warheads were placed, it was still a major agreement between the two nations with the most nuclear weapons. After Nixon resigned due to the Watergate scandal in August 1974, President Gerald Ford continued negotiations with the Soviets over similar measures and in 1979 President Jimmy Carter and Brezhnev signed SALT II, which imposed additional caps and limits on nuclear weapons and related items. As will be discussed below, however, SALT II was never put into force due first to Senate opposition to Carter's foreign policy and then due to Carter's own anger over the Soviet invasion of Afghanistan in December 1979. Overall, the 1970s, despite economic

THE VIEW AFTER: VICTORIES AND COSTS

problems at home, are seen as a period in which the risk of general or nuclear war between the superpowers seemed to recede, at least until the very end of the decade.

One historian, however, has argued that the beginning of détente, and by implication all that occurred during the period, actually came at a high cost. In his book, *Power and Protest: Global Revolution and the Rise of Détente*, Jeremi Suri analyzes the various threats that leaders in the United States, the Soviet Union, China, France, West Germany, and elsewhere felt from their own domestic populations, who, he claims, became increasingly unrestful in the postwar era as leaders promised much while delivering little. As protests erupted in Prague, Paris, Chicago, and other cities in the late 1960s, Suri claims, "Governments could no longer assume that they commanded legitimacy in the eyes of their citizens. Local and national authorities frequently resorted to force against protestors. Police power assured regime continuity, but it also deepened resentment among many domestic groups. Politics became noticeably more contentious for the leaders of the largest states."[19] As a result, leaders turned to new types of engagement with former adversaries and then, as Suri points out regarding Nixon, "used the prospects of great-power cooperation to argue that . . . opponents threatened international peace."[20] The message was that domestic opposition groups should end their protests because such unrest undermined new agreements being put together on the international stage, which, leaders claimed, would benefit everybody. Therefore, Suri's central claim is that "détente was a profoundly conservative response to internal disorder. It sacrificed domestic reform for the sake of international stability. Leaders abandoned their hopes for political change in order to smother the challenges they faced at home."[21] Not only was domestic reform stymied, according to Suri, but "international collaboration among leaders furthered international disillusion among citizens. To this day, large segments of each nation's population remain politically alienated as a consequence of détente."[22] Regarding NSC–68 specifically, Suri notes that its main author, Paul Nitze, was in the 1960s the assistant secretary of defense for international security affairs and while he still believed in the central precepts of the document, he "advised [Secretary of Defense Robert] McNamara and Kennedy that the United States could pursue a more energetic foreign policy only if it developed more diverse instruments for the projection of force."[23] This attitude shows that, while Nitze was a bit more wary by this point of unilateral or ill-planned American actions abroad, his "judgment of the Kremlin's intentions did not change in the 1960s."[24] In addition to the domestic costs stemming from the ways leaders practiced détente in the late 1960s and 1970s, the core ideas of NSC–68 remained operative. The Soviets still needed to be blocked from their

THE VIEW AFTER: VICTORIES AND COSTS   101

attempt to dominate the world and Nitze's idea of "a broader mobilization of American resources against the Soviet Union" was still followed.[25] The way to do this had simply changed, temporarily, from international lines drawn in the sand to new forms of high-level engagement. Most important here is Suri's argument that even détente inflicted high costs on the United States, mostly in the domestic realm.

THE 1970s IN LATIN AMERICA AND AFRICA

Even with détente proceeding at the superpower level, the United States did not end its pattern of intervening in Latin America. With the failure of the Bay of Pigs invasion and a communist Cuba now a fact of life in the Western Hemisphere, U.S. officials considered any left-leaning national leader as a potential communist who might allow an additional Soviet foothold in the region. So when an admitted Marxist, Cheddi Jagan, won a series of popular votes as British Guiana moved toward independence, first Kennedy and then Johnson, using the CIA and American labor unions, funneled money to opposition parties and convinced the British government to alter the electoral scheme in such a way that Jagan's opponent emerged victorious in 1964. Guiana then "safely" moved on to independence two years later, but, according to historian Stephen Rabe, "Guyana suffered misrule until 1992, principally under the autocratic Forbes Burnham (1964–1985). Burnham developed a personality cult, pillaged the national economy, and trampled on civil liberties and human rights. Burnham and his henchmen also discriminated against Indians, denying Guyana's majority population political and economic opportunities."[26] Similarly in Chile a few years later, the Marxist Salvador Allende emerged with the most votes in an election in 1970. Since, however, he had only "won a plurality of votes in a three-way election . . . the outcome rested with the Chilean congress."[27] Once again the CIA stepped in and moved money around to try to prevent an Allende victory, although this achieved nothing and in October 1970 he became president.[28] Nixon and the CIA continued to undermine Allende's government, however, and helped cause political and economic chaos in Chile until "in September 1973, the Chilean military overthrew the government; Allende committed suicide or was murdered."[29] As historian George Herring points out, Allende's ouster may have happened anyways due to his bungled nationalization programs, "but there can be no doubt that U.S. intervention between 1970 and 1973 helped create the conditions in which the coup took place."[30] The subsequent leader, General Augusto Pinochet, ruled from 1973 until 1990. His dictatorial government killed thousands of

THE VIEW AFTER: VICTORIES AND COSTS

Chileans and jailed and tortured tens of thousands more. During the 1960s and the 1970s, the pattern of American intervention in Latin America, and the enormous human, social, and economic costs incurred by people in the region due to America's Cold War ideology, continued.

Africa also became a region of U.S. interest and involvement in the mid-1970s. The Ogaden War of 1977–1978 pitted the U.S.-supported Siad Barre of Somalia against the Soviet-supported Mengistu Haile Mariam, who took power after a 1974 leftist overthrow of Ethiopia's pro-U.S. Emperor Haile Selassie. The most overt example of U.S. intervention in Africa in the 1970s, however, occurred in Angola during Ford's presidency. Fighting in Angola against Portuguese colonizers began in the early 1960s, but independence only came in 1975, a year after the Portuguese military, tired of endless guerrilla war, deposed the fascist dictator at home and moved Portugal toward democracy. In Angola, however, the Marxist MPLA (in English the Popular Front for the Liberation of Angola) assumed power and faced a rightist insurgency by the FNLA (the National Front for the Liberation of Angola). As fighting increased, the Soviets sent aid and Cuba sent thousands of soldiers to assist the MPLA. The Ford administration then secretly provided money to both the FNLA and another group opposed to the MPLA known as UNITA (the National Union for the Total Independence of Angola). This money coincided with an invasion of Angola by South African forces from Namibia, located to the south of Angola and controlled until 1990 by the apartheid government of South Africa, that was designed to topple the MPLA. Between October and December 1975 white South African troops moved north, slowly but methodically taking land and towns from the MPLA. They and their Angolan allies, however, could not capture the capital and were eventually checked by Cuban forces. When Congress learned what Ford had done and that apartheid South Africa was involved, it forced the president to suspend his activities against the MPLA in December 1975.[31] The South African forces then withdrew in January 1976. While American involvement did not lead to the overthrow of a government in this instance, it at least prolonged, and perhaps intensified, the fighting. Angola was a true proxy situation with regional-level allies of the United States and the Soviet Union fighting alongside local ones. While President Carter refused to approve any white minority government in Southern Rhodesia (Zimbabwe today) until a true black majority government was in place, which occurred in 1980, the intervention in Angola under Ford meant that the U.S. record in southern Africa during the second half of the 1970s was mixed at best. Marxists appeared again in a place not economically, strategically, or even politically important to the United States, but U.S. intervention still occurred.

REAGAN AND LATIN AMERICA

Likewise, the election of Ronald Reagan in 1980 led to a continuation of U.S. intervention in Latin America due to Cold War concerns. The combination of the February 1979 Iranian Revolution, which overthrew the pro-U.S. Shah and removed Iran as a U.S. ally in the Middle East, and the Soviet invasion of Afghanistan in December 1979 made President Carter's foreign policy appear adrift. Another problem he faced in Central America involved Nicaragua, where a leftist movement overthrew the pro-U.S. Anastosio Somoza in July 1979. The Sandinistas were named after Augusto Sandino, who had opposed the U.S. occupation of Nicaragua in the late 1920s and early 1930s. He was killed by the U.S.-backed Somoza family, who then ruled Nicaragua until 1979. According to historian Alan McPherson, Carter recognized the repressive nature of Somoza's rule and tried to use aid to control his behavior, so when the Sandinistas took power, Carter at first still tried to use American money to influence them.[32] As McPherson notes, however, "To the Sandinistas, this was too little, too late; the aid did not address the deeper causes of poverty."[33] Still, McPherson points out that despite some nationalization, U.S. businesses were allowed to operate and the Sandinistas "kept their foreign policy relatively separate from that of the Soviets and Cubans."[34] President Reagan, however, did not see it that way. According to historian George Herring, "Reagan and most of his top advisers expressed grave concern about a new 'Soviet beachhead' in the hemisphere, 'another Cuba.'"[35] He authorized the CIA to fund, and then direct on the ground, the training of anti-Sandinista Nicaraguans, known as "contras," who were to keep Nicaragua unstable and eventually overthrow the Sandinistas. As with Angola, however, Congress learned of these measures and in October 1984 passed legislation that ended Reagan's legal avenues for funding the contras. What followed was the murky Iran-Contra affair during which some of Reagan's officials, notably NSC member Lieutenant Colonel Oliver North, constructed a deal whereby the United States sold weapons to Iran and used the money to fund the Nicaraguan contras. When the scheme was discovered, Congress simply reprimanded Reagan for a general failure to properly supervise his officials, several of whom received convictions, although none experienced harsh sentencing.[36] Most important for the discussion here, some thirty thousand people died in Nicaragua as a result of the Contra War stimulated by the Reagan administration and in the end the Sandinistas still held power, although Nicaragua eventually moved toward democracy in the 1990s.[37]

One of Nicaragua's neighbors, El Salvador, fared even worse in the 1980s. By early 1980 a broad coalition of opposition groups had united to conduct a guerilla war against the authoritarian right-wing government, which often used right-wing death squads in response.[38] These squads committed a number of atrocities, including killing American nuns in December 1980, and President Carter, who had turned the aid spigot on and off as with Nicaragua, cut aid to the government again at that point.[39] The new Reagan administration, however, believed all leftist movements in Central America were connected both to each other and to the Soviet Union. For instance, as George Herring notes, "In February [1981], the [State] department released a white paper purporting to contain 'definitive evidence' that Nicaragua, Cuba, and the Soviet Union were making El Salvador a key Cold War battleground."[40] Reagan increased military aid to El Salvador to such high-levels that by 1984, according to Alan McPherson, "The tiny nation was now the third best-funded U.S. ally in the world, behind Israel and Egypt. Each Salvadoran received on average one dollar per day in U.S. aid."[41] All this did, though, was lead to more fighting, resulting in a flood of refugees to the United States.[42] By the time a peace agreement was put in place in late 1991, more than 75,000 had perished and the countryside of El Salvador was largely destroyed.[43] Atrocities had been committed on both sides, but the right-wing death squads were by far the most extreme, sometimes massacring whole villages of peasants. Under Reagan U.S. forces also invaded the Caribbean island nation of Grenada in October 1983. Ostensibly it was to protect American medical students after a Marxist hardline coup, but the invasion also had the effect of removing the Marxist government from power because, as Herring notes, the administration was "nervous about a Cuba–Grenada–Nicaragua axis in the hemisphere."[44] During the 1980s, the United States also worked with the Haitian strongman Jean-Claude Duvalier and the Panamanian dictator and CIA informant Manuel Noriega, although in December 1989 President George H.W. Bush directed U.S. troops to invade Panama, capture Noriega, and bring him to the United States to stand trial for drug trafficking.[45] Although each of these Central American countries had their own internal conflicts, U.S. involvement usually prolonged the fighting and led to increased levels of violence and death, especially in the cases of Nicaragua and El Salvador. American fears of a Cuban repeat or more "Soviet beachheads" in the region produced interventionism in the 1980s on a scale not seen since the 1910s and 1920s.

THE COLD WAR ENDS

As the list of U.S. interventions outside Europe grew during the forty five years of the Cold War, the situation in Europe remained stalemated. Each

THE VIEW AFTER: VICTORIES AND COSTS 105

side pointed armed divisions and nuclear missiles at each other, but did not use them. In the end, communism collapsed in Eastern and Central Europe, and then in Russia itself, because it failed to deliver on its promises of a better world. Although uprisings against local communist parties were put down by Soviet forces in Budapest, Hungary in 1956 and Prague, Czechoslovakia in 1968, by the 1980s the region was beginning to slip away from the Soviets. In the 1970s, the Soviet Union allowed increased trade with the West and western loans were extended to help communist nations modernize. Yet when these loans came due in the 1980s and created debt problems in Eastern European countries, the communist parties running those nations tried to extract even more from their people, leading to unrest. Poland became the center of opposition to the Soviets, where after a widespread series of strikes in the late summer of 1980 Lech Walesa helped found Solidarity, the first non-communist trade union in the Soviet sphere. Although the communist Polish government imposed martial law in late 1981 and tried to dismantle Solidarity by arresting its leaders, the movement remained active and would ultimately triumph by the end of the decade. 1989, of course, was the year communism came crashing down in Central and Eastern Europe. In May, Hungary began to take down fences along its border with Austria, which allowed people in the Eastern bloc to easily get into neutral Austria, and from there to the West. Protests grew against communist rule in East Germany, Czechoslovakia, Hungary, Poland, and the Baltic States of Latvia, Lithuania, and Estonia. In Poland, in August, the Solidarity movement united with other groups to form the first government not led by communists in the region. The most dramatic moment was the night of November 9–10 when communist officials in East Berlin declared they would no longer prevent movement across the Berlin Wall and Berliners from both sides began to destroy the longstanding Cold War symbol. Over the course of November and December, communism then collapsed in the rest of Eastern Europe, including Bulgaria and Romania. It would take two more years, including both democratic elections and a failed hardline communist coup attempt, before the Soviet Union officially ceased to exist on December 25, 1991 and the Russian Federation, along with fourteen other nations that had previously been "socialist republics," took its place. It all happened without a western invasion or World War III. Kennan's containment had kept communism in check in Europe until it collapsed internally, just as he had predicted in early 1946.

But why did the Soviet Union abandon its control of Eastern Europe and why did communism ultimately collapse in the region? Asked another way, why and how did the United States win the Cold War? Historians widely debate the fundamental reasons, but they can be divided into five

THE VIEW AFTER: VICTORIES AND COSTS

Lech Walesa

Lech Walesa was born in 1943 and by the 1970s was involved in organizing workers against communist policies. In 1980 he helped create the first non-communist trade union in the Soviet sphere in Eastern Europe and was instrumental in leading a series of strikes in Gdansk, a city on the shore of the Baltic Sea in northern Poland. After some initial successes, his union, Solidarity, was shut down and Walesa and others were arrested. He spent the rest of the 1980s protesting or under arrest until 1989 when communism finally collapsed in Eastern Europe. He was then president of Poland between 1990 and 1995 and is now retired from public life. Walesa was one of the most prominent anti-communist activists within the Soviet sphere itself and many historians agree that he and his movement played a significant role in weakening the appeal of communism in Eastern Europe, thus undermining the Soviet Union's ability to control the region.

main camps. One group claims the key figure was Ronald Reagan. They argue, generally, that his firm anti-communist rhetoric and his increased defense spending put the Russians on the defensive and forced them to increase their own military spending until the amounts became untenable and led to communism's collapse. A second group argues Soviet economic problems resulted only from their own actions as they propped up Third World countries such as Cuba and Angola, conducted a lengthy and expensive war in Afghanistan, and, as noted above, borrowed heavily from the West. With the populations they controlled in Europe increasingly angry over lack of economic growth and reform, the use of funds in other places and the botched attempts to pay back Western loans in the 1980s played central roles in the fall of communism. A third group claims the new Soviet leader in 1985, Mikhail Gorbachev, was central to the end of the Cold War. Since he realized the Soviet Union could no longer compete with the West in terms of technological advances and economic power, he instituted policies of "glasnost," or political openness, and "perestroika," or economic restructuring, to allow more private economic activity. Ironically, Gorbachev set out to reform and save communism, but in the end unleashed forces that ultimately caused its demise. In addition, as communist governments in Eastern Europe faced mounting protests in 1989, he announced the Red Army would not act, further accelerating the end of communism. A fourth group of historians see Reagan and Gorbachev as equally important and claim their relationship was key to ending the Cold War. Among the several meetings between the two leaders, the two most important were in Reykjavik, Iceland

THE VIEW AFTER: VICTORIES AND COSTS   107

in October 1986 and in Washington in December 1987. During these summits they reached agreements to eliminate entire classes of nuclear missiles, significantly reducing superpower stockpiles and, according to this group of historians, building trust between both sides. This allowed Gorbachev to believe he could pursue reforms within the Soviet sphere unmolested by the West, although events still ultimately spun out of his control. Finally, some historians adhere to the "jazz and blue jeans" argument. They claim that as communism proved incapable of delivering any real economic growth or political reform, populations under communist rule were increasingly attracted to the values and prosperity of the West. Another aspect to this argument includes the signing of the 1975 Helsinki Final Act by many Western nations, the Soviet Union, and most Eastern European governments. The agreement emerged from the détente era and while not officially a treaty, it included promises to respect human and individual rights. Although it would take another fourteen years, the Act played a role in undermining communist rule because activists within the Soviet bloc sought to force communist leaders to implement reforms in line with its ideals. Overall, this group of historians sees causation for the end of the Cold War coming from both sides, because while attractive values and economic prosperity stemmed from the West, it took active pressure on communist governments by large segments of Eastern European populations to end communism. Ultimately, the debate over the fundamental cause for the collapse of communism in Europe will, as with so many Cold War topics, continue.

COSTS AND CONTINGENCY

Historians Campbell Craig and Fredrik Logevall have provided the most provocative claims regarding the price of the Cold War. Other historians have challenged their conclusions, to be sure, but their arguments are a good starting point to discuss the costs incurred by America's Cold War foreign policy. First of all, on the positive side of the ledger, tens of millions of people emerged from under authoritarian communist rule by 1991, an aspect of the Cold War that must not be forgotten. In addition, another good outcome was that no major conflict at the continental or global level erupted between two superpowers conducting world-wide ideological warfare for more than four decades. The negative side of the ledger, however, weighs heavier for Craig and Logevall. To restate their core idea from the beginning of the chapter, they argue, "The weight of the evidence, together with Kennan's clear geopolitical reasoning, suggests strongly that the mission of containment as originally conceived was

THE VIEW AFTER: VICTORIES AND COSTS

largely accomplished by about 1950. If one adds to it the task of dissuading the Soviet Union from ever imagining that it could win the Cold War by launching a nuclear attack, the mission was completed by 1960."[46] Yet the United States pursued a global, militarized containment strategy aimed at removing or defeating communists, or their allies, all over the world during the next several decades. American lives were lost unnecessarily. The national debt spiraled upward due to defense spending spurred by the growth of Eisenhower's famous "military-industrial complex." In addition, Craig and Logevall note a severe cost in "the militarization of American politics," with the "end result" being "a remarkable transformation of American political culture, whereby a people that before 1940 had been, on the whole, opposed to standing armies and suspicious of power politics now seemed tempted so often to choose the military option and revel in American power, to regard diplomacy, sophisticated debate, and consideration of the other side's position as policies of the timid."[47] Essentially, since they argued that containment in Europe was achieved at the latest by 1960, the price of involvement elsewhere was "fundamentally unnecessary."[48] In fact, U.S. interventions even "prolonged the Cold War" because, they claim,

> By exacerbating and globalizing the Cold War rather than confidently sticking with defensive containment, the United States gave Kremlin leaders an excuse to use American belligerence as a justification for its continued obsession with external threats. The arms race sustained the power and legitimacy of Soviet oligarchs, who were terrified by the prospect that the American bogeyman might recede and force them to attend to the deep structural problems of their domestic economy, not to mention the growing restiveness among eastern Europeans. . . . By providing the USSR with such convenient foreign challenges, U.S. militarism bolstered the Soviet Union's own military-industrial complex and protracted the Cold War.[49]

In the end, defeating communism in Europe was a laudable and necessary goal, but it could have been achieved at a much lower price in blood, treasure, social cohesion, and political norms. In addition, as Craig and Logevall point out, "Accurate numbers are hard to come by, but certainly U.S. policies in the Third World after 1945 led to the death or maiming of several million civilians who had never raised a hand against the United States."[50] Odd Arne Westad agrees and notes that in American and Soviet interventions in the Third World, "The *cultural* [emphasis his] violence was sometimes as bad as the physical: millions were forced to change their

THE VIEW AFTER: VICTORIES AND COSTS   109

religion, their language, their family structure, and even their names in order to fit in with progress."[51] Westad also claims, "Seen from a Third World perspective, the results of America's interventions are truly dismal. Instead of being a force for good—which they were no doubt intended to be—these incursions have devastated many societies and left them more vulnerable to further disasters of their own making. So far, the combination of stable growth and stable democracies that Washington has ostensibly sought may be visible in two half-states (South Korea and Taiwan), but is absent in around thirty other countries in which the United States has intervened, directly or indirectly, since 1945."[52] A number of other historians generally agree with these tenets and there is no debating the number of human lives wrecked and the steady increase in the U.S. national debt over the course of several decades due to American actions in the Cold War.

What is debated is the necessity of such human and financial costs, as well as whether or not the political costs were truly incurred. On the latter point, as noted earlier, historian Aaron Friedberg claims, "Powerful countervailing forces inoculated America against the worst extremes of statism during the critical opening stages of the Cold War" and "made it easier for the United States to preserve its economic vitality and techno-logical dynamism, to maintain domestic political support for a protracted strategic competition and to stay the course in that competition better than its supremely statist rival," all "without at the same time transforming itself into a garrison state."[53] In the final analysis, whereas Craig and Logevall find domestic influences on foreign policy to be more insidious and costly, Friedberg in fact finds them beneficial, given the scope of what lay before the United States in 1945 and what the country had to do to match the power of its ideological enemy. Even regarding the "much-reviled members of the 'military industrial complex,'" Friedberg argues they "perhaps after all . . . did good by doing well" in their spending on research and other areas of the economy that ended up producing technological innovation and economic growth.[54] Historians such as John Lewis Gaddis, noted earlier as one who blames Stalin for the onset of the Cold War, extend such analyses to America's international actions during the Cold War. Gaddis argues that in American Third World interventions "the existence of a rival superpower 'center' placed 'peripheries' in a position to manipulate Washington about as often as the other way around."[55] Thus U.S. leaders should not shoulder all the blame for harmful events outside Europe. Much good historical work has been done that shows the agency of Third World leaders and even Westad agrees they played an active role in events, although he still mostly blames the United States for the costs that occurred because it intervened in the first place.

On the issue of why the standoff between superpowers lasted as long as it did, Gaddis argues, "The Cold War went on much longer than it might have had nuclear weapons never been invented. Given the fact that they did exist, the Cold War could have ended with a bang at just about any point. It took decades to arrange a whimper."[56] Such statements not only give an alternative view as to why the Cold War lasted several decades, versus the domestic influences noted by Craig and Logevall, but they also counter those authors' claims that U.S. leaders should have recognized that the Soviet threat to Western Europe was entirely contained by 1950 or 1960. As long as the Soviets, an ideological and geopolitical enemy, had nuclear weapons, American policymakers deemed them a dangerous threat. Gaddis argues, "Nuclear weapons preserved the image of a formidable Soviet Union long after it had entered into its terminal decline. We will never know whether the USSR could have been successfully— but also safely—confronted at an earlier date; for the Cuban missile crisis convinced western leaders, perhaps correctly, that their own nations' survival depended upon that of their adversary. Efforts to shake the other side seemed far too dangerous to undertake. There was, therefore, a trade-off: we avoided *destruction*, but at the price of *duration* [both emphases his]."[57] For Gaddis, nuclear weapons played a key role in prolonging the Cold War because the doctrine of mutually assured destruction meant neither side could safely destroy the other and emerge unscathed, thus convincing U.S. leaders to avoid unnecessary confrontations with the Soviets that may in fact have sped up their collapse. This suggests it would have been very hard for U.S. leaders to avoid seeing the Soviets as a dangerous enemy who continued to present a threat to Western Europe, as well as other places around the world, and were thus not fully contained at any time. Overall, while historians such as Gaddis do criticize some American Cold War actions, most often Vietnam, they tend to deem more of the costs incurred by the United States necessary at some level, or at least unavoidable, in order to defeat the Soviet Union and win the Cold War.[58] Or, as with Friedberg, sometimes some of the costs are not considered costs at all.

As described earlier, there are also ongoing conversations over a number of questions involving the why, who, how, when, and what of the Cold War. Why did it start? Who was responsible? When did it really deepen? What was at stake for the United States in Korea? In Vietnam? In other areas of the Third World? Even in Europe? Why did the Cold War end? Of course, this book has been most concerned with why it lasted as long as it did and whether or not the costs incurred, in the United States and elsewhere, were necessary to achieve western victory by 1991. Methodologically, the debates over these questions point to the concept of historical contingency. Things did not inevitably have to turn out the way they did. Were all the numerous and extensive U.S. interventions around the world ultimately required to inflict Soviet defeat? Could the United States have followed a different path in the Cold War? Could it have incurred fewer costs, and imposed fewer costs on others, while still achieving its ultimate objective of containing and defeating communism in Europe? Although some historians argue international and domestic conditions would have moved any individual U.S. leader toward the foreign policies that were eventually adopted, there were in fact alternative directions open for the United States in the Cold War. It would not have been easy, but had the warnings of figures such as Henry Wallace or George Kennan been heeded, perhaps the United States may have conducted a less global, less militaristic Cold War foreign policy during the four decades between 1950 and 1989. The costs discussed above would then likely have been much reduced or even eliminated. While foreign policy options did narrow between 1945 and 1950, the door was never completely shut on alternative choices during the early Cold War. Wallace may have been more easily dismissed by Truman and his officials, but Kennan's warnings, due to his stature as the father of containment, held more possibility of having an impact. Although he was never able to convince the president to change direction, his cautions against a global, militarized foreign policy received significant attention as debates progressed within the Truman administration over how to deal with the Soviet threat. The reasons Wallace and Kennan were not heeded are for the individual historian, and student, to determine, as are conclusions on the other major debates on Cold War causation, duration, nature, and end. Ultimately, critically analyzing alternative paths that were available in the past, and why they never came to be, can help us more carefully consider policies and courses of action, both domestic and international, in the present. We will become better trained to look for the existence of multiple paths forward and to weigh their merits in order to consider which outcomes might be better, for the United States and for the world.

NOTES

1 George F. Kennan, *American Diplomacy, 1900–1950* (Chicago, IL: The University of Chicago Press, 1951), 107.
2 Ibid., 119.
3 Ibid., 124.
4 Ibid., 125–126.
5 Craig and Logevall, *America's Cold War*, 366.
6 LaFeber, *America, Russia*, 106.

112 THE VIEW AFTER: VICTORIES AND COSTS

7   Craig and Logevall, *America's Cold War*, 129.
8   Ibid., 129.
9   *NSC-68*, 240.
10 Craig and Logevall, *America's Cold War*, 225.
11 Ibid., 226.
12 Herring, *Colony to Superpower*, 732–733.
13 Ibid., 717, 733–735.
14 Craig and Logevall, *America's Cold War*, 273.
15 David L. Anderson, "The Vietnam War," in Robert D. Schulzinger, ed., *A Companion to American Foreign Relations* (Malden, MA: Blackwell Publishing Ltd., 2006), 313.
16 Ibid., 314
17 Craig and Logevall, *America's Cold War*, 274.
18 Ibid., 274.
19 Jeremi Suri, *Power and Protest: Global Revolution and the Rise of Détente* (Cambridge, MA: Harvard University Press, 2003), 4.
20 Ibid., 5.
21 Ibid., 5.
22 Ibid., 5.
23 Ibid., 19.
24 Ibid., 19.
25 Ibid., 19.
26 Stephen G. Rabe, *U.S. Intervention in British Guiana: A Cold War Story* (Chapel Hill, NC: The University of North Carolina Press, 2005), 5.
27 Herring, *Colony to Superpower*, 787.
28 Ibid., 787–788.
29 Ibid., 788.
30 Ibid., 788.
31 Ibid., 825.
32 Alan McPherson, *Intimate Ties, Bitter Struggles: The United States and Latin America Since 1945* (Washington, D.C.: Potomac Books, 2006), 85.
33 Ibid., 85.
34 Ibid., 85.
35 Herring, *Colony to Superpower*, 886.
36 McPherson, *Intimate Ties*, 105.
37 Herring, *Colony to Superpower*, 893.
38 McPherson, *Intimate Ties*, 86–87.
39 Ibid., 86–87.
40 Herring, *Colony to Superpower*, 887.
41 McPherson, *Intimate Ties*, 94.
42 Ibid., 94.
43 Ibid., 101.
44 Herring, *Colony to Superpower*, 888.
45 McPherson, *Intimate Ties*, 108–109.
46 Craig and Logevall, *America's Cold War*, 366.
47 Ibid., 362–365.
48 Ibid., 365.

THE VIEW AFTER: VICTORIES AND COSTS 113

49 Ibid., 365, 367.
50 Ibid., 361.
51 Odd Arne Westad, *The Global Cold War: Third World Interventions and the Making of Our Times* (New York: Cambridge University Press, 2007), 400.
52 Ibid., 404.
53 Friedberg, *Garrison State*, 4, 340, 350.
54 Ibid., 341–345.
55 Gaddis, *We Now Know*, 187.
56 Ibid., 292.
57 Ibid., 292.
58 Ibid., 189, 292–294.

Documents

DOCUMENT 1

The "Long Telegram"

Immediately after World War II, as it became clear that the two most powerful Allies had different visions for the postwar world, the Truman administration did not have a coherent description of the Soviet Union's foreign policy or a clear concept of how to deal with it. George Kennan, a Soviet expert stationed in Moscow when he wrote the Long Telegram, provided the president with both, launching the doctrine of containment that would largely guide American foreign policy in the Cold War for the next forty years.

861.00/2—2246: Telegram

The Charge in the Soviet Union (Kennan) to the Secretary of State

SECRET

Moscow, February 22, 1946–9 p.m. [Received February 22–3: 52 p.m.]

511. Answer to Dept's 284, Feb 3 [13] involves questions so intricate, so delicate, so strange to our form of thought, and so important to analysis of our international environment that I cannot compress answers into single brief message without yielding to what I feel would be dangerous degree of over-simplification. I hope, therefore, Dept will bear with me if I submit in answer to this question five parts, subjects of which will be roughly as follows:

1. Basic features of post-war Soviet outlook.
2. Background of this outlook.
3. Its projection in practical policy on official level.

118 DOCUMENTS

4. Its projection on unofficial level.
5. Practical deductions from standpoint of US policy.

I apologize in advance for this burdening of telegraphic channel; but questions involved are of such urgent importance, particularly in view of recent events, that our answers to them, if they deserve attention at all, seem to me to deserve it at once. There follows:

PART 1: BASIC FEATURES OF POST WAR SOVIET OUTLOOK, AS PUT FORWARD BY OFFICIAL PROPAGANDA MACHINE

Are as Follows:

a. USSR still lives in antagonistic "capitalist encirclement" with which in the long run there can be no permanent peaceful coexistence. As stated by Stalin in 1927 to a delegation of American workers:

> "In course of further development of international revolution there will emerge two centers of world significance: a socialist center, drawing to itself the countries which tend toward socialism, and a capitalist center, drawing to itself the countries that incline toward capitalism. Battle between these two centers for command of world economy will decide fate of capitalism and of communism in entire world."

b. Capitalist world is beset with internal conflicts, inherent in nature of capitalist society. These conflicts are insoluble by means of peaceful compromise. Greatest of them is that between England and US.
c. Internal conflicts of capitalism inevitably generate wars. Wars thus generated may be of two kinds: intra-capitalist wars between two capitalist states, and wars of intervention against socialist world. Smart capitalists, vainly seeking escape from inner conflicts of capitalism, incline toward latter.
d. Intervention against USSR, while it would be disastrous to those who undertook it, would cause renewed delay in progress of Soviet socialism and must therefore be forestalled at all costs.
e. Conflicts between capitalist states, though likewise fraught with danger for USSR, nevertheless hold out great possibilities for advancement of socialist cause, particularly if USSR remains militarily powerful, ideologically monolithic and faithful to its present brilliant leadership.

DOCUMENTS   119

f.   It must be borne in mind that capitalist world is not all bad. In addition to hopelessly reactionary and bourgeois elements, it includes (1) certain wholly enlightened and positive elements united in acceptable communistic parties and (2) certain other elements (now described for tactical reasons as progressive or democratic) whose reactions, aspirations, and activities happen to be "objectively" favorable to interests of USSR. These last must be encouraged and utilized for Soviet purposes.

g.   Among negative elements of bourgeois-capitalist society, most dangerous of all are those whom Lenin called false friends of the people, namely moderate-socialist or social-democratic leaders (in other words, non-Communist left-wing). These are more dangerous than out-and-out reactionaries, for latter at least march under their true colors, whereas moderate left-wing leaders confuse people by employing devices of socialism to serve interests of reactionary capital.

So much for premises. To what deductions do they lead from standpoint of Soviet policy? To following:

a.   Everything must be done to advance relative strength of USSR as factor in international society. Conversely, no opportunity must be missed to reduce strength and influence, collectively as well as individually, of capitalist powers.

b.   Soviet efforts, and those of Russia's friends abroad, must be directed toward deepening and exploiting of differences and conflicts between capitalist powers. If these eventually deepen into an "imperialist" war, this war must be turned into revolutionary upheavals within the various capitalist countries.

c.   "Democratic-progressive" elements abroad are to be utilized to maximum to bring pressure to bear on capitalist governments along lines agreeable to Soviet interests.

d.   Relentless battle must be waged against socialist and social-democratic leaders abroad.

PART 2: BACKGROUND OF OUTLOOK

Before examining ramifications of this party line in practice there are certain aspects of it to which I wish to draw attention.

First, it does not represent natural outlook of Russian people. Latter are, by and large, friendly to outside world, eager for experience of it, eager to measure against it talents they are conscious of possessing, eager

DOCUMENTS

above all to live in peace, and enjoy fruits of their own labor. Party line only represents thesis which official propaganda machine puts forward with great skill and persistence to a public often remarkably resistant in the stronghold of its innermost thoughts. But party line is binding for outlook and conduct of people who make up apparatus of power—party, secret police and Government—and it is exclusively with these that we have to deal.

Second, please note that premises on which this party line is based are for most part simply not true. Experience has shown that peaceful and mutually profitable coexistence of capitalist and socialist states is entirely possible. Basic internal conflicts in advanced countries are no longer primarily those arising out of capitalist ownership of means of production, but are ones arising from advanced urbanism and industrialism as such, which Russia has thus far been spared not by socialism but only by her own backwardness. Internal rivalries of capitalism do not always generate wars; and not all wars are attributable to this cause. To speak of possibility of intervention against USSR today, after elimination of Germany and Japan and after example of recent war, is sheerest nonsense. If not provoked by forces of intolerance and subversion "capitalist" world of today is quite capable of living at peace with itself and with Russia. Finally, no sane person has reason to doubt sincerity of moderate socialist leaders in Western countries. Nor is it fair to deny success of their efforts to improve conditions for working population whenever, as in Scandinavia, they have been given chance to show what they could do.

Falseness of those premises, every one of which predates recent war, was amply demonstrated by that conflict itself Anglo-American differences did not turn out to be major differences of Western World. Capitalist countries, other than those of Axis, showed no disposition to solve their differences by joining in crusade against USSR. Instead of imperialist war turning into civil wars and revolution, USSR found itself obliged to fight side by side with capitalist powers for an avowed community of aim.

Nevertheless, all these theses, however baseless and disproven, are being boldly put forward again today. What does this indicate? It indicates that Soviet party line is not based on any objective analysis of situation beyond Russia's borders; that it has, indeed, little to do with conditions outside of Russia; that it arises mainly from basic inner-Russian necessities which existed before recent war and exist today.

At bottom of Kremlin's neurotic view of world affairs is traditional and instinctive Russian sense of insecurity. Originally, this was insecurity of a peaceful agricultural people trying to live on vast exposed plain in neighborhood of fierce nomadic peoples. To this was added, as Russia came into contact with economically advanced West, fear of more

DOCUMENTS   121

competent, more powerful, more highly organized societies in that area. But this latter type of insecurity was one which afflicted rather Russian rulers than Russian people; for Russian rulers have invariably sensed that their rule was relatively archaic in form fragile and artificial in its psychological foundation, unable to stand comparison or contact with political systems of Western countries. For this reason they have always feared foreign penetration, feared direct contact between Western world and their own, feared what would happen if Russians learned truth about world without or if foreigners learned truth about world within. And they have learned to seek security only in patient but deadly struggle for total destruction of rival power, never in compacts and compromises with it.

It was no coincidence that Marxism, which had smoldered ineffectively for half a century in Western Europe, caught hold and blazed for first time in Russia. Only in this land which had never known a friendly neighbor or indeed any tolerant equilibrium of separate powers, either internal or international, could a doctrine thrive which viewed economic conflicts of society as insoluble by peaceful means. After establishment of Bolshevist regime, Marxist dogma, rendered even more truculent and intolerant by Lenin's interpretation, became a perfect vehicle for sense of insecurity with which Bolsheviks, even more than previous Russian rulers, were afflicted. In this dogma, with its basic altruism of purpose, they found justification for their instinctive fear of outside world, for the dictatorship without which they did not know how to rule, for cruelties they did not dare not to inflict, for sacrifice they felt bound to demand. In the name of Marxism they sacrificed every single ethical value in their methods and tactics. Today they cannot dispense with it. It is fig leaf of their moral and intellectual respectability. Without it they would stand before history, at best, as only the last of that long succession of cruel and wasteful Russian rulers who have relentlessly forced country on to ever new heights of military power in order to guarantee external security of their internally weak regimes. This is why Soviet purposes must always be solemnly clothed in trappings of Marxism, and why no one should underrate importance of dogma in Soviet affairs. Thus Soviet leaders are driven by necessities of their own past and present position to put forward which [apparent omission] outside world as evil, hostile and menacing, but as bearing within itself germs of creeping disease and destined to be wracked with growing internal convulsions until it is given final Coup de grace by rising power of socialism and yields to new, and better world. This thesis provides justification for that increase of military and police power of Russian state, for that isolation of Russian population from outside world, and for that fluid and constant pressure to extend limits of Russian police power which are together the natural and instinctive urges of Russian rulers. Basically this is only the

DOCUMENTS

steady advance of uneasy Russian nationalism, a centuries old movement in which conceptions of offense and defense are inextricably confused. But in new guise of international Marxism, with its honeyed promises to a desperate and war torn outside world, it is more dangerous and insidious than ever before.

It should not be thought from above that Soviet party line is necessarily disingenuous and insincere on part of all those who put it forward. Many of them are too ignorant of outside world and mentally too dependent to question [apparent omission] self-hypnotism, and who have no difficulty making themselves believe what they find it comforting and convenient to believe. Finally we have the unsolved mystery as to who, if anyone, in this great land actually receives accurate and unbiased information about outside world. In atmosphere of oriental secretiveness and conspiracy which pervades this Government, possibilities for distorting or poisoning sources and currents of information are infinite. The very disrespect of Russians for objective truth—indeed, their disbelief in its existence—leads them to view all stated facts as instruments for furtherance of one ulterior purpose or another. There is good reason to suspect that this Government is actually a conspiracy within a conspiracy; and I for one am reluctant to believe that Stalin himself receives anything like an objective picture of outside world. Here there is ample scope for the type of subtle intrigue at which Russians are past masters. Inability of foreign governments to place their case squarely before Russian policy makers— extent to which they are delivered up in their relations with Russia to good graces of obscure and unknown advisors whom they never see and cannot influence—this to my mind is most disquieting feature of diplomacy in Moscow, and one which Western statesmen would do well to keep in mind if they would understand nature of difficulties encountered here.

PART 3: PROJECTION OF SOVIET OUTLOOK IN PRACTICAL POLICY ON OFFICIAL LEVEL

We have now seen nature and background of Soviet program. What may we expect by way of its practical implementation?

Soviet policy, as Department implies in its query under reference, is conducted on two planes: (1) official plane represented by actions undertaken officially in name of Soviet Government; and (2) subterranean plane of actions undertaken by agencies for which Soviet Government does not admit responsibility.

DOCUMENTS   123

Policy promulgated on both planes will be calculated to serve basic policies (a) to (d) outlined in part 1. Actions taken on different planes will differ considerably, but will dovetail into each other in purpose, timing and effect.

On official plane we must look for following:

a. Internal policy devoted to increasing in every way strength and prestige of Soviet state: intensive military-industrialization; maximum development of armed forces; great displays to impress outsiders; continued secretiveness about internal matters, designed to conceal weaknesses and to keep opponents in dark.

b. Wherever it is considered timely and promising, efforts will be made to advance official limits of Soviet power. For the moment, these efforts are restricted to certain neighboring points conceived of here as being of immediate strategic necessity, such as Northern Iran, Turkey, possibly Bornholm. However, other points may at any time come into question, if and as concealed Soviet political power is extended to new areas. Thus a "friendly Persian Government might be asked to grant Russia a port on Persian Gulf. Should Spain fall under Communist control, question of Soviet base at Gibraltar Strait might be activated. But such claims will appear on official level only when unofficial preparation is complete.

c. Russians will participate officially in international organizations where they see opportunity of extending Soviet power or of inhibiting or diluting power of others. Moscow sees in UNO not the mechanism for a permanent and stable world society founded on mutual interest and aims of all nations, but an arena in which aims just mentioned can be favorably pursued. As long as UNO is considered here to serve this purpose, Soviets will remain with it. But if at any time they come to conclusion that it is serving to embarrass or frustrate their aims for power expansion and if they see better prospects for pursuit of these aims along other lines, they will not hesitate to abandon UNO. This would imply, however, that they felt themselves strong enough to split unity of other nations by their withdrawal to render UNO ineffective as a threat to their aims or security, replace it with an international weapon more effective from their viewpoint. Thus Soviet attitude toward UNO will depend largely on loyalty of other nations to it, and on degree of vigor, decisiveness and cohesion with which those nations defend in UNO the peaceful and hopeful concept of international life, which that organization represents to our way of thinking. I reiterate, Moscow has no abstract devotion to UNO ideals. Its attitude to that organization will remain essentially pragmatic and tactical.

124 DOCUMENTS

d. Toward colonial areas and backward or dependent peoples, Soviet policy, even on official plane, will be directed toward weakening of power and influence and contacts of advanced Western nations, on theory that in so far as this policy is successful, there will be created a vacuum which will favor Communist-Soviet penetration. Soviet pressure for participation in trusteeship arrangements thus represents, in my opinion, a desire to be in a position to complicate and inhibit exertion of Western influence at such points rather than to provide major channel for exerting of Soviet power. Latter motive is not lacking, but for this Soviets prefer to rely on other channels than official trusteeship arrangements. Thus we may expect to find Soviets asking for admission everywhere to trusteeship or similar arrangements and using levers thus acquired to weaken Western influence among such peoples.

e. Russians will strive energetically to develop Soviet representation in, and official ties with, countries in which they sense Strong possibilities of opposition to Western centers of power. This applies to such widely separated points as Germany, Argentina, Middle Eastern countries, etc.

f. In international economic matters, Soviet policy will really be dominated by pursuit of autarchy for Soviet Union and Soviet-dominated adjacent areas taken together. That, however, will be underlying policy. As far as official line is concerned, position is not yet clear. Soviet Government has shown strange reticence since termination hostilities on subject foreign trade. If large scale long term credits should be forthcoming, I believe Soviet Government may eventually again do lip service, as it did in 1930's to desirability of building up international economic exchanges in general. Otherwise I think it possible Soviet foreign trade may be restricted largely to Soviet's own security sphere, including occupied areas in Germany, and that a cold official shoulder may be turned to principle of general economic collaboration among nations.

g. With respect to cultural collaboration, lip service will likewise be rendered to desirability of deepening cultural contacts between peoples, but this will not in practice be interpreted in any way which could weaken security position of Soviet peoples. Actual manifestations of Soviet policy in this respect will be restricted to arid channels of closely shepherded official visits and functions, with superabundance of vodka and speeches and dearth of permanent effects.

h. Beyond this, Soviet official relations will take what might be called "correct" course with individual foreign governments, with great stress being laid on prestige of Soviet Union and its representatives and with punctilious attention to protocol as distinct from good manners.

DOCUMENTS 125

PART 4: FOLLOWING MAY BE SAID AS TO WHAT WE MAY EXPECT BY WAY OF IMPLEMENTATION OF BASIC SOVIET POLICIES ON UNOFFICIAL, OR SUBTERRANEAN PLANE, I.E. ON PLANE FOR WHICH SOVIET GOVERNMENT ACCEPTS NO RESPONSIBILITY

Agencies utilized for promulgation of policies on this plane are following:

1. Inner central core of Communist Parties in other countries. While many of persons who compose this category may also appear and act in unrelated public capacities, they are in reality working closely together as an underground operating directorate of world communism, a concealed Comintern tightly coordinated and directed by Moscow. It is important to remember that this inner core is actually working on underground lines, despite legality of parties with which it is associated.
2. Rank and file of Communist Parties. Note distinction is drawn between those and persons defined in paragraph 1. This distinction has become much sharper in recent years. Whereas formerly foreign Communist Parties represented a curious (and from Moscow's standpoint often inconvenient) mixture of conspiracy and legitimate activity, now the conspiratorial element has been neatly concentrated in inner circle and ordered underground, while rank and file—no longer even taken into confidence about realities of movement—are thrust forward as bona fide internal partisans of certain political tendencies within their respective countries, genuinely innocent of conspiratorial connection with foreign states. Only in certain countries where communists are numerically strong do they now regularly appear and act as a body. As a rule they are used to penetrate, and to influence or dominate, as case may be, other organizations less likely to be suspected of being tools of Soviet Government, with a view to accomplishing their purposes through [apparent omission] organizations, rather than by direct action as a separate political party.
3. A wide variety of national associations or bodies which can be dominated or influenced by such penetration. These include: labor unions, youth leagues, women's organizations, racial societies, religious societies, social organizations, cultural groups, liberal magazines, publishing houses, etc.
4. International organizations which can be similarly penetrated through influence over various national components. Labor, youth, and women's organizations are prominent among them. Particular, almost vital

126   DOCUMENTS

importance is attached in this connection to international labor movement. In this, Moscow sees possibility of sidetracking western governments in world affairs and building up international lobby capable of compelling governments to take actions favorable to Soviet interests in various countries and of paralyzing actions disagreeable to USSR

5. Russian Orthodox Church, with its foreign branches, and through it the Eastern Orthodox Church in general.

6. Pan-Slav movement and other movements (Azerbaijan, Armenian, Turcoman, etc.) based on racial groups within Soviet Union.

7. Governments or governing groups willing to lend themselves to Soviet purposes in one degree or another, such as present Bulgarian and Yugoslav Governments, North Persian regime, Chinese Communists, etc. Not only propaganda machines but actual policies of these regimes can be placed extensively at disposal of USSR

It may be expected that component parts of this far-flung apparatus will be utilized in accordance with their individual suitability, as follows:

a. To undermine general political and strategic potential of major Western powers. Efforts will be made in such countries to disrupt national self confidence, to hamstring measures of national defense, to increase social and industrial unrest, to stimulate all forms of disunity. All persons with grievances, whether economic or racial, will be urged to spelt redress not in mediation and compromise, but in defiant violent struggle for destruction of other elements of society. Here poor will be set against rich, black against white, young against old, newcomers against established residents, etc.

b. On unofficial plane particularly violent efforts will be made to weaken power and influence of Western Powers of [on] colonial backward, or dependent peoples. On this level, no holds will be barred. Mistakes and weaknesses of western colonial administration will be mercilessly exposed and exploited. Liberal opinion in Western countries will be mobilized to weaken colonial policies. Resentment among dependent peoples will be stimulated. And while latter are being encouraged to seek independence of Western Powers, Soviet dominated puppet political machines will be undergoing preparation to take over domestic power in respective colonial areas when independence is achieved.

c. Where individual governments stand in path of Soviet purposes pressure will be brought for their removal from office. This can happen where governments directly oppose Soviet foreign policy aims (Turkey, Iran), where they seal their territories off against Communist penetration (Switzerland, Portugal), or where they compete too strongly, like Labor Government in England, for moral domination

DOCUMENTS   127

among elements which it is important for Communists to dominate. (Sometimes, two of these elements are present in a single case. Then Communist opposition becomes particularly shrill and savage.)

d. In foreign countries Communists will, as a rule, work toward destruction of all forms of personal independence, economic, political or moral. Their system can handle only individuals who have been brought into complete dependence on higher power. Thus, persons who are financially independent—such as individual businessmen, estate owners, successful farmers, artisans, and all those who exercise local leadership or have local prestige, such as popular local clergymen or political figures, are anathema. It is not by chance that even in USSR local officials are kept constantly on move from one job to another, to prevent their taking root.

e. Everything possible will be done to set major Western Powers against each other. Anti-British talk will be plugged among Americans, anti-American talk among British. Continentals, including Germans, will be taught to abhor both Anglo -Saxon powers. Where suspicions exist, they will be fanned; where not, ignited. No effort will be spared to discredit and combat all efforts which threaten to lead to any sort of unity or cohesion among other [apparent omission] from which Russia might be excluded. Thus, all forms of international organization not amenable to Communist penetration and control, whether it be the Catholic [apparent omission] international economic concerns, or the international fraternity of royalty and aristocracy, must expect to find themselves under fire from many, and often [apparent omission].

f. In general, all Soviet efforts on unofficial international plane will be negative and destructive in character, designed to tear down sources of strength beyond reach of Soviet control. This is only in line with basic Soviet instinct that there can be no compromise with rival power and that constructive work can start only when Communist power is doming But behind all this will be applied insistent, unceasing pressure for penetration and command of key positions in administration and especially in police apparatus of foreign countries. The Soviet regime is a police regime par excellence, reared in the dim half world of Tsarist police intrigue, accustomed to think primarily in terms of police power. This should never be lost sight of in ganging Soviet motives.

PART 5: PRACTICAL DEDUCTIONS FROM STANDPOINT OF US POLICY

In summary, we have here a political force committed fanatically to the belief that with US there can be no permanent modus vivendi that it is

128 DOCUMENTS

desirable and necessary that the internal harmony of our society be disrupted, our traditional way of life be destroyed, the international authority of our state be broken, if Soviet power is to be secure. This political force has complete power of disposition over energies of one of world's greatest peoples and resources of world's richest national territory, and is borne along by deep and powerful currents of Russian nationalism. In addition, it has an elaborate and far flung apparatus for exertion of its influence in other countries, an apparatus of amazing flexibility and versatility, managed by people whose experience and skill in underground methods are presumably without parallel in history. Finally, it is seemingly inaccessible to considerations of reality in its basic reactions. For it, the vast fund of objective fact about human society is not, as with us, the measure against which outlook is constantly being tested and re-formed, but a grab bag from which individual items are selected arbitrarily and tendentiously to bolster an outlook already preconceived. This is admittedly not a pleasant picture. Problem of how to cope with this force in [is] undoubtedly greatest task our diplomacy has ever faced and probably greatest it will ever have to face. It should be point of departure from which our political general staff work at present juncture should proceed. It should be approached with same thoroughness and care as solution of major strategic problem in war, and if necessary, with no smaller outlay in planning effort. I cannot attempt to suggest all answers here. But I would like to record my conviction that problem is within our power to solve— and that without recourse to any general military conflict. And in support of this conviction there are certain observations of a more encouraging nature I should like to make:

1. Soviet power, unlike that of Hitlerite Germany, is neither schematic nor adventuristic. It does not work by fixed plans. It does not take unnecessary risks. Impervious to logic of reason, and it is highly sensitive to logic of force. For this reason it can easily withdraw—and usually does when strong resistance is encountered at any point. Thus, if the adversary has sufficient force and makes clear his readiness to use it, he rarely has to do so. If situations are properly handled there need be no prestige-engaging showdowns.
2. Gauged against Western World as a whole, Soviets are still by far the weaker force. Thus, their success will really depend on degree of cohesion, firmness and vigor which Western World can muster. And this is factor which it is within our power to influence.
3. Success of Soviet system, as form of internal power, is not yet finally proven. It has yet to be demonstrated that it can survive supreme test of successive transfer of power from one individual or group to

DOCUMENTS   129

another. Lenin's death was first such transfer, and its effects wracked Soviet state for 15 years. After Stalin's death or retirement will be second. But even this will not be final test. Soviet internal system will now be subjected, by virtue of recent territorial expansions, to series of additional strains which once proved severe tax on Tsardom. We here are convinced that never since termination of civil war have mass of Russian people been emotionally farther removed from doctrines of Communist Party than they are today. In Russia, party has now become a great and—for the moment—highly successful apparatus of dictatorial administration, but it has ceased to be a source of emotional inspiration. Thus, internal soundness and permanence of movement need not yet be regarded as assured.

4.   All Soviet propaganda beyond Soviet security sphere is basically negative and destructive. It should therefore be relatively easy to combat it by any intelligent and really constructive program.

For those reasons I think we may approach calmly and with good heart problem of how to deal with Russia. As to how this approach should be made, I only wish to advance, by way of conclusion, following comments:

1.   Our first step must be to apprehend, and recognize for what it is, the nature of the movement with which we are dealing. We must study it with same courage, detachment, objectivity, and same determination not to be emotionally provoked or unseated by it, with which doctor studies unruly and unreasonable individual.

2.   We must see that our public is educated to realities of Russian situation. I cannot over-emphasize importance of this. Press cannot do this alone. It must be done mainly by Government, which is necessarily more experienced and better informed on practical problems involved. In this we need not be deterred by ugliness of the picture. I am convinced that there would be far less hysterical anti-Sovietism in our country today if realities of this situation were better understood by our people. There is nothing as dangerous or as terrifying as the unknown. It may also be argued that to reveal more information on our difficulties with Russia would reflect unfavorably on Russian - American relations. I feel that if there is any real risk here involved, it is one which we should have courage to face, and sooner the better. But I cannot see what we would be risking. Our stake in this country, even coming on heels of tremendous demonstrations of our friendship for Russian people, is remarkably small. We have here no investments to guard, no actual trade to lose, virtually no citizens to protect, few

cultural contacts to preserve. Our only stake lies in what we hope rather than what we have; and I am convinced we have better chance of realizing those hopes if our public is enlightened and if our dealings with Russians are placed entirely on realistic and matter-of-fact basis.

3. Much depends on health and vigor of our own society. World communism is like malignant parasite which feeds only on diseased tissue. This is point at which domestic and foreign policies meets Every courageous and incisive measure to solve internal problems of our own society, to improve self-confidence, discipline, morale, and community spirit of our own people, is a diplomatic victory over Moscow worth a thousand diplomatic notes and joint communiqués. If we cannot abandon fatalism and indifference in face of deficiencies of our own society, Moscow will profit—Moscow cannot help profiting by them in its foreign policies.

4. We must formulate and put forward for other nations a much more positive and constructive picture of sort of world we would like to see than we have put forward in past. It is not enough to urge people to develop political processes similar to our own. Many foreign peoples, in Europe at least, are tired and frightened by experiences of past, and are less interested in abstract freedom than in security. They are seeking guidance rather than responsibilities. We should be better able than Russians to give them this. And unless we do, Russians certainly will.

5. Finally we must have courage and self-confidence to cling to our own methods and conceptions of human society. After all, the greatest danger that can befall us in coping with this problem of Soviet communism, is that we shall allow ourselves to become like those with whom we are coping.

KENNAN

Source: U.S. Department of State. Foreign Relations of the United States, 1946, Volume VI: Eastern Europe: The Soviet Union (Washington, D.C.: U.S. Government Printing Office, 1969).

DOCUMENT 2

Letter from Henry Wallace to Harry S. Truman, July 23, 1946

Contrary to Kennan's ideas, Secretary of Commerce Henry Wallace urged the president in early 1946 to try to see the world through Russian eyes. He claimed the Soviet Union merely sought recovery and reconstruction after the devastation of the war years. An antagonistic reaction to every Soviet move by the United States would only make tensions worse, Wallace believed. He represented those who wanted to preserve the sense of wartime cooperation with the Soviet Union.

July 23, 1946

My Dear Mr. President:

I hope you will excuse this long letter. Personally I hate to write long letters, and I hate to receive them.

My only excuse is that this subject is a very important one—probably the most important in the world today. I checked with you about this last Thursday and you suggested after the Cabinet meeting on Friday that you would like to have my views.

I have been increasingly disturbed about the trend of international affairs since the end of the war, and I am even more troubled by the apparently growing feeling among the American people that another war is coming and the only way that we can head it off is to arm ourselves to the teeth. Yet all of past history indicates that an armaments race does not lead to peace but to war. The months just ahead may well be the crucial period which will decide whether the civilized world will go down in destruction after the five or ten years needed for several nations to arm themselves with atomic bombs. Therefore, I want to give you my views on how the present trend towards conflict might be averted.

132 DOCUMENTS

You may think it strange, in reading further, that I should express so much concern at this particular time, just after the foreign ministers' conference at which real progress was made on peace treaties for several Eastern European countries and for Italy.

Others have expressed a feeling of increased optimism that still further progress could be made through continued negotiations on the same basis, even though the remaining European issues are much more difficult than those on which a measure of agreement has already been reached.

I am fully appreciative of the efforts that have been made arid the patience that has been exercised by our various representatives with the Russians during the last few years.

I am conscious of the aggravations they have put up with and of the apparent inconsistencies on the part of the Russian representatives.

On the other hand, I feel these very difficulties make it necessary for some of us who, from the outside, are watching the course of events to voice our opinions.

THE BURDEN OF ARMAMENTS

Incidentally, as Secretary of Commerce I talk to a good many business men, and I find them very much concerned over the size of the Federal budget and the burden of the National debt. For the next fiscal year and for the year immediately ahead by far the largest category of Federal spending is the National defence.

For example, the total recommended Federal appropriations for the fiscal year 1947 submitted to the Congress in the official budget amounted to about 36 billion dollars. Of the total budget some 13 billion dollars was for the War and Navy Departments alone. An additional 5 billion dollars was for war liquidation activities. Ten billion represented interest on the public debt and veterans' benefits, which are primarily the continuing costs of past wars. These items total 28 billion dollars, or about 80 per cent, of the total recommended expenditures.

Clearly, a large reduction in the Federal budget would require a cut in military appropriations. These appropriations are now more than ten times as great as they were during the thirties. In the 1938 budget, appropriations for national defence were less than a billion dollars, compared with 13 billion dollars for the present fiscal year. Thus, even from a purely dollars and cents standpoint, American business and the American people have an interest' in organising a peaceful world in which the completely unproductive expenditures on national defence could be reduced.

Of course, dollars and cents are not the most important reason why we all want a peaceful world. The fundamental reason is that we do not wish to go through another war—and especially an atomic war which will undoubtedly be directed primarily against civilian populations and may well mean the end of modern civilisation.

Yet, are we really concentrating all our efforts on a programme to build a lasting peace?

There can be no doubt that the American people want and expect their leaders will work for an enduring peace. But the people must necessarily leave to their leaders the specific ways and means to this objective. I think that at the moment the people feel that the outlook for the elimination of war is dark, that other nations are wilfully obstructing American efforts to achieve a permanent peace.

AMERICA IN FOREIGN EYES

How do American actions since V-J Day appear to other nations?

I mean by actions the concrete things like 13 billion dollars for the War and Navy Departments, the Bikini tests of the atomic bomb and continued production of bombs, the plan to arm Latin America with our weapons, production of B-29's and planned production of B-36's, and the effort to secure air bases spread over half the globe from which the other half of the globe can be bombed. I cannot but feel that these actions must make it look to the rest of the world as if we are only paying lip service to peace at the conference table.

These acts rather make it appear either (1) that we are preparing ourselves to win the war which we regard as inevitable, or (2) that we are trying to build up a predominance of force to intimidate the rest of mankind.

How would it look to us if Russia had the atomic bomb and we did not, if Russia had 10,000-mile bombers and air bases within a thousand miles of our coastlines and we did not?

Some of the military men and self-styled "realists" are saying:

"What's wrong with trying to build up a predominance of force? The only way to preserve peace is for this country to be so well armed that no one will dare attack us. We know that America will never start a war."

The flaw in this policy is simply that it will not work. In a world of atomic bombs and other revolutionary new weapons, such as radioactive poison gases and biological warfare, a peace maintained by a predominance of forces is no longer possible.

PEACE CANNOT BE DICTATED

Why is this so? The reasons are clear: First: Atomic warfare is cheap and easy compared with old fashioned war. Within a very few years several countries can have atomic bombs and other atomic weapons. Compared with the cost of large armies and the manufacture of old fashioned weapons, atomic bombs cost very little and require only a relatively small part of a nation's production plant and labor force.

Second: So far as winning a war is concerned, having more bombs— even many more bombs—than the other fellow is no longer a decisive advantage. If another nation had enough bombs to eliminate all our principal cities and our heavy industry, it wouldn't help us very much if we had ten times as many bombs as we needed to do the same to them.

Third, and most important: The very fact that several nations have atomic bombs will inevitably result in a neurotic, fear-ridden, itching-trigger psychology in all peoples of the world, and because of our wealth and vulnerability we would be among the most seriously affected. Atomic war will not require vast and time consuming preparations, the mobilisation of large armies, the conversion of a large proportion of a country's industrial plants to the manufacture of weapons. In a world armed with atomic weapons, some incident will lead to the use of those weapons.

There is a school of military thinking which recognises these facts, recognises that when several nations have atomic bombs, a war which will destroy modern civilisation will result and that no nation or combination of nations can win such a war. This school of thought therefore advocates a "preventive war," an attack on Russia now before Russia has atomic bombs. This scheme is not only immoral but stupid. If we should attempt to destroy all the principal Russian cities and her heavy industry, we might well succeed. But the immediate counter-measure which such an attack would call for is the prompt occupation of all continental Europe by the Red Army. Would we be prepared to destroy the cities of all Europe in trying to finish what we started? This idea is so contrary to all the basic instincts and principles of the American people that any such action would be possible only under a dictatorship at home.

Thus the "predominance of force," idea, and the notion of a "defensive attack" are both unworkable. The only solution is the one which you have so wisely advanced and which forms the basis of the Moscow statement on atomic energy.

The solution consists of mutual trust and confidence among nations, atomic disarmament, and an effective system of enforcing that disarmament.

DOCUMENTS 135

ATOM MONOPOLY

There is, however, a fatal defect in the Moscow statement, in the Acheson report, and in the American plan recently presented to the United Nations Atomic Energy Commission. That defect is the scheme, as it is generally understood, of arriving at international agreements by "easy stages," of requiring other nations to enter into binding commitments not to conduct research into the military uses of atomic energy and to disclose their uranium and thorium resources while the United States retains the right to withhold its technical knowledge of atomic energy until the international control and inspection system is working to our satisfaction.

In other words, we are telling the Russians that if they are "good boys" we may eventually turn over our knowledge of atomic energy to them and to the other nations. But there is no objective standard of what will qualify them as being "good" nor any specified time for sharing our knowledge. Is it any wonder that the Russians did not show any great enthusiasm for our plan?

Would we have been enthusiastic if the Russians had a monopoly of atomic energy, and offered to share the information with us at some indefinite time in the future at their discretion if we agreed now not to try to make a bomb and give them information on our secret resources of uranium and thorium?

I think we would react as the Russians appear to have done. We would have put up counter-proposals for the record, but our real effort would go into trying to make a bomb so that our bargaining position would be equalised. That is the essence of the Russian position, which is very clearly stated in the "Pravda" article of June 24, 1946.

It is perfectly clear that the "step-by-step" plan in any such one-sided form is not workable. The entire agreement will have to be worked out and wrapped up in a single package. This may involve certain steps or stages, but the timing of such steps must be agreed to in the initial master treaty.

RUSSIA'S REACTIONS

Realistically, Russia has two cards which she can use in negotiating with us:

1. Our lack of information on the state of her scientific and technical progress on atomic energy;
2. Our ignorance of her uranium and thorium resources.

These cards are nothing like as powerful as our cards—a stockpile of bombs, manufacturing plants in actual production, B-29's and B-36's, and our bases covering half the globe. Yet we are in effect asking her to reveal her only two cards immediately—telling her that after we have seen her cards we will decide whether we want to continue to play the game. Insistence on our part that the game must be played our way will only lead to a deadlock. The Russians will redouble their efforts to manufacture bombs, and they may also decide to expand their "security zone" in a serious way. Up to now, despite all our outcries against it, their efforts to develop a security zone in Eastern Europe and in the Middle East are small change from the point of view of military power as compared with our air bases in Greenland, Okinawa, and many other places thousands of miles from our shores.

RIVAL CONTROL PLANS

We may feel very self-righteous if we refuse to budge on our plan and the Russians refuse to accept it, but that means only one thing—the atomic armament race is on in deadly earnest.

I am convinced, therefore, that if we are to achieve our hopes of negotiating a treaty which will result in effective international atomic disarmament, we must abandon the impractical form of "step-by-step" idea which was presented to the United Nations Atomic Energy Commission. We must be prepared to reach an agreement which will commit us to disclosing information and destroying our bombs at a specified time or in terms of specified actions by other countries, rather than at our unfettered discretion. If we are willing to negotiate on this basis, I believe the Russians will also negotiate seriously with a view to reaching an agreement. There can be, of course, no absolute assurance the Russians will finally agree to a workable plan if we adopt this view. They may prefer to stall until they also have bombs and can negotiate on a more equal basis, not realising the danger to themselves as well as the rest of the world in a situation in which several nations have atomic bombs.

But we must make to head off the atomic bomb race. We have everything to gain by doing so, and do not give up anything by adopting this policy as the fundamental basis for our negotiation. During the transition period toward full-scale international control we retain our technical know-how and only existing production plants for fissionable materials and bombs remain within our borders. The Russian counter-proposal itself is an indication that they may be willing to negotiate seriously if we are. In some respects their counter-proposal goes even farther than

DOCUMENTS   137

our plan and is in agreement with the basic principles of our plan, which is to make violations of the proposed treaty a national and international crime for which individuals can be punished.

THE QUESTION OF THE VETO

It will have been noted that in the preceding discussion I have not mentioned the question of the so-called "veto." I have not done so because the veto issue is completely irrelevant, because the proposal to "abolish the veto," which means something in the general activities of the Security Council, has no meaning with respect to a treaty on atomic energy. If we sign a treaty with other nations, we will all have agreed to do certain things. Until we arrive at such a treaty, we as well as the other major powers will have the power of veto. Once the treaty is ratified, however, the question of the veto becomes meaningless. If any nation violates the treaty provision, of permitting inspection of suspected illegal bomb-making activities, what action is there that can be vetoed? As in the case of any other treaty violation, the remaining signatory nations are free to take what action they feel is necessary, including the ultimate step of declaring war.

I believe that for the United States and Russia to live together in peace is the most important single problem facing the world today.

Many people, in view of the relatively satisfactory outcome of the recent Paris Conference, feel that good progress is being made on the problem of working out relations between the Anglo-Saxon powers and Russia. This feeling seems to me to be resting on superficial appearances more productive of a temporary truce than of final peace.

On the whole, as we look beneath the surface in late July of 1946, our actions and those of the Western Powers in general carry with them the ultimate danger of a third world war—this time an atomic war. As the strongest single nation, and the nation whose leadership is followed by the entire world with the exception of Russia and a few weak neighbouring countries in Eastern Europe, I believe that we have the opportunity to lead the world to peace.

In general, there are two over-all points of view which can be taken in approaching the problem of United States-Russian relations.

The first is that it is not possible to get along with the Russians, and therefore war is inevitable.

The second is that war with Russia would bring catastrophe to all mankind, and therefore we must find a way of living in peace.

It is clear that our own welfare as well as that of the entire world requires that we maintain the latter point of view. I am sure that this is also your opinion, and the radio address of the Secretary of State on July 15 clearly indicates that he is prepared to negotiate as long as may be necessary to work out a solution on this basis.

We should try to get an honest answer to the question of what the factors are which cause Russia to distrust us, in addition to the question of what factors lead us to distrust Russia.

I am not sure that we have as a nation or an administration found an adequate answer to either question, although we have recognised that both questions are of critical importance.

WHY AMERICA DISTRUSTS RUSSIA

Our basic distrust of the Russians, which has been greatly intensified in recent months by the playing up of conflict in the press, stems from differences in political and economic organisation. For the first time in our history defeatists among us have raised the fear of another system as a successful rival to democracy and free enterprise in other countries and perhaps even our own. I am convinced that we can meet that challenge as we have in the past by demonstrating that economic abundance can be achieved without sacrificing personal, political, and religious liberties. We cannot meet it as Hitler tried to by an anti-Comintern alliance. It is perhaps too easy to forget that despite the deep-seated differences in our cultures and intensive anti-Russian propaganda of some twenty-five years standing, the American people reversed their attitudes during the crises of war. Today, under the pressure of seemingly insoluble international problems and continuing deadlocks, the tide of American public opinion is again turning against Russia. In this reaction lies one of the dangers to which this letter is addressed. I should list the factors which make for Russian distrust of the United States and of the Western World as follows: The first is Russian history, which we must take into account because it is the setting in which Russians see all actions and policies of the rest of the world. Russian history for over a thousand years has been a succession of attempts, often unsuccessful, to resist invasion and conquest—by the Mongols, the Turks, the Swedes, the Germans, and the Poles.

HOW RUSSIA VIEWS THE WEST

The scant thirty years of the existence of the Soviet Government has in Russian eyes been a continuation of their historical struggle for national existence. The first four years of the new regime, from 1917 through 1921, were spent in resisting attempts at destruction by the Japanese, British, and French, with some American assistance, and by the several White Russian armies encouraged and financed by the Western powers. Then, in 1941, the Soviet State was almost conquered by the Germans after a period during which the Western European powers had apparently acquiesced in the rearming of Germany in the belief that the Nazis would seek to expand eastward rather than westward. The Russians, therefore, obviously see themselves as fighting for their existence in a hostile world. Second, it follows that to the Russians all of the defence and security measures of the Western powers seem to have an aggressive intent. Our actions to expand our military security system—such steps as extending the Monroe Doctrine to include the arming of the western hemisphere nations, our present monopoly of the atomic bomb, our interest in outlying bases and our general support of the British Empire—appear to them as going far beyond the requirements of defence. I think we might feel the same if the United States were the only capitalistic country in the world, and the principal socialistic countries were creating a level of armed strength far exceeding anything in their previous history. From the Russian point of view, also, the granting of a loan to Britain and the lack of tangible results on their request to borrow for rehabilitation purposes may be regarded as another evidence of strengthening of an anti-Soviet bloc.

UNFRIENDLY ENCIRCLEMENT

Finally, our resistance to her attempts to obtain warm water ports and her own security system in the form of "friendly" neighbouring States seems, from the Russian point of view, to clinch the case. After twenty-five years of isolation and having achieved the status of a major power, Russia believes that she is entitled to recognition of her new status. Our interest in establishing democracy in Eastern Europe, where democracy, by and large has never existed, seems to her an attempt to re-establish the encirclement of unfriendly neighbours which was created after the last war and which might serve as a springboard of still another effort to destroy her.

   If this analysis is correct—and there is ample evidence to support it—the action to improve the situation is clearly indicated. The fundamental objective of such action should be to allay any reasonable Russian grounds for fear, suspicion, and distrust. We must recognise that the world has changed and that today there can be no "One World" unless the United States and Russia can find some way of living together. For example, most of us are firmly convinced of the soundness of our position when we suggest the internationalisation and defortification of the Danube or of

140 DOCUMENTS

the Dardanelles, but we would be horrified and angered by any Russian counter-proposal that would involve also the internationalising and disarming of Suez or Panama. We must recognise that to the Russians these seem to be identical situations.

We should ascertain from a fresh point of view what Russia believes to be essential to her own security as a prerequisite to the writing of the peace and to the co-operation in the construction of a world order. We should be prepared to judge her requirements against the background of what we ourselves and the British have insisted upon as essential to our respective security. The progress made during June and July on the Italian and other treaties indicates that we can hope to arrive at understanding and agreement on this aspect of the problem.

TWO SYSTEMS CAN EXIST

We should not pursue further the question of the veto in connection with atomic energy, a question which is irrelevant and should never have been raised. We should be prepared to negotiate a treaty which will establish a definite sequence of events for the establishment of international control and development of atomic energy. This, I believe, is the most important single question, and the one on which the present trend is definitely toward deadlock rather than ultimate agreement.

We should make an effort to counteract the irrational fear of Russia which is being systematically built up in the American people by certain individuals and publications. The slogan that Communism and capitalism, regimentation, and democracy, cannot continue to exist in the same world is, from a historical point of view, pure propaganda. Several religious doctrines, all claiming to be the only true gospel and salvation, have existed side by side with a reasonable degree of tolerance for centuries. This country was for the first half of its national life a democratic island in a world dominated by absolutist governments.

We should not act as if we, too, felt that we were threatened in today's world. We are by far the most powerful nation in the world, the only Allied Nation which came out of the war without devastation and much stronger than before the war. Any talk on our part about the need for strengthening our defences further is bound to appear hypocritical to other nations.

We should also be prepared to enter into economic discussion without demanding that the Russians agree in advance to discussion of a series of what are to them difficult and somewhat unrelated political and economic concessions. Although this is the field in which my Department is most directly concerned, I must say that in my opinion this aspect of the problem is not as critical as some of the others, and certainly is far less important than the question of atomic energy control. But successful negotiations in this field might help considerably to bridge the chasm that separates us.

The question of a loan should be approached on economic and commercial grounds and should be disassociated as much as possible from the current misunderstandings which flow from the basic differences between their system and ours. You have already clearly disassociated yourself and the American people from the expressions of anti-Soviet support for the British loan If we could have followed up your statement on signing the British Loan Bill with a loan to the U.S.S.R. on a commercial basis and on similar financial terms, I believe that it would have clearly demonstrated that this country is not attempting to use its economic resources in the game of power politics. In the light of the present Export-Import Bank situation, it is now of the greatest importance that we undertake general economic discussions at an early date.

MUTUAL TRADE

It is of the greatest importance that we should discuss with the Russians in a friendly way their long-range economic problems and the future of our co-operation in matters of trade. The reconstruction programme of the U.S.S.R. and the plans for the full development of the Soviet Union offer tremendous opportunities for American goods and American technicians. American products, especially machines of all kinds, are well established in the Soviet Union. For example, American equipment, practices and methods are standard in coal mining, iron and steel, oil, and non-ferrous metals.

Nor would this trade be one-sided. Although the Soviet Union has been an excellent credit risk in the past, eventually the goods and services exported from this country must be paid for by the Russians by exports to us and to other countries. Russian products which are either definitely needed or which are noncompetitive in this country are various non-ferrous metal ores, furs, linen products, lumber products, vegetable drugs, paper and pulp, and native handicrafts.

I feel that negotiations on the establishment of active trade might well help to clear away the fog of political misunderstanding. Such discussions might well be initiated while we are endeavouring to reach a common ground on security issues, and if conducted in an understanding manner, could only serve to make that problem easier.

142   DOCUMENTS

In the memorandum which I sent to you in March and which I suggested should be given to General Walter Bedell Smith (U.S. Ambassador) to take to Moscow, I made certain suggestions for trade discussions in this country, I want to renew my original proposal and urge the appointment of a mission to Moscow. Such a mission might have as its objective the drafting of a proposal involving Russian reconstruction and collaboration with Russia in the industrial and economic development of areas in which we have joint interests, such as the Middle East. As I stated at that time, I am prepared to make suggestions for the composition of the mission and some of the specific economic questions to be discussed.

INVITATION TO STALIN

The Department of Commerce has already arranged, with the co-operation of the State Department, to send two representatives to Moscow for the months of July and August for preliminary discussions of a much more limited scope. I think it is very significant that most of the more optimistic reports about the possibilities of getting along with the Russians have come from American observers who were business men. I have in mind such men as Wendell Wilkie, Eric Johnston, and former Ambassador Joe Davies. The Russians seem to be friendly to, and seem to have respect for, capitalist business men.

A number of observers have reported that the Soviet leaders are "isolationists" and appear to be lacking a true insight into the principles, motives, and ways of thinking in other nations. We must admit, however, that they pointed out the symptoms and the way to present World War II in their promotion of the concept of collective security. And aside from that, it seems to me we should try to do something constructive about their isolationism and ignorance, and I believe the aforementioned trade mission could accomplish much in that direction. I gather, too, that is part of what you have had in mind in inviting Premier Stalin to visit America.

PRACTICAL COLLABORATION

Many of the problems relating to the countries bordering on Russia could more readily be solved once an atmosphere of mutual trust and confidence is established and some form of economic arrangements are worked out with Russia. These problems also might be helped by discussions of an economic nature. Russian economic penetration of the

DOCUMENTS 143

Danube area, for example, might be countered by concrete proposals for economic collaboration in the development of the resources of this area, rather than by insisting that the Russians should cease their unilateral penetration and offering no solution to the present economic chaos there.

This proposal admittedly calls for a shift in some of our thinking about international matters. It is imperative that we make this shift. We have little time to lose. Our post-war actions have not yet been adjusted to the lessons to be gained from experience of Allied co-operation during the war and the facts of the atomic age.

It is certainly desirable that, as far as possible, we achieve unity on the home front with respect to our international relations; but unity on the basis of building up conflict abroad would prove to be not only unsound but disastrous. I think there is some reason to fear that in our earnest efforts to achieve bipartisan unity in this country we may have given way too much to isolationism masquerading as tough realism in international affairs.

The real test lies in the achievement of international unity. It will be fruitless to continue to seek solutions for the many specific problems that face us in the making of the peace and in the establishment of an enduring international order without first achieving an atmosphere of mutual trust and confidence. The task admittedly is not an easy one. There is no question, as the Secretary of State has indicated, that negotiations with the Russians are difficult because of cultural differences, their traditional isolationism, and their insistence on a visible "quid pro quo" in all agreements.

REAL SECURITY

But the task is not an insuperable one if we take into account that to other nations our foreign policy consists not only of the principles that we advocate but of the actions we take. Fundamentally, this comes down to the point discussed earlier in this letter, that even our own security in the sense that we have known it in the past, cannot be preserved by military means in a world armed with atomic weapons. The only type of security which can be maintained by our own military force is the type described by a military man before the Senate atomic energy committee—a security against invasion after all our cities and perhaps 40 million of our city population have been destroyed by atomic weapons. That is the best that "security" on the basis of armaments has to offer us. It is not the kind of security that our people and the people of the other United Nations are striving for.

144 DOCUMENTS

I think that progressive leadership along the lines suggested above would represent and best serve the interests of the large majority of our people, would reassert the forward looking position of the Democratic Party in international affairs, and, finally, would arrest the new trend towards isolationism and a disastrous atomic world war.

Respectfully,

H. A. WALLACE.

DOCUMENT 3

The Truman Doctrine

As moves by the Soviet Union appeared more ominous to American observers in the year after Kennan penned his containment doctrine, President Truman became more convinced that he had to block any potential Russian advance. When the British announced they could no longer help the Greek government against an internal communist movement in early 1947, Truman feared the potential loss of Greece, and maybe Turkey as well, to communism. He declared the United States would help and asked Congress for a substantial sum. Yet Truman's language widened the promise of American help far beyond the eastern Mediterranean and set the stage for U.S. interventions against many kinds of actual or perceived communist threats over the subsequent decades.

PRESIDENT HARRY S. TRUMAN'S ADDRESS BEFORE A JOINT SESSION OF CONGRESS, MARCH 12, 1947

Mr. President, Mr. Speaker, Members of the Congress of the United States:

The gravity of the situation which confronts the world today necessitates my appearance before a joint session of the Congress. The foreign policy and the national security of this country are involved.

One aspect of the present situation, which I wish to present to you at this time for your consideration and decision, concerns Greece and Turkey.

The United States has received from the Greek Government an urgent appeal for financial and economic assistance. Preliminary reports from the

146 DOCUMENTS

American Economic Mission now in Greece and reports from the American Ambassador in Greece corroborate the statement of the Greek Government that assistance is imperative if Greece is to survive as a free nation.

I do not believe that the American people and the Congress wish to turn a deaf ear to the appeal of the Greek Government.

Greece is not a rich country. Lack of sufficient natural resources has always forced the Greek people to work hard to make both ends meet. Since 1940, this industrious and peace loving country has suffered invasion, four years of cruel enemy occupation, and bitter internal strife.

When forces of liberation entered Greece they found that the retreating Germans had destroyed virtually all the railways, roads, port facilities, communications, and merchant marine. More than a thousand villages had been burned. Eighty-five percent of the children were tubercular. Livestock, poultry, and draft animals had almost disappeared. Inflation had wiped out practically all savings.

As a result of these tragic conditions, a militant minority, exploiting human want and misery, was able to create political chaos which, until now, has made economic recovery impossible.

Greece is today without funds to finance the importation of those goods which are essential to bare subsistence. Under these circumstances the people of Greece cannot make progress in solving their problems of reconstruction. Greece is in desperate need of financial and economic assistance to enable it to resume purchases of food, clothing, fuel and seeds. These are indispensable for the subsistence of its people and are obtainable only from abroad. Greece must have help to import the goods necessary to restore internal order and security, so essential for economic and political recovery.

The Greek Government has also asked for the assistance of experienced American administrators, economists and technicians to insure that the financial and other aid given to Greece shall be used effectively in creating a stable and self-sustaining economy and in improving its public administration.

The very existence of the Greek state is today threatened by the terrorist activities of several thousand armed men, led by Communists, who defy the government's authority at a number of points, particularly along the northern boundaries. A Commission appointed by the United Nations Security Council is at present investigating disturbed conditions in northern Greece and alleged border violations along the frontier between Greece on the one hand and Albania, Bulgaria, and Yugoslavia on the other.

Meanwhile, the Greek Government is unable to cope with the situation. The Greek army is small and poorly equipped. It needs supplies and equipment if it is to restore the authority of the government

DOCUMENTS   147

throughout Greek territory. Greece must have assistance if it is to become a self-supporting and self-respecting democracy.

The United States must supply that assistance. We have already extended to Greece certain types of relief and economic aid but these are inadequate.

There is no other country to which democratic Greece can turn.

No other nation is willing and able to provide the necessary support for a democratic Greek government.

The British Government, which has been helping Greece, can give no further financial or economic aid after March 31. Great Britain finds itself under the necessity of reducing or liquidating its commitments in several parts of the world, including Greece.

We have considered how the United Nations might assist in this crisis. But the situation is an urgent one requiring immediate action and the United Nations and its related organizations are not in a position to extend help of the kind that is required.

It is important to note that the Greek Government has asked for our aid in utilizing effectively the financial and other assistance we may give to Greece, and in improving its public administration. It is of the utmost importance that we supervise the use of any funds made available to Greece; in such a manner that each dollar spent will count toward making Greece self-supporting, and will help to build an economy in which a healthy democracy can flourish.

No government is perfect. One of the chief virtues of a democracy, however, is that its defects are always visible and under democratic processes can be pointed out and corrected. The Government of Greece is not perfect. Nevertheless it represents eighty-five per cent of the members of the Greek Parliament who were chosen in an election last year. Foreign observers, including 692 Americans, considered this election to be a fair expression of the views of the Greek people.

The Greek Government has been operating in an atmosphere of chaos and extremism. It has made mistakes. The extension of aid by this country does not mean that the United States condones everything that the Greek Government has done or will do. We have condemned in the past, and we condemn now, extremist measures of the right or the left. We have in the past advised tolerance, and we advise tolerance now.

Greece's neighbor, Turkey, also deserves our attention.

The future of Turkey as an independent and economically sound state is clearly no less important to the freedom-loving peoples of the world than the future of Greece. The circumstances in which Turkey finds itself today are considerably different from those of Greece. Turkey has been spared the disasters that have beset Greece. And during the war, the United States and Great Britain furnished Turkey with material aid.

148   DOCUMENTS

Nevertheless, Turkey now needs our support.

Since the war Turkey has sought financial assistance from Great Britain and the United States for the purpose of effecting that modernization necessary for the maintenance of its national integrity.

That integrity is essential to the preservation of order in the Middle East.

The British government has informed us that, owing to its own difficulties can no longer extend financial or economic aid to Turkey.

As in the case of Greece, if Turkey is to have the assistance it needs, the United States must supply it. We are the only country able to provide that help.

I am fully aware of the broad implications involved if the United States extends assistance to Greece and Turkey, and I shall discuss these implications with you at this time.

One of the primary objectives of the foreign policy of the United States is the creation of conditions in which we and other nations will be able to work out a way of life free from coercion. This was a fundamental issue in the war with Germany and Japan. Our victory was won over countries which sought to impose their will, and their way of life, upon other nations.

To ensure the peaceful development of nations, free from coercion, the United States has taken a leading part in establishing the United Nations, The United Nations is designed to make possible lasting freedom and independence for all its members. We shall not realize our objectives, however, unless we are willing to help free peoples to maintain their free institutions and their national integrity against aggressive movements that seek to impose upon them totalitarian regimes. This is no more than a frank recognition that totalitarian regimes imposed on free peoples, by direct or indirect aggression, undermine the foundations of international peace and hence the security of the United States.

The peoples of a number of countries of the world have recently had totalitarian regimes forced upon them against their will. The Government of the United States has made frequent protests against coercion and intimidation, in violation of the Yalta agreement, in Poland, Rumania, and Bulgaria. I must also state that in a number of other countries there have been similar developments.

At the present moment in world history nearly every nation must choose between alternative ways of life. The choice is too often not a free one.

One way of life is based upon the will of the majority, and is distinguished by free institutions, representative government, free elections, guarantees of individual liberty, freedom of speech and religion, and freedom from political oppression.

DOCUMENTS 149

The second way of life is based upon the will of a minority forcibly imposed upon the majority. It relies upon terror and oppression, a controlled press and radio; fixed elections, and the suppression of personal freedoms.

I believe that it must be the policy of the United States to support free peoples who are resisting attempted subjugation by armed minorities or by outside pressures.

I believe that we must assist free peoples to work out their own destinies in their own way.

I believe that our help should be primarily through economic and financial aid which is essential to economic stability and orderly political processes.

The world is not static, and the status quo is not sacred. But we cannot allow changes in the status quo in violation of the Charter of the United Nations by such methods as coercion, or by such subterfuges as political infiltration. In helping free and independent nations to maintain their freedom, the United States will be giving effect to the principles of the Charter of the United Nations.

It is necessary only to glance at a map to realize that the survival and integrity of the Greek nation are of grave importance in a much wider situation. If Greece should fall under the control of an armed minority, the effect upon its neighbor, Turkey, would be immediate and serious. Confusion and disorder might well spread throughout the entire Middle East.

Moreover, the disappearance of Greece as an independent state would have a profound effect upon those countries in Europe whose peoples are struggling against great difficulties to maintain their freedoms and their independence while they repair the damages of war.

It would be an unspeakable tragedy if these countries, which have struggled so long against overwhelming odds, should lose that victory for which they sacrificed so much. Collapse of free institutions and loss of independence would be disastrous not only for them but for the world. Discouragement and possibly failure would quickly be the lot of neighboring peoples striving to maintain their freedom and independence.

Should we fail to aid Greece and Turkey in this fateful hour, the effect will be far reaching to the West as well as to the East.

We must take immediate and resolute action.

I therefore ask the Congress to provide authority for assistance to Greece and Turkey in the amount of $400,000,000 for the period ending June 30, 1948. In requesting these funds, I have taken into consideration the maximum amount of relief assistance which would be furnished to

Greece out of the $350,000,000 which I recently requested that the Congress authorize for the prevention of starvation and suffering in countries devastated by the war.

In addition to funds, I ask the Congress to authorize the detail of American civilian and military personnel to Greece and Turkey, at the request of those countries, to assist in the tasks of reconstruction, and for the purpose of supervising the use of such financial and material assistance as may be furnished. I recommend that authority also be provided for the instruction and training of selected Greek and Turkish personnel.

Finally, I ask that the Congress provide authority which will permit the speediest and most effective use, in terms of needed commodities, supplies, and equipment, of such funds as may be authorized.

If further funds, or further authority, should be needed for purposes indicated in this message, I shall not hesitate to bring the situation before the Congress. On this subject the Executive and Legislative branches of the Government must work together.

This is a serious course upon which we embark.

I would not recommend it except that the alternative is much more serious. The United States contributed $341,000,000,000 toward winning World War II. This is an investment in world freedom and world peace.

The assistance that I am recommending for Greece and Turkey amounts to little more than 1 tenth of 1 per cent of this investment. It is only common sense that we should safeguard this investment and make sure that it was not in vain.

The seeds of totalitarian regimes are nurtured by misery and want. They spread and grow in the evil soil of poverty and strife. They reach their full growth when the hope of a people for a better life has died. We must keep that hope alive.

The free peoples of the world look to us for support in maintaining their freedoms.

If we falter in our leadership, we may endanger the peace of the world—and we shall surely endanger the welfare of our own nation.

Great responsibilities have been placed upon us by the swift movement of events.

I am confident that the Congress will face these responsibilities squarely.

Source: Truman, Harry S. "Truman Doctrine." Delivered before a joint session of Congress, March 12, 1947. Lillian Goldman Law Library, 2008. http://avalon.law.yale.edu/20th_century/trudoc.asp. Accessed March 30, 2017.

DOCUMENT 4

Speech on the Truman Doctrine

As he had done a year earlier in private, Wallace again put forth an alternative vision of what he hoped the American stance toward Russia would be. He warned against the temptations he saw in the Truman Doctrine for the United States to pursue unnecessary and unproductive adventures abroad. He again pleaded, this time with the American public, for a more conciliatory tone toward the Soviet Union, and again represented a potentially different path forward for American foreign policy. While his views were not adopted, his ideas, and those of others who thought like him, have prompted historians to wonder if the United States could have won the Cold War at less cost to itself, and to other countries.

March 12, 1947, marked a turning point in American history. It is not a Greek crisis that we face, it is an American crisis. It is a crisis in the American spirit . . . Only the American people fully aroused and promptly acting can prevent disaster.

President Truman, in the name of democracy and humanitarianism, proposed a military lend-lease program. He proposed a loan of $400,000,000 to Greece and Turkey as a down payment on an unlimited expenditure aimed at opposing Communist expansion. He proposed, in effect, that America police Russia's every border. There is no regime too reactionary for us provided it stands in Russia's expansionist path. There is no country too remote to serve as the scene of a contest which may widen until it becomes a world war.

President Truman calls for action to combat a crisis. What is this crisis that necessitates Truman going to Capitol Hill as though a Pearl Harbor has suddenly hit us? How many more of these Pearl Harbors will there be? How can they be foreseen? What will they cost? [. . .]

One year ago at Fulton, Mo., Winston Churchill called for a diplomatic offensive against Soviet Russia. By sanctioning that speech, Truman committed us to a policy of combating Russia with British sources. That policy proved to be so bankrupt that Britain can no longer maintain it. Now President Truman proposes we take over Britain's hopeless task. Today Americans are asked to support the Governments of Greece and Turkey. Tomorrow we shall be asked to support the Governments of China and Argentina.

I say that this policy is utterly futile. No people can be bought. America cannot afford to spend billions and billions of dollars for unproductive purposes. The world is hungry and insecure, and the peoples of all lands demand change. President Truman cannot prevent change in the world any more than he can prevent the tide from coming in or the sun from setting. But once America stands for opposition to change, we are lost. America will become the most-hated nation in the world.

Russia may be poor and unprepared for war, but she knows very well how to reply to Truman's declaration of economic and financial pressure. All over the world Russia and her ally, poverty, will increase the pressure against us. Who among us is ready to predict that in this struggle American dollars will outlast the grievances that lead to communism? I certainly don't want to see communism spread. I predict that Truman's policy will spread communism in Europe and Asia. You can't fight something with nothing. When Truman offers unconditional aid to King George of Greece, he is acting as the best salesman communism ever had. In proposing this reckless adventure, Truman is betraying the great tradition of America and the leadership of the great American who preceded him . . .

When President Truman proclaims the world-wide conflict between East and West, he is telling the Soviet leaders that we are preparing for eventual war. They will reply by measures to strengthen their position in the event of war. Then the task of keeping the world at peace will pass beyond the power of the common people everywhere who want peace. Certainly it will not be freedom that will be victorious in this struggle. Psychological and spiritual preparation for war will follow financial preparation; civil liberties will be restricted; standards of living will be forced downward; families will be divided against each other; none of the values that we hold worth fighting for will be secure . . .

This is the time for an all-out worldwide reconstruction program for peace. This is America's opportunity. The peoples of all lands say to America: Send us plows for our fields instead of tanks and guns to be used against us. . . . The dollars that are spent will be spent for the production of goods and will come back to us in a thousand different ways. Our programs will be based on service instead of the outworn ideas of

DOCUMENTS 153

imperialism and power politics. It is a fundamental law of life that a strong idea is merely strengthened by persecution. The way to handle communism is by what William James called the replacing power of the higher affection. In other words, we give the common man all over the world something better than communism. I believe we have something better than communism here in America. But President Truman has not spoken for the American ideal. It is now the turn of the American people to speak.

Common sense is required of all of us in realizing that helping militarism never brings peace. Courage is required of all of us in carrying out a program that can bring peace. Courage and common sense are the qualities that made America great. Let's keep those qualities now.

Source: Wallace, Henry A. "Speech on the Truman Doctrine: March 27, 1947." Ashland University: Ashbrook Center, 2006–2017. http://teachingamericanhistory.org/library/document/speech-on-the-truman-doctrine/. Accessed March 30, 2017.

DOCUMENT 5

NSC-68

*W*ith both sides digging in for a long standoff by the end of the 1940s, the Truman administration undertook a full review of American foreign policy and produced NSC-68, which laid out the specific ways the United States would finance and conduct the globalized containment strategy of the Truman Doctrine. The document reinforced the view of the Soviet Union as a dangerous ideological enemy bent on world conquest and called for a larger American military presence around the globe. Critics, however, have noted that this militarization of American foreign policy narrowed the options for future presidents and made them susceptible to the use of either covert or overt force to achieve American objectives over the next several decades.

NSC 68: UNITED STATES OBJECTIVES AND PROGRAMS FOR NATIONAL SECURITY (APRIL 14, 1950)

A Report to the President Pursuant to the President's Directive of January 31, 1950

TOP SECRET
[Washington,] April 7, 1950

Contents

Terms of Reference
Analysis

I.   Background of the Present World Crisis
II.   The Fundamental Purpose of the United States
III.   The Fundamental Design of the Kremlin
IV.   The Underlying Conflict in the Realm of Ideas and Values Between the U.S. Purpose and the Kremlin Design

      1.   Nature of the Conflict
      2.   Objectives
      3.   Means

V.   Soviet Intentions and Capabilities—Actual and Potential
VI.   U.S. Intentions and Capabilities—Actual and Potential
VII.   Present Risks
VIII. Atomic Armaments

      A.   Military Evaluation of U.S. and U.S.S.R. Atomic Capabilities
      B.   Stockpiling and Use of Atomic Weapons
      C.   International Control of Atomic Energy

IX.   Possible Courses of Action

Introduction
The Role of Negotiation

A.   The First Course—Continuation of Current Policies, with Current and Currently Projected Programs for Carrying Out These Projects
B.   The Second Course—Isolation
C.   The Third Course—War
D.   The Remaining Course of Action—A Rapid Build-up of Political, Economic, and Military Strength in the Free World

Conclusions
Recommendations

TERMS OF REFERENCE

The following report is submitted in response to the President's directive of January 31 which reads:

That the President direct the Secretary of State and the Secretary of Defense to undertake a reexamination of our objectives in peace and war and of the effect of these objectives on our strategic plans, in the light of the probable fission bomb capability and possible thermonuclear bomb capability of the Soviet Union.

The document which recommended that such a directive be issued reads in part:

It must be considered whether a decision to proceed with a program directed toward determining feasibility prejudges the more fundamental decisions (a) as to whether, in the event that a test of a thermonuclear weapon proves successful, such weapons should be stockpiled, or (b) if stockpiled, the conditions under which they might be used in war. If a test of a thermonuclear weapon proves successful, the pressures to produce and stockpile such weapons to be held for the same purposes for which fission bombs are then being held will be greatly increased. The question of use policy can be adequately assessed only as a part of a general reexamination of this country's strategic plans and its objectives in peace and war. Such reexamination would need to consider national policy not only with respect to possible thermonuclear weapons, but also with respect to fission weapons—viewed in the light of the probable fission bomb capability and the possible thermonuclear bomb capability of the Soviet Union. The moral, psychological, and political questions involved in this problem would need to be taken into account and be given due weight. The outcome of this reexamination would have a crucial bearing on the further question as to whether there should be a revision in the nature of the agreements, including the international control of atomic energy, which we have been seeking to reach with the U.S.S.R.

ANALYSIS

I. Background of the Present Crisis

Within the past thirty-five years the world has experienced two global wars of tremendous violence. It has witnessed two revolutions—the Russian and the Chinese—of extreme scope and intensity. It has also seen the collapse of five empires–the Ottoman, the Austro-Hungarian, German, Italian, and Japanese—and the drastic decline of two major imperial systems, the British and the French. During the span of one generation, the international distribution of power has been fundamentally altered. For several centuries it had proved impossible for any one nation to gain such preponderant strength that a coalition of other nations could not in time face it with greater strength. The international scene was marked by recurring periods of violence and war, but a system of sovereign and independent states was maintained, over which no state was able to achieve hegemony.

Two complex sets of factors have now basically altered this historic distribution of power. First, the defeat of Germany and Japan and the decline of the British and French Empires have interacted with the development of the United States and the Soviet Union in such a way that power increasingly gravitated to these two centers. Second, the Soviet Union, unlike previous aspirants to hegemony, is animated by a new fanatic faith, anti-thetical to our own, and seeks to impose its absolute authority over the rest of the world. Conflict has, therefore, become endemic and is waged, on the part of the Soviet Union, by violent or non-violent methods in accordance with the dictates of expediency. With the development of increasingly terrifying weapons of mass destruction, every individual faces the ever-present possibility of annihilation should the conflict enter the phase of total war.

On the one hand, the people of the world yearn for relief from the anxiety arising from the risk of atomic war. On the other hand, any substantial further extension of the area under the domination of the Kremlin would raise the possibility that no coalition adequate to confront the Kremlin with greater strength could be assembled. It is in this context that this Republic and its citizens in the ascendancy of their strength stand in their deepest peril.

The issues that face us are momentous, involving the fulfillment or destruction not only of this Republic but of civilization itself. They are issues which will not await our deliberations. With conscience and resolution this Government and the people it represents must now take new and fateful decisions.

II. Fundamental Purpose of the United States

The fundamental purpose of the United States is laid down in the Preamble to the Constitution: ". . . to form a more perfect Union, establish justice, insure domestic Tranquility, provide for the common defence, promote the general Welfare, and secure the Blessings of Liberty to ourselves and our Posterity." In essence, the fundamental purpose is to assure the integrity and vitality of our free society, which is founded upon the dignity and worth of the individual.

Three realities emerge as a consequence of this purpose: Our determination to maintain the essential elements of individual freedom, as set forth in the Constitution and Bill of Rights; our determination to create conditions under which our free and democratic system can live and prosper; and our determination to fight if necessary to defend our way of

158 DOCUMENTS

life, for which as in the Declaration of Independence, "with a firm reliance on the protection of Divine Providence, we mutually pledge to each other our lives, our Fortunes, and our sacred Honor."

III. Fundamental Design of the Kremlin

The fundamental design of those who control the Soviet Union and the international communist movement is to retain and solidify their absolute power, first in the Soviet Union and second in the areas now under their control. In the minds of the Soviet leaders, however, achievement of this design requires the dynamic extension of their authority and the ultimate elimination of any effective opposition to their authority.

The design, therefore, calls for the complete subversion or forcible destruction of the machinery of government and structure of society in the countries of the non-Soviet world and their replacement by an apparatus and structure subservient to and controlled from the Kremlin. To that end Soviet efforts are now directed toward the domination of the Eurasian land mass. The United States, as the principal center of power in the non-Soviet world and the bulwark of opposition to Soviet expansion, is the principal enemy whose integrity and vitality must be subverted or destroyed by one means or another if the Kremlin is to achieve its fundamental design.

IV. The Underlying Conflict in the Realm of Ideas and Values between the U.S. Purpose and the Kremlin Design

A. NATURE OF CONFLICT

The Kremlin regards the United States as the only major threat to the conflict between idea of slavery under the grim oligarchy of the Kremlin, which has come to a crisis with the polarization of power described in Section I, and the exclusive possession of atomic weapons by the two protagonists. The idea of freedom, moreover, is peculiarly and intolerably subversive of the idea of slavery. But the converse is not true. The implacable purpose of the slave state to eliminate the challenge of freedom has placed the two great powers at opposite poles. It is this fact which gives the present polarization of power the quality of crisis.

The free society values the individual as an end in himself, requiring of him only that measure of self-discipline and self-restraint which make the rights of each individual compatible with the rights of every other individual. The freedom of the individual has as its counterpart, therefore, the negative responsibility of the individual not to exercise his freedom in ways inconsistent with the freedom of other individuals and the positive responsibility to make constructive use of his freedom in the building of a just society.

From this idea of freedom with responsibility derives the marvelous diversity, the deep tolerance, the lawfulness of the free society. This is the explanation of the strength of free men. It constitutes the integrity and the vitality of a free and democratic system. The free society attempts to create and maintain an environment in which every individual has the opportunity to realize his creative powers. It also explains why the free society tolerates those within it who would use their freedom to destroy it. By the same token, in relations between nations, the prime reliance of the free society is on the strength and appeal of its idea, and it feels no compulsion sooner or later to bring all societies into conformity with it.

For the free society does not fear, it welcomes, diversity. It derives its strength from its hospitality even to antipathetic ideas. It is a market for free trade in ideas, secure in its faith that free men will take the best wares, and grows to a fuller and better realization of their powers in exercising their choice.

The idea of freedom is the most contagious idea in history, more contagious than the idea of submission to authority. For the breadth of freedom cannot be tolerated in a society which has come under the domination of an individual or group of individuals with a will to absolute power. Where the despot holds absolute power—the absolute power of the absolutely powerful will—all other wills must be subjugated in an act of willing submission, a degradation willed by the individual upon himself under the compulsion of a perverted faith. It is the first article of this faith that he finds and can only find the meaning of his existence in serving the ends of the system. The system becomes God, and submission to the will of God becomes submission to the will of the system. It is not enough to yield outwardly to the system—even Gandhian non-violence is not acceptable—for the spirit of resistance and the devotion to a higher authority might then remain, and the individual would not be wholly submissive.

The same compulsion which demands total power over all men within the Soviet state without a single exception, demands total power over all Communist Parties and all states under Soviet domination. Thus Stalin has said that the theory and tactics of Leninism as expounded by the Bolshevik party are mandatory for the proletarian parties of all countries. A true internationalist is defined as one who unhesitatingly upholds the position of the Soviet Union and in the satellite states true patriotism is love of the Soviet Union. By the same token the "peace policy" of the

160 DOCUMENTS

Soviet Union, described at a Party Congress as "a more advantageous form of fighting capitalism," is a device to divide and immobilize the non-Communist world, and the peace the Soviet Union seeks is the peace of total conformity to Soviet policy.

The antipathy of slavery to freedom explains the iron curtain, the isolation, the autarchy of the society whose end is absolute power. The existence and persistence of the idea of freedom is a permanent and continuous threat to the foundation of the slave society; and it therefore regards as intolerable the long continued existence of freedom in the world. What is new, what makes the continuing crisis, is the polarization of power which now inescapably confronts the slave society with the free.

The assault on free institutions is world-wide now, and in the context of the present polarization of power a defeat of free institutions anywhere is a defeat everywhere. The shock we sustained in the destruction of Czechoslovakia was not in the measure of Czechoslovakia's material importance to us. In a material sense, her capabilities were already at Soviet disposal. But when the integrity of Czechoslovak institutions was destroyed, it was in the intangible scale of values that we registered a loss more damaging than the material loss we had already suffered.

Thus unwillingly our free society finds itself mortally challenged by the Soviet system. No other value system is so wholly irreconcilable with ours, so implacable in its purpose to destroy ours, so capable of turning to its own uses the most dangerous and divisive trends in our own society, no other so skillfully and powerfully evokes the elements of irrationality in human nature everywhere, and no other has the support of a great and growing center of military power.

B. OBJECTIVES

The objectives of a free society are determined by its fundamental values and by the necessity for maintaining the material environment in which they flourish. Logically and in fact, therefore, the Kremlin's challenge to the United States is directed not only to our values but to our physical capacity to protect their environment. It is a challenge which encompasses both peace and war and our objectives in peace and war must take account of it.

1. Thus we must make ourselves strong, both in the way in which we affirm our values in the conduct of our national life, and in the development of our military and economic strength.
2. We must lead in building a successfully functioning political and economic system in the free world. It is only by practical affirmation,

DOCUMENTS 161

abroad as well as at home, of our essential values, that we can preserve our own integrity, in which lies the real frustration of the Kremlin design.

3. But beyond thus affirming our values our policy and actions must be such as to foster a fundamental change in the nature of the Soviet system, a change toward which the frustration of the design is the first and perhaps the most important step. Clearly it will not only be less costly but more effective if this change occurs to a maximum extent as a result of internal forces in Soviet society.

In a shrinking world, which now faces the threat of atomic warfare, it is not an adequate objective merely to seek to check the Kremlin design, for the absence of order among nations is becoming less and less tolerable. This fact imposes on us, in our own interests, the responsibility of world leadership. It demands that we make the attempt, and accept the risks inherent in it, to bring about order and justice by means consistent with the principles of freedom and democracy. We should limit our requirement of the Soviet Union to its participation with other nations on the basis of equality and respect for the rights of others. Subject to this requirement, we must with our allies and the former subject peoples seek to create a world society based on the principle of consent. Its framework cannot be inflexible. It will consist of many national communities of great and varying abilities and resources, and hence of war potential. The seeds of conflicts will inevitably exist or will come into being. To acknowledge this is only to acknowledge the impossibility of a final solution. Not to acknowledge it can be fatally dangerous in a world in which there are no final solutions.

All these objectives of a free society are equally valid and necessary in peace and war. But every consideration of devotion to our fundamental values and to our national security demands that we seek to achieve them by the strategy of the cold war. It is only by developing the moral and material strength of the free world that the Soviet regime will become convinced of the falsity of its assumptions and that the pre-conditions for workable agreements can be created. By practically demonstrating the integrity and vitality of our system the free world widens the area of possible agreement and thus can hope gradually to bring about a Soviet acknowledgement of realities which in sum will eventually constitute a frustration of the Soviet design. Short of this, however, it might be possible to create a situation which will induce the Soviet Union to accommodate itself, with or without the conscious abandonment of its design, to coexistence on tolerable terms with the non-Soviet world. Such a development would be a triumph for the idea of freedom and democracy. It must be an immediate objective of United States policy.

162   DOCUMENTS

There is no reason, in the event of war, for us to alter our overall objectives. They do not include unconditional surrender, the subjugation of the Russian peoples or a Russia shorn of its economic potential. Such a course would irrevocably unite the Russian people behind the regime which enslaves them. Rather these objectives contemplate Soviet acceptance of the specific and limited conditions requisite to an international environment in which free institutions can flourish, and in which the Russian peoples will have a new chance to work out their own destiny. If we can make the Russian people our allies in the enterprise we will obviously have made our task easier and victory more certain.

The objectives outlined in NSC 20/4 (November 23, 1948) . . . are fully consistent with the objectives stated in this paper, and they remain valid. The growing intensity of the conflict which has been imposed upon us, however, requires the changes of emphasis and the additions that are apparent. Coupled with the probable fission bomb capability and possible thermonuclear bomb capability of the Soviet Union, the intensifying struggle requires us to face the fact that we can expect no lasting abatement of the crisis unless and until a change occurs in the nature of the Soviet system.

C. MEANS

The free society is limited in its choice of means to achieve its ends.

Compulsion is the negation of freedom, except when it is used to enforce the rights common to all. The resort to force, internally or externally, is therefore a last resort for a free society. The act is permissible only when one individual or groups of individuals within it threaten the basic rights of other individuals or when another society seeks to impose its will upon it. The free society cherishes and protects as fundamental the rights of the minority against the will of a majority, because these rights are the inalienable rights of each and every individual.

The resort to force, to compulsion, to the imposition of its will is therefore a difficult and dangerous act for a free society, which is warranted only in the face of even greater dangers. The necessity of the act must be clear and compelling; the act must commend itself to the overwhelming majority as an inescapable exception to the basic idea of freedom; or the regenerative capacity of free men after the act has been performed will be endangered.

The Kremlin is able to select whatever means are expedient in seeking to carry out its fundamental design. Thus it can make the best of several possible worlds, conducting the struggle on those levels where it considers it profitable and enjoying the benefits of a pseudo-peace on those levels where it is not ready for a contest. At the ideological or psychological level, in the struggle for men's minds, the conflict is worldwide. At the political and economic level, within states and in the relations between states, the struggle for power is being intensified. And at the military level, the Kremlin has thus far been careful not to commit a technical breach of the peace, although using its vast forces to intimidate its neighbors, and to support an aggressive foreign policy, and not hesitating through its agents to resort to arms in favorable circumstances. The attempt to carry out its fundamental design is being pressed, therefore, with all means which are believed expedient in the present situation, and the Kremlin has inextricably engaged us in the conflict between its design and our purpose.

We have no such freedom of choice, and least of all in the use of force. Resort to war is not only a last resort for a free society, but it is also an act which cannot definitively end the fundamental conflict in the realm of ideas. The idea of slavery can only be overcome by the timely and persistent demonstration of the superiority of the idea of freedom. Military victory alone would only partially and perhaps only temporarily affect the fundamental conflict, for although the ability of the Kremlin to threaten our security might be for a time destroyed, the resurgence of totalitarian forces and the re-establishment of the Soviet system or its equivalent would not be long delayed unless great progress were made in the fundamental conflict.

Practical and ideological considerations therefore both impel us to the conclusion that we have no choice but to demonstrate the superiority of the idea of freedom by its constructive application, and to attempt to change the world situation by means short of war in such a way as to frustrate the Kremlin design and hasten the decay of the Soviet system.

For us the role of military power is to serve the national purpose by deterring an attack upon us while we seek by other means to create an environment in which our free society can flourish, and by fighting, if necessary, to defend the integrity and vitality of our free society and to defeat any aggressor. The Kremlin uses Soviet military power to back up and serve the Kremlin design. It does not hesitate to use military force aggressively if that course is expedient in the achievement of its design. The differences between our fundamental purpose and the Kremlin design, therefore, are reflected in our respective attitudes toward and use of military force.

Our free society, confronted by a threat to its basic values, naturally will take such action, including the use of military force, as may be required to protect those values. The integrity of our system will not be jeopardized by any measures, covert or overt, violent or non-violent, which serve the purposes of frustrating the Kremlin design, nor does the necessity for conducting ourselves so as to affirm our values in actions as well as words forbid such measures, provided only they are appropriately calculated to that end and are not so excessive or misdirected as to make us enemies of the people instead of the evil men who have enslaved them.

But if war comes, what is the role of force? Unless we so use it that the Russian people can perceive that our effort is directed against the regime and its power for aggression, and not against their own interests, we will unite the regime and the people in the kind of last ditch fight in which no underlying problems are solved, new ones are created, and where our basic principles are obscured and compromised. If we do not in the application of force demonstrate the nature of our objectives we will, in fact, have compromised from the outset our fundamental purpose. In the words of the *Federalist* (No. 28) "The means to be employed must be proportioned to the extent of the mischief." The mischief may be a global war or it may be a Soviet campaign for limited objectives. In either case we should take no avoidable initiative which would cause it to become a war of annihilation, and if we have the forces to defeat a Soviet drive for limited objectives it may well be to our interest not to let it become a global war. Our aim in applying force must be to compel the acceptance of terms consistent with our objectives, and our capabilities for the application of force should, therefore, within the limits of what we can sustain over the long pull, be congruent to the range of tasks which we may encounter.

V. Soviet Intentions and Capabilities—Actual and Potential

A. POLITICAL AND PSYCHOLOGICAL

The Kremlin's design for world domination begins at home. The first concern of a despotic oligarchy is that the local base of its power and authority be secure. The massive fact of the iron curtain isolating the Soviet peoples from the outside world, the repeated political purges within the USSR and the institutionalized crimes of the MVD [the Soviet Ministry of Internal Affairs] are evidence that the Kremlin does not feel secure at home and that "the entire coercive force of the socialist state" is more than ever one of seeking to impose its absolute authority over "the economy, manner of life, and consciousness of people" (Vyshinski, *The Law of the Soviet State,* p. 74). Similar evidence in the satellite states of Eastern Europe leads to the conclusion that this same policy, in less advanced phases, is being applied to the Kremlin's colonial areas.

Being a totalitarian dictatorship, the Kremlin's objectives in these policies is the total subjective submission of the peoples now under its

DOCUMENTS   165

control. The concentration camp is the prototype of the society which these policies are designed to achieve, a society in which the personality of the individual is so broken and perverted that he participates affirmatively in his own degradation.

The Kremlin's policy toward areas not under its control is the elimination of resistance to its will and the extension of its influence and control. It is driven to follow this policy because it cannot, for the reasons set forth in Chapter IV, tolerate the existence of free societies; to the Kremlin the most mild and inoffensive free society is an affront, a challenge and a subversive influence. Given the nature of the Kremlin, and the evidence at hand, it seems clear that the ends toward which this policy is directed are the same as those where its control has already been established.

The means employed by the Kremlin in pursuit of this policy are limited only by considerations of expediency. Doctrine is not a limiting factor; rather it dictates the employment of violence, subversion, and deceit, and rejects moral considerations. In any event, the Kremlin's conviction of its own infallibility has made its devotion to theory so subjective that past or present pronouncements as to doctrine offer no reliable guide to future actions. The only apparent restraints on resort to war are, therefore, calculations of practicality.

With particular reference to the United States, the Kremlin's strategic and tactical policy is affected by its estimate that we are not only the greatest immediate obstacle which stands between it and world domination, we are also the only power which could release forces in the free and Soviet worlds which could destroy it. The Kremlin's policy toward us is consequently animated by a peculiarly virulent blend of hatred and fear. Its strategy has been one of attempting to undermine the complex of forces, in this country and in the rest of the free world, on which our power is based. In this it has both adhered to doctrine and followed the sound principle of seeking maximum results with minimum risks and commitments. The present application of this strategy is a new form of expression for traditional Russian caution. However, there is no justification in Soviet theory or practice for predicting that, should the Kremlin become convinced that it could cause our downfall by one conclusive blow, it would not seek that solution.

In considering the capabilities of the Soviet world, it is of prime importance to remember that, in contrast to ours, they are being drawn upon close to the maximum possible extent. Also in contrast to us, the Soviet world can do more with less—it has a lower standard of living, its economy requires less to keep it functioning, and its military machine operates effectively with less elaborate equipment and organization.

166 DOCUMENTS

The capabilities of the Soviet world are being exploited to the full because the Kremlin is inescapably militant. It is inescapably militant because it possesses and is possessed by a world-wide revolutionary movement, because it 'is the inheritor of Russian imperialism, and because it is a totalitarian dictatorship. Persistent crisis, conflict, and expansion are the essence of the Kremlin's militancy. This dynamism serves to intensify all Soviet capabilities.

Two enormous organizations, the Communist Party and the secret police, are an outstanding source of strength to the Kremlin. In the Party, it has an apparatus designed to impose at home an ideological uniformity among its people and to act abroad as an instrument of propaganda, subversion and espionage. In its police apparatus, it has a domestic repressive instrument guaranteeing under present circumstances the continued security of the Kremlin. The demonstrated capabilities of these two basic organizations, operating openly or in disguise, in mass or through single agents, is unparalleled in history. The party, the police and the conspicuous might of the Soviet military machine together tend to create an overall impression of irresistible Soviet power among many peoples of the free world.

The ideological pretensions of the Kremlin are another great source of strength. Its identification of the Soviet system with communism, its peace campaigns and its championing of colonial peoples may be viewed with apathy, if not cynicism, by the oppressed totalitariat of the Soviet world, but in the free world these ideas find favorable responses in vulnerable segments of society. They have found a particularly receptive audience in Asia, especially as the Asiatics have been impressed by what has been plausibly portrayed to them as the rapid advance of the USSR from a backward society to a position of great world power. Thus, in its pretensions to being (a) the source of a new universal faith and (b) the model "scientific" society, the Kremlin cynically identifies itself with the genuine aspirations of large numbers of people, and places itself at the head of an international crusade with all of the benefits which derive there from.

Finally, there is a category of capabilities, strictly speaking neither institutional nor ideological, which should be taken into consideration. The extraordinary flexibility of Soviet tactics is certainly a strength. It derives from the utterly amoral and opportunistic conduct of Soviet policy. Combining this quality with the elements of secrecy, the Kremlin possesses a formidable capacity to act with the widest tactical latitude, with stealth, and with speed.

The greatest vulnerability of the Kremlin lies in the basic nature of its relations with the Soviet people.

That relationship is characterized by universal suspicion, fear, and denunciation. It is a relationship in which the Kremlin relies, not only for its power but its very survival, on intricately devised mechanisms of coercion. The Soviet monolith is held together by the iron curtain around it and the iron bars within it, not by any force of natural cohesion. These artificial mechanisms of unity have never been intelligently challenged by a strong outside force. The full measure of their vulnerability is therefore not yet evident.

The Kremlin's relations with its satellites and their peoples is likewise a vulnerability. Nationalism still remains the most potent emotional-political force. The well-known ills of colonialism are compounded, however, by the excessive demands of the Kremlin that its satellites accept not only the imperial authority of Moscow but that they believe in and proclaim the ideological primacy and infallibility of the Kremlin. These excessive requirements can be made good only through extreme coercion. The result is that if a satellite feels able to effect its independence of the Kremlin, as Tito was able to do, it is likely to break away.

In short, Soviet ideas and practices run counter to the best and potentially the strongest instincts of men, and deny their most fundamental aspirations. Against an adversary which effectively affirmed the constructive and hopeful instincts of men and was capable of fulfilling their fundamental aspirations, the Soviet system might prove to be fatally weak.

The problem of succession to Stalin is also a Kremlin vulnerability. In a system where supreme power is acquired and held through violence and intimidation, the transfer of that power may well produce a period of instability.

In a very real sense, the Kremlin is a victim of, its own dynamism. This dynamism can become a weakness if it is frustrated, if in its forward thrusts it encounters a superior force which halts the expansion and exerts a superior counter pressure. Yet the Kremlin cannot relax the condition of crisis and mobilization, for to do so would be to lose its dynamism, whereas the seeds of decay within the Soviet system would begin to flourish and fructify.

The Kremlin is, of course, aware of these weaknesses. It must know that in the present world situation they are of secondary significance. So long as the Kremlin retains the initiative, so long as it can keep on the offensive unchallenged by clearly superior counter-force—spiritual as well as material—its vulnerabilities are largely inoperative and even concealed by its successes. The Kremlin has not yet been given real reason to fear and be diverted by the rot within its system.

B. ECONOMIC

The Kremlin has no economic intentions unrelated to its overall policies. Economics in the Soviet world is not an end in itself. The Kremlin's policy,

168 DOCUMENTS

in so far as it has to do with economics, is to utilize economic processes to contribute to the overall strength, particularly the war-making capacity of the Soviet system. The material welfare of the totalitariat is severely subordinated to the interest of the system.

As for capabilities, even granting optimistic Soviet reports of production, the total economic strength of the U.S.S.R. compares with that of the U.S. as roughly one to four. This is reflected not only in gross national product (1949: USSR $65 billion; U.S. $250 billion), but in production of key commodities in 1949:

	U.S.	USSR	USSR and EUROPEAN ORBIT COMBINED
Ingot Steel (million met. tons)	80.4	21.5	28.0
Primary aluminum (thousand met. tons)	617.6	130–135	140–145
Electric power (billion kwh)	410	72	112
Crude oil (million met. tons)	276.5	33.0	38.9

Assuming the maintenance of present policies, while a large U.S. advantage is likely to remain, the Soviet Union will be steadily reducing the discrepancy between its overall economic strength and that of the U.S. by continuing to devote proportionately more to capital investment than the U.S.

But a full-scale effort by the U.S. would be capable of precipitately altering this trend. The USSR today is on a near maximum production basis. No matter what efforts Moscow might make, only a relatively slight change in the rate of increase in overall production could be brought about. In the U.S., on the other hand, a very rapid absolute expansion could be realized. The fact remains, however, that so long as the Soviet Union is virtually mobilized, and the United States has scarcely begun to summon up its forces, the greater capabilities of the U.S. are to that extent inoperative in the struggle for power. Moreover, as the Soviet attainment of an atomic capability has demonstrated, the totalitarian state, at least in time of peace, can focus its efforts on any given project far more readily than the democratic state.

In other fields—general technological competence, skilled labor resources, productivity of labor force, etc.—the gap between the USSR

DOCUMENTS 169

and the U.S. roughly corresponds to the gap in production. In the field of scientific research, however, the margin of United States superiority is unclear, especially if the Kremlin can utilize European talents.

C. MILITARY

The Soviet Union is developing the military capacity to support its design for world domination. The Soviet Union actually possesses armed forces far in excess of those necessary to defend its national territory. These armed forces are probably not yet considered by the Soviet Union to be sufficient to initiate a war which would involve the United States. This excessive strength, coupled now with an atomic capability, provides the Soviet Union with great coercive power for use in time of peace in furtherance of its objectives and serves as a deterrent to the victims of its aggression from taking any action in opposition to its tactics which would risk war.

Should a major war occur in 1950 the Soviet Union and its satellites are considered by the Joint Chiefs of Staff to be in a sufficiently advanced state of preparation immediately to undertake and carry out the following campaigns.

a. To overrun Western Europe, with the possible exception of the Iberian and Scandinavian Peninsulas; to drive toward the oil-bearing areas of the Near and Middle East; and to consolidate Communist gains in the Far East;
b. To launch air attacks against the British Isles and air and sea attacks against the lines of communications of the Western Powers in the Atlantic and the Pacific;
c. To attack selected targets with atomic weapons, now including the likelihood of such attacks against targets in Alaska, Canada, and the United States. Alternatively, this capability, coupled with other actions open to the Soviet Union, might deny the United Kingdom as an effective base of operations for allied forces. It also should be possible for the Soviet Union to prevent any allied "Normandy" type amphibious operations intended to force a reentry into the continent of Europe.

After the Soviet Union completed its initial campaigns and consolidated its positions in the Western European area, it could simultaneously conduct:

a. Full-scale air and limited sea operations against the British Isles;
b. Invasions of the Iberian and Scandinavian Peninsulas;

170 DOCUMENTS

c. Further operations in the Near and Middle East, continued air operations against the North American continent, and air and sea operations against Atlantic and Pacific lines of communication; and

d. Diversionary attacks in other areas.

During the course of the offensive operations listed in the second and third paragraphs above, the Soviet Union will have an air defense capability with respect to the vital areas of its own and its satellites' territories which can oppose but cannot prevent allied air operations against these areas.

It is not known whether the Soviet Union possesses war reserves and arsenal capabilities sufficient to supply its satellite armies or even its own forces throughout a long war. It might not be in the interest of the Soviet Union to equip fully its satellite armies, since the possibility of defections would exist.

It is not possible at this time to assess accurately the finite disadvantages to the Soviet Union which may accrue through the implementation of the Economic Cooperation Act of 1948, as amended, and the Mutual Defense Assistance Act of 1949. It should be expected that, as this implementation progresses, the internal security situation of the recipient nations should improve concurrently. In addition, a strong United States military position, plus increases in the armaments of the nations of Western Europe, should strengthen the determination of the recipient nations to counter Soviet moves and in event of war could be considered as likely to delay operations and increase the time required for the Soviet Union to overrun Western Europe. In all probability, although United States backing will stiffen their determination, the armaments increase under the present aid programs will not be of any major consequence prior to 1952. Unless the military strength of the Western European nations is increased on a much larger scale than under current programs and at an accelerated rate, it is more than likely that those nations will not be able to oppose even by 1960 the Soviet armed forces in war with any degree of effectiveness. Considering the Soviet Union military capability, the long-range allied military objective in Western Europe must envisage an increased military strength in that area sufficient possibly to deter the Soviet Union from a major war or, in any event, to delay materially the over-running of Western Europe and, if feasible, to hold a bridgehead on the continent against Soviet Union offensives.

We do not know accurately what the Soviet atomic capability is but the Central Intelligence Agency intelligence estimates, concurred in by State, Army, Navy, Air Force, and Atomic Energy Commission, assign to the Soviet Union a production capability giving it a fission bomb stockpile within the following ranges:

By mid-1950	10–20
By mid-1951	25–45
By mid-1952	45–90
By mid-1953	70–135
By mid-1954	200

This estimate is admittedly based on incomplete coverage of Soviet activities and represents the production capabilities of known or deducible Soviet plants. If others exist, as is possible, this estimate could lead us into a feeling of superiority in our atomic stockpile that might be dangerously misleading, particularly with regard to the timing of a possible Soviet offensive. On the other hand, if the Soviet Union experiences operating difficulties, this estimate would be reduced. There is some evidence that the Soviet Union is acquiring certain materials essential to research on and development of thermonuclear weapons.

The Soviet Union now has aircraft able to deliver the atomic bomb. Our Intelligence estimates assign to the Soviet Union an atomic bomber capability already in excess of that needed to deliver available bombs. We have at present no evaluated estimate regarding the Soviet accuracy of delivery on target. It is believed that the Soviets cannot deliver their bombs on target with a degree of accuracy comparable to ours, but a planning estimate might well place it at 40–60 percent of bombs sorted. For planning purposes, therefore, the date the Soviets possess an atomic stockpile of 200 bombs would be a critical date for the United States, for the delivery of 100 atomic bombs on targets in the United States would seriously damage this country.

At the time the Soviet Union has a substantial atomic stockpile and if it is assumed that it will strike a strong surprise blow and if it is assumed further that its atomic attacks will be met with no more effective defense opposition than the United States and its allies have programmed, results of those attacks could include:

a. Laying waste to the British Isles and thus depriving the Western Powers of their use as a base;

b. Destruction of the vital centers and of the communications of Western Europe, thus precluding effective defense by the Western Powers; and

c. Delivering devastating attacks on certain vital centers of the United States and Canada.

The possession by the Soviet Union of a thermonuclear capability in addition to this substantial atomic stockpile would result in tremendously increased damage.

During this decade, the defensive capabilities of the Soviet Union will probably be strengthened, particularly by the development and use of modem aircraft, aircraft warning and communications devices, and defensive guided missiles.

VI. U.S. Intentions and Capabilities—Actual and Potential

A. POLITICAL AND PSYCHOLOGICAL

Our overall policy at the present time may be described as one designed to foster a world environment in which the American system can survive and flourish. It therefore rejects the concept of isolation and affirms the necessity of our positive participation in the world community.

This broad intention embraces two subsidiary policies. One is a policy which we would probably pursue even if there were no Soviet threat. It is a policy of attempting to develop a healthy international community. The other is the policy of "containing" the Soviet system. These two policies are closely interrelated and interact on one another. Nevertheless, the distinction between them is basically valid and contributes to a clearer understanding of what we are trying to do.

The policy of striving to develop a healthy international community is the long-term constructive effort which we are engaged in. It was this policy which gave rise to our vigorous sponsorship of the United Nations. It is of course the principal reason for our long continuing endeavors to create and now develop the Inter-American system. It, as much as containment, underlay our efforts to rehabilitate Western Europe. Most of our international economic activities can likewise be explained in terms of this policy.

In a world of polarized power, the policies designed to develop a healthy international community are more than ever necessary to our own strength.

As for the policy of "containment," it is one which seeks by all means short of war to (1) block further expansion of Soviet power, (2) expose the falsities of Soviet pretensions, (3) induce a retraction of the Kremlin's control and influence, and (4) in general, so foster the seeds of destruction within the Soviet system that the Kremlin is brought at least to the point of modifying its behavior to conform to generally accepted international standards.

DOCUMENTS   173

It was and continues to be cardinal in this policy that we possess superior overall power in ourselves or in dependable combination with other like-minded nations. One of the most important ingredients of power is military strength. In the concept of "containment," the maintenance of a strong military posture is deemed to be essential for two reasons: (1) as an ultimate guarantee of our national security and (2) as an indispensable backdrop to the conduct of the policy of "containment." Without superior aggregate military strength, in being and readily mobilizable, a policy of "containment"—which is in effect a policy of calculated and gradual coercion—is no more than a policy of bluff.

At the same time, it is essential to the successful conduct of a policy of "containment" that we always leave open the possibility of negotiation with the USSR. A diplomatic freeze—and we are in one now—tends to defeat the very purposes of "containment" because it raises tensions at the same time that it makes Soviet retractions and adjustments in the direction of moderated behavior more difficult. It also tends to inhibit our initiative and deprives us of opportunities for maintaining a moral ascendancy in our struggle with the Soviet system.

In "containment" it is desirable to exert pressure in a fashion which will avoid so far as possible directly challenging Soviet prestige, to keep open the possibility for the USSR to retreat before pressure with a minimum loss of face and to secure political advantage from the failure of the Kremlin to yield or take advantage of the openings we leave it.

We have failed to implement adequately these two fundamental aspects of "containment." In the face of obviously mounting Soviet military strength ours has declined relatively. Partly as a byproduct of this, but also for other reasons, we now find ourselves at a diplomatic impasse with the Soviet Union, with the Kremlin growing bolder, with both of us holding on grimly to what we have, and with ourselves facing difficult decisions.

In examining our capabilities it is relevant to ask at the outset—capabilities for what? The answer cannot be stated solely in the negative terms of resisting the Kremlin design. It includes also our capabilities to attain the fundamental purpose of the United States, and to foster a world environment in which our free society can survive and flourish.

Potentially we have these capabilities. We know we have them in the economic and military fields. Potentially we also have them in the political and psychological fields. The vast majority of Americans are confident that the system of values which animates our society—the principles of freedom, tolerance, the importance of the individual, and the supremacy of reason over will—are valid and more vital than the ideology which is the fuel of Soviet dynamism. Translated into terms relevant to the lives of other peoples—our system of values can become perhaps a powerful appeal to millions who now seek or find in authoritarianism a refuge from anxieties, bafflement, and insecurity.

Essentially, our democracy also possesses a unique degree of unity. Our society is fundamentally more cohesive than the Soviet system, the solidarity of which is artificially created through force, fear, and favor. This means that expressions of national consensus in our society are soundly and solidly based. It means that the possibility of revolution in this country is fundamentally less than that in the Soviet system.

These capabilities within us constitute a great potential force in our international relations. The potential within us of bearing witness to the values by which we live holds promise for a dynamic manifestation to the rest of the world of the vitality of our system. The essential tolerance of our world outlook, our generous and constructive impulses, and the absence of covetousness in our international relations are assets of potentially enormous influence.

These then are our potential capabilities. Between them and our capabilities currently being utilized is a wide gap of unactualized power. In sharp contrast is the situation of the Soviet world. Its capabilities are inferior to those of our allies and to our own. But they are mobilized close to the maximum possible extent.

The full power which resides within the American people will be evoked only through the traditional democratic process: This process requires, firstly, that sufficient information regarding the basic political, economic, and military elements of the present situation be made publicly available so that an intelligent popular opinion may be formed. Having achieved a comprehension of the issues now confronting this Republic, it will then be possible for the American people, and the American Government to arrive at a consensus. Out of this common view will develop a determination of the national will and a solid resolute expression of that will. The initiative in this process lies with the Government.

The democratic way is harder than the authoritarian way because, in seeking to protect and fulfill the individual, it demands of him understanding, judgment, and positive participation in the increasingly complex, and exacting problems of the modern world. It demands that he exercise discrimination: that while pursuing through free inquiry the search for truth he knows when he should commit an act of faith; that he distinguish between the necessity for tolerance and the necessity for just suppression. A free society is vulnerable in that it is easy for people to lapse into excesses—the excesses of a permanently open mind wishfully waiting for evidence that evil design may become noble purpose, the excess of faith becoming prejudice, the excess of tolerance degenerating into

DOCUMENTS   175

indulgence of conspiracy and the excess of resorting to suppression when more moderate measures are not only more appropriate but more effective.

In coping with dictatorial governments acting in secrecy and with speed, we are also vulnerable in that the democratic process necessarily operates in the open and at a deliberate tempo. Weaknesses in our situation are readily apparent and subject to immediate exploitation. This Government therefore cannot afford in the face of the totalitarian challenge to operate on a narrow margin of strength. A democracy can compensate for its natural vulnerability only if it maintains clearly superior overall power in its most inclusive sense.

The very virtues of our system likewise handicap us in certain respects in our relations with our allies. While it is a general source of strength to us that our relations with our allies are conducted on a basis of persuasion and consent rather than compulsion and capitulation, it is also evident that dissent among us can become a vulnerability. Sometimes the dissent has its principal roots abroad in situations about which we can do nothing. Sometimes it arises largely out of certain weaknesses within ourselves, about which we can do something—our native impetuosity and a tendency to expect too much from people widely divergent from us.

The full capabilities of the rest of the free world are a potential increment to our own capabilities. It may even be said that the capabilities of the Soviet world, specifically the capabilities of the masses who have nothing to lose but their Soviet chains, are a potential which can be enlisted on our side.

Like our own capabilities, those of the rest of the free world exceed the capabilities of the Soviet system. Like our own they are far from being effectively mobilized and employed in the struggle against the Kremlin design. This is so because the rest of the free world lacks a sense of unity, confidence, and common purpose. This is true in even the most homogeneous and advanced segment of the free world—Western Europe.

As we ourselves demonstrate power, confidence, and a sense of moral and political direction, so those same qualities will be evoked in Western Europe. In such a situation, we may also anticipate a general improvement in the political tone in Latin America, Asia, and Africa and the real beginnings of awakening among the Soviet totalitariat.

In the absence of affirmative decision on our part, the rest of the free world is almost certain to become demoralized. Our friends will become more than a liability to us; they can eventually become a positive increment to Soviet power.

In sum, the capabilities of our allies are, in an important sense, a function of our own. An affirmative decision to summon up the potential

176 DOCUMENTS

within ourselves would evoke the potential strength within others and add it to our own.

B. ECONOMIC

1. *Capabilities*. In contrast to the war economy of the Soviet world (cf. Ch. V–B), the American economy (and the economy of the free world as a whole) is at present directed to the provision of rising standards of living. The military budget of the United States represents 6 to 7 percent of its gross national product (as against 13.8 percent for the Soviet Union). Our North Atlantic Treaty [NAT] allies devoted 4.8 percent of their national product to military purposes in 1949.

This difference in emphasis between the two economies means that the readiness of the free world to support a war effort is tending to decline relative to that of the Soviet Union. There is little direct investment in production facilities for military end-products and in dispersal. There are relatively few men receiving military training and a relatively low rate of production of weapons. However, given time to convert to a war effort, the capabilities of the United States economy and also of the Western European economy would be tremendous. In the light of Soviet military capabilities, a question which may be of decisive importance in the event of war is the question whether there will be time to mobilize our superior human and material resources for a war effort (cf. Chs. VIII and IX).

The capability of the American economy to support a build-up of economic and military strength at home and to assist a build-up abroad is limited not, as in the case of the Soviet Union, so much by the ability to produce as by the decision on the proper allocation of resources to this and other purposes. Even Western Europe could afford to assign a substantially larger proportion of its resources to defense, if the necessary foundation in public understanding and will could be laid, and if the assistance needed to meet its dollar deficit were provided.

A few statistics will help to clarify this point [Table 1].

The Soviet Union is now allocating nearly 40 percent of its gross available resources to military purposes and investment, much of which is in war-supporting industries. It is estimated that even in an emergency the Soviet Union could not increase this proportion to much more than 50 percent, or by one-fourth. The United States, on the other hand, is allocating only about 20 percent of its resources to defense and investment (or 22 percent including foreign assistance), and little of its investment outlays are directed to war-supporting industries. In an emergency the United States could allocate more than 50 percent of its resources to military purposes and foreign assistance, or five to six times as much as at present.

DOCUMENTS   177

Table 1 Percentage of Gross Available Resources Allocated to Investment, National Defense, and Consumption in East and West, 1949 (in percent of total)

COUNTRY	GROSS INVESTMENT	DEFENSE	CONSUMPTION
USSR	25.4	13.8	60.8
Soviet Orbit	22.0 (a)	4.0 (b)	74.0 (a)
U.S.	13.6	6.5	79.9
European NAT countries	20.4	4.8	74.8

(a) crude estimate. [Footnote in the source text.]
(b) Includes Soviet Zone of Germany; otherwise 5 percent. [Footnote in the source text.]

The same point can be brought out by statistics on the use of important products. The Soviet Union is using 14 percent of its ingot steel, 47 percent of its primary aluminum, and 18.5 percent of its crude oil for military purposes, while the corresponding percentages for the United States are 1.7, 8.6, and 5.6. Despite the tremendously larger production of these goods in the United States than the Soviet Union, the latter is actually using, for military purposes, nearly twice as much steel as the United States and 8 to 26 percent more aluminum.

Perhaps the most impressive indication of the economic superiority of the free world over the Soviet world which can be made on the basis of available data is provided in comparisons (based mainly on the *Economic Survey of Europe, 1948*) [Table 2].

It should be noted that these comparisons understate the relative position of the NAT countries for several reasons: (1) Canada is excluded because comparable data were not available; (2) the data for the USSR are the 1950 targets (as stated in the fourth five-year plan) rather than actual rates of production and are believed to exceed in many cases the production actually achieved; (3) the data for the European NAT countries are actual data for 1948, and production has generally increased since that time.

Furthermore, the United States could achieve a substantial absolute increase in output and could thereby increase the allocation of resources to a build-up of the economic and military strength of itself and its allies without suffering a decline in its real standard of living. Industrial production declined by 10 percent between the first quarter of 1948 and the last quarter of 1949, and by approximately one-fourth between 1944 and 1949. In March 1950 there were approximately 4,750,000 unemployed, as compared to 1,070,000 in 1943 and 670,000 in 1944. The gross national product declined slowly in 1949 from the peak reached in 1948

Table 2 Comparative Statistics on Economic Capabilities of East and West

	U.S. 1948–49	EUROPEAN NAT COUNTRIES	TOTAL	USSR (1950 PLAN)	SATELLITES 1948–49	TOTAL
Population (millions)	149	173	322	198 (a)	75	273
Employment in non-agricultural establishments (millions)	45	—	—	31 (a)	—	—
Gross National Production (billion dollars)	250	84	334	65 (a)	21	86
National income per capita (current dollars)	1700	480	1040	330	280	315
Production data (b):						
Coal (million tons)	582	306	888	250	88	338
Electric power (billion kwh)	356	124	480	82	15	97
Crude petroleum (million tons)	277	1	278	35	5	40
Pig iron (million tons)	55	24	79	19.5	3.2	22.7
Steel (million tons)	80	32	112	25	6	31
Cement (million tons)	35	21	56	10.5	2.1	12.6
Motor vehicles (thousands)	5273	580	5853	500	25	525

(a) 1949 data. [Footnote in the source text.]
(b) for the European NAT countries and for the satellites, the data include output by major producers. [Footnote in the source text.]

DOCUMENTS 179

($262 billion in 1948 to an annual rate of $256 billion in the last six months of 1949), and in terms of constant prices declined by about 20 percent between 1944 and 1948.

With a high level of economic activity, the United States could soon attain a gross national product of $300 billion per year, as was pointed out in the President's Economic Report (January 1950). Progress in this direction would permit, and might itself be aided by, a buildup of the economic and military strength of the United States and the free world; furthermore, if a dynamic expansion of the economy were achieved, the necessary build-up could be accomplished without a decrease in the national standard of living because the required resources could be obtained by siphoning off a part of the annual increment in the gross national product. These are facts of fundamental importance in considering the courses of action open to the United States (cf. Ch. IX).

2. *Intentions.* Foreign economic policy is a major instrument in the conduct of United States foreign relations. It is an instrument which can powerfully influence the world environment in ways favorable to the security and welfare of this country. It is also an instrument which, if unwisely formulated and employed, can do actual harm to our national interests. It is an instrument uniquely suited to our capabilities, provided we have the tenacity of purpose and the understanding requisite to a realization of its potentials. Finally, it is an instrument peculiarly appropriate to the cold war.

The preceding analysis has indicated that an essential element in a program to frustrate the Kremlin design is the development of a successfully functioning system among the free nations. It is clear that economic conditions are among the fundamental determinants of the will and the strength to resist subversion and aggression.

United States foreign economic policy has been designed to assist in the building of such a system and such conditions in the free world. The principal features of this policy can be summarized as follows:

1. assistance to Western Europe in recovery and the creation of a viable economy (the European Recovery Program);
2. assistance to other countries because of their special needs arising out of the war or the cold war and our special interests in or responsibility for meeting them (grant assistance to Japan, the Philippines, and Korea, loans and credits by the Export-Import Bank, the International Monetary Fund, and the International Bank to Indonesia, Yugoslavia, Iran, etc.);
3. assistance in the development of underdeveloped areas (the Point IV program and loans and credits to various countries, overlapping to some extent with those mentioned under 2);

180 DOCUMENTS

4. military assistance to the North Atlantic Treaty countries, Greece, Turkey, etc.;
5. restriction of East-West trade in items of military importance to the East;
6. purchase and stockpiling of strategic materials; and
7. efforts to reestablish an international economy based on multilateral trade, declining trade barriers, and convertible currencies (the GATT-ITO program, the Reciprocal Trade Agreements program, the IMF-IBRD program, and the program now being developed to solve the problem of the United States balance of payments).

In both their short and long term aspects, these policies and programs are directed to the strengthening of the free world and therefore to the frustration of the Kremlin design. Despite certain inadequacies and inconsistencies, which are now being studied in connection with the problem of the United States balance of payments, the United States has generally pursued a foreign economic policy which has powerfully supported its overall objectives. The question must nevertheless be asked whether current and currently projected programs will adequately support this policy in the future, in terms both of need and urgency.

The last year has been indecisive in the economic field. The Soviet Union has made considerable progress in integrating the satellite economies of Eastern Europe into the Soviet economy, but still faces very large problems, especially with China. The free nations have important accomplishments to record, but also have tremendous problems still ahead. On balance, neither side can claim any great advantage in this field over its relative position a year ago. The important question therefore becomes: what are the trends?

Several conclusions seem to emerge. First, the Soviet Union is widening the gap between its preparedness for war and the unpreparedness of the free world for war. It is devoting a far greater *proportion* of its resources to military purposes than are the free nations and, in significant components of military power, a greater *absolute* quantity of resources. Second, the Communist success in China, taken with the politico-economic situation in the rest of South and South-East Asia, provides a springboard for a further incursion in this troubled area. Although Communist China faces serious economic problems which may impose some strains on the Soviet economy, it is probable that the social and economic problems faced by the free nations in this area present more than offsetting opportunities for Communist expansion. Third, the Soviet Union holds positions in Europe which, if it maneuvers skillfully, could be used to do great damage to the Western European economy and to the maintenance of the Western

DOCUMENTS 181

orientation of certain countries, particularly Germany and Austria. Fourth, despite (and in part because of) the Titoist' defection, the Soviet Union has accelerated its efforts to integrate satellite economy with its own and to increase the degree of autarchy within the areas under its control.

Fifth, meanwhile, Western Europe, with American (and Canadian) assistance, has achieved a record level of production. However, it faces the prospect of a rapid tapering off of American assistance without the possibility of achieving, by its own efforts, a satisfactory equilibrium with the dollar area. It has also made very little progress toward "economic integration," which would in the long run tend to improve its productivity and to provide an economic environment conducive to political stability. In particular, the movement toward economic integration does not appear to be rapid enough to provide Western Germany with adequate economic opportunities in the West. The United Kingdom still faces economic problems which may require a moderate but politically difficult decline in the British standard of living or more American assistance than is contemplated. At the same time, a strengthening of the British position is needed if the stability of the Commonwealth is not to be impaired and if it is to be a focus of resistance to Communist expansion in South and South-East Asia. Improvement of the British position is also vital in building up the defensive capabilities of Western Europe.

Sixth, throughout Asia the stability of the present moderate governments, which are more in sympathy with our purposes than any probable successor regimes would be, is doubtful. The problem is only in part an economic one. Assistance in economic development is important as a means of holding out to the peoples of Asia some prospect of improvement in standards of living under their present governments. But probably more important are a strengthening of central institutions, an improvement in administration, and generally a development of an economic and social structure within which the peoples of Asia can make more effective use of their great human and material resources.

Seventh, and perhaps most important, there are indications of a letdown of United States efforts under the pressure of the domestic budgetary situation, disillusion resulting from excessively optimistic expectations about the duration and results of our assistance programs, and doubts about the wisdom of continuing to strengthen the free nations as against preparedness measures in light of the intensity of the cold war.

Eighth, there are grounds for predicting that the United States and other free nations will within a period of a few years at most experience a decline in economic activity of serious proportions unless more positive governmental programs are developed than are now available.

182   DOCUMENTS

In short, as we look into the future, the programs now planned will not meet the requirements of the free nations. The difficulty does not lie so much in the inadequacy or misdirection of policy as in the inadequacy of planned programs, in terms of timing or impact, to achieve our objectives. The risks inherent in this situation are set forth in the following chapter and a course of action designed to reinvigorate our efforts in order to reverse the present trends and to achieve our fundamental purpose is outlined in Chapter IX.

C. MILITARY

The United States now possesses the greatest military potential of any single nation in the world. The military weaknesses of the United States vis-à-vis the Soviet Union, however, include its numerical inferiority in forces in being and in total manpower. Coupled with the inferiority of forces in being, the United States also lacks tenable positions from which to employ its forces in event of war and munitions power in being and readily available.

It is true that the United States armed forces are now stronger than ever before in other times of apparent peace; it is also true that there exists a sharp disparity between our actual military strength and our commitments. The relationship of our strength to our present commitments, however, is not alone the governing factor. The world situation, as well as commitments, should govern; hence, our military strength more properly should be related to the world situation confronting us. When our military strength is related to the world situation and balanced against the likely exigencies of such a situation, it is clear that our military strength is becoming dangerously inadequate.

If war should begin in 1950, the United States and its allies will have the military capability of conducting defensive operations to provide a reasonable measure of protection to the Western Hemisphere, bases in the Western Pacific, and essential military lines of communication; and an inadequate measure of protection to vital military bases in the United Kingdom and in the Near and Middle East. We will have the capability of conducting powerful offensive air operations against vital elements of the Soviet war-making capacity.

The scale of the operations listed in the preceding paragraph is limited by the effective forces and material in being of the United States and its allies vis-à-vis the Soviet Union. Consistent with the aggressive threat facing us and in consonance with overall strategic plans, the United States must provide to its allies on a continuing basis as large amounts of military assistance as possible without serious detriment to the United States operational requirements.

If the potential military capabilities of the United States and its allies were rapidly and effectively developed, sufficient forces could be produced probably to deter war, or if the Soviet Union chooses war, to withstand the initial Soviet attacks, to stabilize supporting attacks, and to retaliate in turn with even greater impact on the Soviet capabilities. From the military point of view alone, however, this would require not only the generation of the necessary military forces but also the development and stockpiling of improved weapons of all types.

Under existing peacetime conditions, a period of from two to three years is required to produce a material increase in military power. Such increased power could be provided in a somewhat shorter period in a declared period of emergency or in wartime through a full-out national effort. Any increase in military power in peacetime, however, should be related both to its probable military role in war, to the implementation of immediate and long-term United States foreign policy vis-à-vis the Soviet Union, and to the realities of the existing situation. If such a course of increasing our military power is adopted now, the United States would have the capability of eliminating the disparity between its military strength and the exigencies of the situation we face; eventually of gaining the initiative in the "cold" war and of materially delaying if not stopping the Soviet offensives in war itself.

VII. Present Risks

A. GENERAL

It is apparent from the preceding sections that the integrity and vitality of our system is in greater jeopardy than ever before in our history. Even if there were no Soviet Union we would face the great problem of the free society, accentuated many fold in this industrial age, of reconciling order, security, the need for participation, with the requirement of freedom. We would face the fact that in a shrinking world the absence of order among nations is becoming less and less tolerable. The Kremlin design seeks to impose order among nations by means which would destroy our free and democratic system. The Kremlin's possession of atomic weapons puts new power behind its design, and increases the jeopardy to our system. It adds new strains to the uneasy equilibrium-without-order which exists in the world and raises new doubts in men's minds whether the world will long tolerate this tension without moving toward some kind of order, on somebody's terms.

184 DOCUMENTS

The risks we face are of a new order of magnitude, commensurate with the total struggle in which we are engaged. For a free society there is never total victory, since freedom and democracy are never wholly attained, are always in the process of being attained. But defeat at the hands of the totalitarian is total defeat. These risks crowd in on us, in a shrinking world of polarized power, so as to give us no choice, ultimately, between meeting them effectively or being overcome by them.

B. SPECIFIC

It is quite clear from Soviet theory and practice that the Kremlin seeks to bring the free world under its dominion by the methods of the cold war. The preferred technique is to subvert by infiltration and intimidation. Every institution of our society is an instrument which it is sought to stultify and turn against our purposes. Those that touch most closely our material and moral strength are obviously the prime targets, labor unions, civic enterprises, schools, churches, and all media for influencing opinion. The effort is not so much to make them serve obvious Soviet ends as to prevent them from serving our ends, and thus to make them sources of confusion in our economy, our culture, and our body politic. The doubts and diversities that in terms of our values are part of the merit of a free system, the weaknesses and the problems that are peculiar to it, the rights and privileges that free men enjoy, and the disorganization and destruction left in the wake of the last attack on our freedoms, all are but opportunities for the Kremlin to do its evil work. Every advantage is taken of the fact that our means of prevention and retaliation are limited by those principles and scruples which are precisely the ones that give our freedom and democracy its meaning for us. None of our scruples deter those whose only code is "morality is that which serves the revolution."

Since everything that gives us or others respect for our institutions is a suitable object for attack, it also fits the Kremlin's design that where, with impunity, we can be insulted and made to suffer indignity the opportunity shall not be missed, particularly in any context which can be used to cast dishonor on our country, our system, our motives, or our methods. Thus the means by which we sought to restore our own economic health in the '30's, and now seek to restore that of the free world, come equally under attack. The military aid by which we sought to help the free world was frantically denounced by the Communists in the early days of the last war, and of course our present efforts to develop adequate military strength for ourselves and our allies are equally denounced.

At the same time the Soviet Union is seeking to create overwhelming military force, in order to back up infiltration with intimidation. In the only terms in which it understands strength, it is seeking to demonstrate to the free world that force and the will to use it are on the side of the Kremlin, that those who lack it are decadent and doomed. In local incidents it threatens and encroaches both for the sake of local gains and to increase anxiety and defeatism in all the free world.

The possession of atomic weapons at each of the opposite poles of power, and the inability (for different reasons) of either side to place any trust in the other, puts a premium on a surprise attack against us. It equally puts a premium on a more violent and ruthless prosecution of its design by cold war, especially if the Kremlin is sufficiently objective to realize the improbability of our prosecuting a preventive war. It also puts a premium on piecemeal aggression against others, counting on our unwillingness to engage in atomic war unless we are directly attacked. We run all these risks and the added risk of being confused and immobilized by our inability to weigh and choose, and pursue a firm course based on a rational assessment of each.

The risk that we may thereby be prevented or too long delayed in taking all needful measures to maintain the integrity and vitality of our system is great. The risk that our allies will lose their determination is greater. And the risk that in this manner a descending spiral of too little and too late, of doubt and recrimination, may present us with ever narrower and more desperate alternatives, is the greatest risk of all. For example, it is clear that our present weakness would prevent us from offering effective resistance at any of several vital pressure points. The only deterrent we can present to the Kremlin is the evidence we give that we may make any of the critical points which we cannot hold the occasion for a global war of annihilation.

The risk of having no better choice than to capitulate or precipitate a global war at any of a number of pressure points is bad enough in itself, but it is multiplied by the weakness it imparts to our position in the cold war. Instead of appearing strong and resolute we are continually at the verge of appearing and being alternately irresolute and desperate; yet it is the cold war which we must win, because both the Kremlin design, and our fundamental purpose give it the first priority.

The frustration of the Kremlin design, however, cannot be accomplished by us alone, as will appear from the analysis in Chapter IX, B. Strength at the center, in the United States, is only the first of two essential elements. The second is that our allies and potential allies do not as a result of a sense of frustration or of Soviet intimidation drift into a course of neutrality eventually leading to Soviet domination. If this were to happen in Germany the effect upon Western Europe and eventually upon us might be catastrophic.

But there are risks in making ourselves strong. A large measure of sacrifice and discipline will be demanded of the American people. They will be asked to give up some of the benefits which they have come to associate with their freedoms. Nothing could be more important than that they fully understand the reasons for this. The risks of a superficial understanding or of an inadequate appreciation of the issues are obvious and might lead to the adoption of measures which in themselves would jeopardize the integrity of our system. At any point in the process of demonstrating our will to make good our fundamental purpose, the Kremlin may decide to precipitate a general war, or in testing us, may go too far. These are risks we will invite by making ourselves strong, but they are lesser risks than those we seek to avoid. Our fundamental purpose is more likely to be defeated from lack of the will to maintain it, than from any mistakes we may make or assault we may undergo because of asserting that will. No people in history have preserved their freedom who thought that by not being strong enough to protect themselves they might prove inoffensive to their enemies.

VIII. Atomic Armaments

A. MILITARY EVALUATION OF U.S. AND USSR ATOMIC CAPABILITIES

1. The United States now has an atomic capability, including both numbers and deliverability, estimated to be adequate, if effectively utilized, to deliver a serious blow against the war-making capacity of the USSR. It is doubted whether such a blow, even if it resulted in the complete destruction of the contemplated target systems, would cause the USSR to sue for terms or prevent Soviet forces from occupying Western Europe against such ground resistance as could presently be mobilized. A very serious initial blow could, however, so reduce the capabilities of the USSR to supply and equip its military organization and its civilian population as to give the United States the prospect of developing a general military superiority in a war of long duration.
2. As the atomic capability of the USSR increases, it will have an increased ability to hit at our atomic bases and installations and thus seriously hamper the ability of the United States to carry out an attack such as that outlined above. It is quite possible that in the near future the USSR will have a sufficient number of atomic bombs and a sufficient deliverability to raise a question whether Britain with its

DOCUMENTS 187

present inadequate air defense could be relied upon as an advance base from which a major portion of the U.S. attack could be launched.

It is estimated that, within the next four years, the USSR will attain the capability of seriously damaging vital centers of the United States, provided it strikes a surprise blow and provided further that the blow is opposed by no more effective opposition than we now have programmed. Such a blow could so seriously damage the United States as to greatly reduce its superiority in economic potential.

Effective opposition to this Soviet capability will require among other measures greatly increased air warning systems, air defenses, and vigorous development and implementation of a civilian defense program which has been thoroughly integrated with the military defense systems.

In time the atomic capability of the USSR can be expected to grow to a point where, given surprise and no more effective opposition than we now have programmed, the possibility of a decisive initial attack cannot be excluded.

3. In the initial phases of an atomic war, the advantages of initiative and surprise would be very great. A police state living behind an iron curtain has an enormous advantage in maintaining the necessary security and centralization of decision required to capitalize on this advantage.

4. For the moment our atomic retaliatory capability is probably adequate to deter the Kremlin from a deliberate direct military attack against ourselves or other free peoples. However, when it calculates that it has a sufficient atomic capability to make a surprise attack on us, nullifying our atomic superiority and creating a military situation decisively in its favor, the Kremlin might be tempted to strike swiftly and with stealth. The existence of two large atomic capabilities in such a relationship might well act, therefore, not as a deterrent, but as an incitement to war.

5. A further increase in the number and power of our atomic weapons is necessary in order to assure the effectiveness of any U.S. retaliatory blow, but would not of itself seem to change the basic logic of the above points. Greatly increased general air, ground, and sea strength, and increased air defense and civilian defense programs would also be necessary to provide reasonable assurance that the free world could survive an initial surprise atomic attack of the weight which it is estimated the USSR will be capable of delivering by 1954 and still permit the free world to go on to the eventual attainment of its objectives. Furthermore, such a build–up of strength could safeguard and increase our retaliatory power, and thus might put off for some

188   DOCUMENTS

time the date when the Soviet Union could calculate that a surprise blow would be advantageous. This would provide additional time for the effects of our policies to produce a modification of the Soviet system.

6. If the USSR develops a thermonuclear weapon ahead of the U.S., the risks of greatly increased Soviet pressure against all the free world, or an attack against the U.S., will be greatly increased.

7. If the U.S. develops a thermonuclear weapon ahead of the USSR, the U.S. should for the time being be able to bring increased pressure on the USSR.

B. STOCKPILING AND USE OF ATOMIC WEAPONS

1. From the foregoing analysis it appears that it would be to the long-term advantage of the United States if atomic weapons were to be effectively eliminated from national peacetime armaments; the additional objectives which must be secured if there is to be a reasonable prospect of such effective elimination of atomic weapons are discussed in Chapter IX. In the absence of such elimination and the securing of these objectives, it would appear that we have no alternative but to increase our atomic capability as rapidly as other considerations make appropriate. In either case, it appears to be imperative to increase as rapidly as possible our general air, ground, and sea strength and that of our allies to a point where we are militarily not so heavily dependent on atomic weapons.

2. As is indicated in Chapter IV, it is important that the United States employ military force only if the necessity for its use is clear and compelling and commends itself to the overwhelming majority of our people. The United States cannot therefore engage in war except as a reaction to aggression of so clear and compelling a nature as to bring the overwhelming majority of our people to accept the use of military force. In the event war comes, our use of force must be to compel the acceptance of our objectives and must be congruent to the range of tasks which we may encounter.

In the event of a general war with the USSR, it must be anticipated that atomic weapons will be used by each side in the manner it deems best suited to accomplish its objectives. In view of our vulnerability to Soviet atomic attack, it has been argued that we might wish to hold our atomic weapons only for retaliation against prior use by the USSR. To be able to do so and still have hope of achieving our objectives, the non-atomic military capabilities of ourselves and our allies would have to be fully developed and the political weaknesses of the Soviet Union fully exploited. In the event of war, however, we could not be sure that we could move toward the attainment of these objectives without the USSR's resorting sooner or later to the use of its atomic weapons. Only if we had overwhelming atomic superiority and obtained command of the air might the USSR be deterred from employing its atomic weapons as we progressed toward the attainment of our objectives.

In the event the USSR develops by 1954 the atomic capability which we now anticipate, it is hardly conceivable that, if war comes, the Soviet leaders would refrain from the use of atomic weapons unless they felt fully confident of attaining their objectives by other means.

In the event we use atomic weapons either in retaliation for their prior use by the USSR or because there is no alternative method by which we can attain our objectives, it is imperative that the strategic and tactical targets against which they are used be appropriate and the manner in which they are used be consistent with those objectives.

It appears to follow from the above that we should produce and stockpile thermonuclear weapons in the event they prove feasible and would add significantly to our net capability. Not enough is yet known of their potentialities to warrant a judgment at this time regarding their use in war to attain our objectives.

3. It has been suggested that we announce that we will not use atomic weapons except in retaliation against the prior use of such weapons by an aggressor. It has been argued that such a declaration would decrease the danger of an atomic attack against the United States and its allies.

In our present situation of relative unpreparedness in conventional weapons, such a declaration would be interpreted by the USSR as an admission of great weakness and by our allies as a clear indication that we intended to abandon them. Furthermore, it is doubtful whether such a declaration would be taken sufficiently seriously by the Kremlin to constitute an important factor in determining whether or not to attack the United States. It is to be anticipated that the Kremlin would weigh the facts of our capability far more heavily than a declaration of what we proposed to do with that capability.

Unless we are prepared to abandon our objectives, we cannot make such a declaration in good faith until we are confident that we will be in a position to attain our objectives without war, or, in the event of war, without recourse to the use of atomic weapons for strategic or tactical purposes.

190 DOCUMENTS

C. INTERNATIONAL CONTROL OF ATOMIC ENERGY

1. A discussion of certain of the basic considerations involved in securing effective international control is necessary to make clear why the additional objectives discussed in Chapter IX must be secured.

2. No system of international control could prevent the production and use of atomic weapons in the event of a prolonged war. Even the most effective system of international control could, of itself, only provide (a) assurance that atomic weapons had been eliminated from national peacetime armaments and (b) immediate notice of a violation. In essence, an effective international control system would be expected to assure a certain amount of time after notice of violation before atomic weapons could be used in war.

3. The time period between notice of violation and possible use of atomic weapons in war which a control system could be expected to assure depends upon a number of factors.

   The dismantling of existing stockpiles of bombs and the destruction of casings and firing mechanisms could by themselves give little assurance of securing time. Casings and firing mechanisms are presumably easy to produce, even surreptitiously, and the assembly of weapons does not take much time.

   If existing stocks of fissionable materials were in some way eliminated and the future production of fissionable materials effectively controlled, war could not start with a surprise atomic attack.

   In order to assure an appreciable time lag between notice of violation and the time when atomic weapons might be available in quantity, it would be necessary to destroy all plants capable of making large amounts of fissionable material. Such action would, however, require a moratorium on those possible peacetime uses which call for large quantities of fissionable materials.

   Effective control over the production and stockpiling of raw materials might further extend the time period which effective international control would assure. Now that the Russians have learned the technique of producing atomic weapons, the time between violation of an international control agreement and production of atomic weapons will be shorter than was estimated in 1946, except possibly in the field of thermonuclear or other new types of weapons.

4. The certainty of notice of violation also depends upon a number of factors. In the absence of good faith, it is to be doubted whether any system can be designed which will give certainty of notice of violation. International ownership of raw materials and fissionable materials and international ownership and operation of dangerous facilities, coupled with inspection based on continuous unlimited

freedom of access to all parts of the Soviet Union (as well as to all parts of the territory of other signatories to the control agreement) appear to be necessary to give the requisite degree of assurance against secret violations. As the Soviet stockpile of fissionable materials grows, the amount which the USSR might secretly withhold and not declare to the inspection agency grows. In this sense, the earlier an agreement is consummated the greater the security it would offer. The possibility of successful secret production operations also increases with developments which may reduce the size and power consumption of individual reactors. The development of a thermonuclear bomb would increase many fold the damage a given amount of fissionable material could do and would, therefore, vastly increase the danger that a decisive advantage could be gained through secret operations.

5. The relative sacrifices which would be involved in international control need also to be considered. If it were possible to negotiate an effective system of international control the United States would presumably sacrifice a much larger stockpile of atomic weapons and a much larger production capacity than would the USSR. The opening up of national territory to international inspection involved in an adequate control and inspection system would have a far greater impact on the USSR than on the United States. If the control system involves the destruction of all large reactors and thus a moratorium on certain possible peacetime uses, the USSR can be expected to argue that it, because of greater need for new sources of energy, would be making a greater sacrifice in this regard than the United States.

6. The United States and the peoples of the world as a whole desire a respite from the dangers of atomic warfare. The chief difficulty lies in the danger that the respite would be short and that we might not have adequate notice of its pending termination. For such an arrangement to be in the interest of the United States, it is essential that the agreement be entered into in good faith by both sides and the probability against its violation high.

7. The most substantial contribution to security of an effective international control system would, of course, be the opening up of the Soviet Union, as required under the UN plan. Such opening up is not, however, compatible with the maintenance of the Soviet system in its present rigor. This is a major reason for the Soviet refusal to accept the UN plan.

The studies which began with the Acheson-Lilienthal committee and culminated in the present UN plan made it clear that inspection of atomic facilities would not alone give the assurance of control; but that ownership and operation by an international authority of the world's atomic energy activities from the mine to the last use of fissionable materials was also essential. The delegation of sovereignty which this implies is necessary for effective control and, therefore, is as necessary for the United States and the rest of the free world as it is presently unacceptable to the Soviet Union.

It is also clear that a control authority not susceptible directly or indirectly to Soviet domination is equally essential. As the Soviet Union would regard any country not under its domination as under the potential if not the actual domination of the United States, it is clear that what the United States and the non-Soviet world must insist on, the Soviet Union at present rejects.

The principal immediate benefit of international control would be to make a surprise atomic attack impossible, assuming the elimination of large reactors and the effective disposal of stockpiles of fissionable materials. But it is almost certain that the Soviet Union would not agree to the elimination of large reactors, unless the impracticability of producing atomic power for peaceful purposes had been demonstrated beyond a doubt. By the same token, it would not now agree to elimination of its stockpile of fissionable materials.

Finally, the absence of good faith on the part of the USSR must be assumed until there is concrete evidence that there has been a decisive change in Soviet policies. It is to be doubted whether such a change can take place without a change in the nature of the Soviet system itself.

The above considerations make it clear that at least a major change in the relative power positions of the United States and the Soviet Union would have to take place before an effective system of international control could be negotiated. The Soviet Union would have had to have moved a substantial distance down the path of accommodation and compromise before such an arrangement would be conceivable. This conclusion is supported by the Third Report of the United Nations Atomic Energy Commission to the Security Council, May 17, 1948, in which it is stated that ". . . the majority of the Commission has been unable to secure . . . their acceptance of the nature and extent of participation in the world community required of all nations in this field. . . . As a result, the Commission has been forced to recognize that agreement on effective measures for the control of atomic energy is itself dependent on cooperation in broader fields of policy."

In short, it is impossible to hope than an effective plan for international control can be negotiated unless and until the Kremlin design has been frustrated to a point at which a genuine and drastic change in Soviet policies has taken place.

IX. Possible Courses of Action

Introduction. Four possible courses of action by the United States in the present situation can be distinguished. They are: a. Continuation of current policies, with current and currently projected programs for carrying out these policies; b. Isolation; c. War; and d. A more rapid building up of the political, economic, and military strength of the free world than provided under a, with the purpose of reaching, if possible, a tolerable state of order among nations without war and of preparing to defend ourselves in the event that the free world is attacked.

The role of negotiation. Negotiation must be considered in relation to these courses of action. A negotiator always attempts to achieve an agreement which is somewhat better than the realities of his fundamental position would justify and which is, in any case, not worse than his fundamental position requires. This is as true in relations among sovereign states as in relations between individuals. The Soviet Union possesses several advantages over the free world in negotiations on any issue: a. It can and does enforce secrecy on all significant facts about conditions within the Soviet Union, so that it can be expected to know more about the realities of the free world's position than the free world knows about its position; b. It does not have to be responsive in any important sense to public opinion; c. It does not have to consult and agree with any other countries on the terms it will offer and accept; and d. It can influence public opinion in other countries while insulating the peoples under its control.

These are important advantages. Together with the unfavorable trend of our power position, they militate, as is shown in Section A below, against successful negotiation of a general settlement at this time. For although the United States probably now possesses, principally in atomic weapons, a force adequate to deliver a powerful blow upon the Soviet Union and to open the road to victory in a long war, it is not sufficient by itself to advance the position of the United States in the cold war.

The problem is to create such political and economic conditions in the free world, backed by force sufficient to inhibit Soviet attack, that the Kremlin will accommodate itself to these conditions, gradually withdraw, and eventually change its policies drastically. It has been shown in Chapter VIII that truly effective control of atomic energy would require such an opening up of the Soviet Union and such evidence in other ways of its good faith and its intent to co-exist in peace as to reflect or at least initiate a change in the Soviet system.

Clearly under present circumstances we will not be able to negotiate a settlement which calls for a change in the Soviet system. What, then, is the role of negotiation?

194 DOCUMENTS

In the first place, the public in the United States and in other free countries will require, as a condition to firm policies and adequate programs directed to the frustration of the Kremlin design, that the free world be continuously prepared to negotiate agreements with the Soviet Union on equitable terms. It is still argued by many people here and abroad that equitable agreements with the Soviet Union are possible, and this view will gain force if the Soviet Union begins to show signs of accommodation, even on unimportant issues.

The free countries must always, therefore, be prepared to negotiate and must be ready to take the initiative at times in seeking negotiation. They must develop a negotiating position which defines the issues and the terms on which they would be prepared—and at what stages—to accept agreements with the Soviet Union. The terms must be fair in the view of popular opinion in the free world. This means that they must be consistent with a positive program for peace—in harmony with the United Nations' Charter and providing, at a minimum, for the effective control of all armaments by the United Nations or a successor organization. The terms must not require more of the Soviet Union than such behavior and such participation in a world organization. The fact that such conduct by the Soviet Union is impossible without such a radical change in Soviet policies as to constitute a change in the Soviet system would then emerge as a result of the Kremlin's unwillingness to accept such terms or of its bad faith in observing them.

A sound negotiating position is, therefore, an essential element in the ideological conflict. For some time after a decision to build up strength, any offer of, or attempt at, negotiation of a general settlement along the lines of the Berkeley speech by the Secretary of State could be only a tactic.' Nevertheless, concurrently with a decision and a start on building up the strength of the free world, it may be desirable to pursue this tactic both to gain public support for the program and to minimize the immediate risks of war. It is urgently necessary for the United States to determine its negotiating position and to obtain agreement with its major allies on the purposes and terms of negotiation.

In the second place, assuming that the United States in cooperation with other free countries decides and acts to increase the strength of the free world and assuming that the Kremlin chooses the path of accommodation, it will from time to time be necessary and desirable to negotiate on various specific issues with the Kremlin as the area of possible agreement widens.

The Kremlin will have three major objectives in negotiations with the United States. The first is to eliminate the atomic capabilities of the United States; the second is to prevent the effective mobilization of the superior potential of the free world in human and material resources; and the third is to secure a withdrawal of United States forces from, and commitments to, Europe and Japan. Depending on its evaluation of its own strengths and weaknesses as against the West's (particularly the ability and will of the West to sustain its efforts), it will or will not be prepared to make important concessions to achieve these major objectives. It is unlikely that the Kremlin's evaluation is such that it would now be prepared to make significant concessions.

The objectives of the United States and other free countries in negotiations with the Soviet Union (apart from the ideological objectives discussed above) are to record, in a formal fashion which will facilitate the consolidation and further advance of our position, the process of Soviet accommodation to the new political, psychological, and economic conditions in the world which will result from adoption of the fourth course of action and which will be supported by the increasing military strength developed as an integral part of that course of action. In short, our objectives are to record, where desirable, the gradual withdrawal of the Soviet Union and to facilitate that process by making negotiation, if possible, always more expedient than resort to force.

It must be presumed that for some time the Kremlin will accept agreements only if it is convinced that by acting in bad faith whenever and wherever there is an opportunity to do so with impunity, it can derive greater advantage from the agreements than the free world. For this reason, we must take care that any agreements are enforceable or that they are not susceptible of violation without detection and the possibility of effective countermeasures.

This further suggests that we will have to consider carefully the order in which agreements can be concluded. Agreement on the control of atomic energy would result in a relatively greater disarmament of the United States than of the Soviet Union, even assuming considerable progress in building up the strength of the free world in conventional forces and weapons. It might be accepted by the Soviet Union as part of a deliberate design to move against Western Europe and other areas of strategic importance with conventional forces and weapons. In this event, the United States would find itself at war, having previously disarmed itself in its most important weapon, and would be engaged in a race to redevelop atomic weapons.

This seems to indicate that for the time being the United States and other free countries would have to insist on concurrent agreement on the control of nonatomic forces and weapons and perhaps on the other elements of a general settlement, notably peace treaties with Germany, Austria, and Japan and the withdrawal of Soviet influence from the

DOCUMENTS

satellites. If, contrary to our expectations, the Soviet Union should accept agreements promising effective control of atomic energy, and conventional armaments, without any other changes in Soviet policies, we would have to consider very carefully whether we could accept such agreements. It is unlikely that this problem will arise.

To the extent that the United States and the rest of the free world succeed in so building up their strength in conventional forces and weapons that a Soviet attack with similar forces could be thwarted or held, we will gain increased flexibility and can seek agreements on the various issues in any order, as they become negotiable.

In the third place, negotiation will play a part in the building up of the strength of the free world, apart from the ideological strength discussed above. This is most evident in the problems of Germany, Austria, and Japan. In the process of building up strength, it may be desirable for the free nations, without the Soviet Union, to conclude separate arrangements with Japan, Western Germany, and Austria which would enlist the energies and resources of these countries in support of the free world. This will be difficult unless it has been demonstrated by attempted negotiation with the Soviet Union that the Soviet Union is not prepared to accept treaties of peace which would leave these countries free, under adequate safeguards, to participate in the United Nations and in regional or broader associations of states consistent with the United Nations' Charter and providing security and adequate opportunities for the peaceful development of their political and economic life.

This demonstrates the importance, from the point of view of negotiation as well as for its relationship to the building up of the strength of the free world (see Section D below), of the problem of closer association—on a regional or a broader basis—among the free countries.

In conclusion, negotiation is not a possible separate course of action but rather a means of gaining support for a program of building strength, of recording, where necessary and desirable, progress in the cold war, and of facilitating further progress while helping to minimize the risks of war. Ultimately, it is our objective to negotiate a settlement with the Soviet Union (or a successor state or states) on which the world can place reliance as an enforceable instrument of peace. But it is important to emphasize that such a settlement can only record the progress which the free world will have made in creating a political and economic system in the world so successful that the frustration of the Kremlin's design for world domination will be complete. The analysis in the following sections indicates that the building of such a system requires expanded and accelerated programs for the carrying out of current policies.

A. THE FIRST COURSE—CONTINUATION OF CURRENT POLICIES, WITH CURRENT AND CURRENTLY PROJECTED PROGRAMS FOR CARRYING OUT THESE POLICIES

1. *Military aspects.* On the basis of current programs, the United States has a large potential military capability but an actual capability which, though improving, is declining relative to the USSR, particularly in light of its probable fission bomb capability and possible thermonuclear bomb capability. The same holds true for the free world as a whole relative to the Soviet world as a whole. If war breaks out in 1950 or in the next few years, the United States and its allies, apart from a powerful atomic blow, will be compelled to conduct delaying actions, while building up their strength for a general offensive. A frank evaluation of the requirements, to defend the United States and its vital interests and to support a vigorous initiative in the cold war, on the one hand, and of present capabilities, on the other, indicates that there is a sharp and growing disparity between them.

   A review of Soviet policy shows that the military capabilities, actual and potential, of the United States and the rest of the free world, together with the apparent determination of the free world to resist further Soviet expansion, have not induced the Kremlin to relax its pressures generally or to give up the initiative in the cold war. On the contrary, the Soviet Union has consistently pursued a bold foreign policy, modified only when its probing revealed a determination and an ability of the free world to resist encroachment upon it. The relative military capabilities of the free world are declining, with the result that its determination to resist may also decline and that the security of the United States and the free world as a whole will be jeopardized.

   From the military point of view, the actual and potential capabilities of the United States, given a continuation of current and projected programs, will become less and less effective as a war deterrent. Improvement of the state of readiness will become more and more important not only to inhibit the launching of war by the Soviet Union but also to support a national policy designed to reverse the present ominous trends in international relations. A building up of the military capabilities of the United States and the free world is a pre-condition to the achievement of the objectives outlined in this report and to the protection of the United States against disaster.

   Fortunately, the United States military establishment has been developed into a unified and effective force as a result of the policies laid down by the Congress and the vigorous carrying out of these

198   DOCUMENTS

policies by the Administration in the fields of both organization and economy. It is, therefore, a base upon which increased strength can be rapidly built with maximum efficiency and economy.

2. *Political aspects.* The Soviet Union is pursuing the initiative in the conflict with the free world. Its atomic capabilities, together with its successes in the Far East, have led to an increasing confidence on its part and to an increasing nervousness in Western Europe and the rest of the free world. We cannot be sure, of course, how vigorously the Soviet Union will pursue its initiative, nor can we be sure of the strength or weakness of the other free countries in reacting to it. There are, however, ominous signs of further deterioration in the Far East. There are also some indications that a decline in morale and confidence in Western Europe may be expected. In particular, the situation in Germany is unsettled. Should the belief or suspicion spread that the free nations are not now able to prevent the Soviet Union from taking, if it chooses, the military actions outlined in Chapter V, the determination of the free countries to resist probably would lessen and there would be an increasing temptation for them to seek a position of neutrality.

Politically, recognition of the military implications of a continuation of present trends will mean that the United States and especially other free countries will tend to shift to the defensive, or to follow a dangerous policy of bluff, because the maintenance of a firm initiative in the cold war is closely related to aggregate strength in being and readily available.

This is largely a problem of the incongruity of the current actual capabilities of the free world and the threat to it, for the free world has an economic and military potential far superior to the potential of the Soviet Union and its satellites. The shadow of Soviet force falls darkly on Western Europe and Asia and supports a policy of encroachment. The free world lacks adequate means—in the form of forces in being—to thwart such expansion locally. The United States will therefore be confronted more frequently with the dilemma of reacting totally to a limited extension of Soviet control or of not reacting at all (except with ineffectual protests and half measures). Continuation of present trends is likely to lead, therefore, to a gradual withdrawal under the direct or indirect pressure of the Soviet Union, until we discover one day that we have sacrificed positions of vital interest. In other words, the United States would have chosen, by lack of the necessary decisions and actions, to fall back to isolation in the Western Hemisphere. This course would at best result in only a relatively brief truce and would be ended either by our capitulation

DOCUMENTS   199

or by a defensive war—on unfavorable terms from unfavorable positions—against a Soviet Empire compromising all or most of Eurasia. (See Section B.)

3. *Economic and social aspects.* As was pointed out in Chapter VI, the present foreign economic policies and programs of the United States will not produce a solution to the problem of international economic equilibrium, notably the problem of the dollar gap, and will not create an economic base conducive to political stability in many important free countries.

    The European Recovery Program has been successful in assisting the restoration and expansion of production in Western Europe and has been a major factor in checking the dry rot of Communism in Western Europe. However, little progress has been made toward the resumption by Western Europe of a position of influence in world affairs commensurate with its potential strength. Progress in this direction will require integrated political, economic, and military policies and programs, which are supported by the United States and the Western European countries and which will probably require a deeper participation by the United States than has been contemplated.

    The Point IV Program and other assistance programs will not adequately supplement, as now projected, the efforts of other important countries to develop effective institutions, to improve the administration of their affairs, and to achieve a sufficient measure of economic development. The moderate regimes now in power in many countries, like India, Indonesia, Pakistan, and the Philippines, will probably be unable to restore or retain their popular support and authority unless they are assisted in bringing about a more rapid improvement of the economic and social structure than present programs will make possible.

    The Executive Branch is now undertaking a study of the problem of the United States balance of payments and of the measures which might be taken by the United States to assist in establishing international economic equilibrium. This is a very important project and work on it should have a high priority. However, unless such an economic program is matched and supplemented by an equally far-sighted and vigorous political and military program, we will not be successful in checking and rolling back the Kremlin's drive.

4. *Negotiation.* In short, by continuing along its present course the free world will not succeed in making effective use of its vastly superior political, economic, and military potential to build a tolerable state of order among nations. On the contrary, the political, economic, and military situation of the free world is already unsatisfactory and will become less favorable unless we act to reverse present trends.

This situation is one which militates against successful negotiations with the Kremlin—for the terms of agreements on important pending issues would reflect present realities and would therefore be unacceptable, if not disastrous, to the United States and the rest of the free world. Unless a decision had been made and action undertaken to build up the strength, in the broadest sense, of the United States and the free world, an attempt to negotiate a general settlement on terms acceptable to us would be ineffective and probably long drawn out, and might thereby seriously delay the necessary measures to build up our strength.

This is true despite the fact that the United States now has the capability of delivering a powerful blow against the Soviet Union in the event of war, for one of the present realities is that the United States is not prepared to threaten the use of our present atomic superiority to coerce the Soviet Union into acceptable agreements. In light of present trends, the Soviet Union will not withdraw and the only conceivable basis for a general settlement would be spheres of influence and of no influenced "settlement" which the Kremlin could readily exploit to its great advantage. The idea that Germany or Japan or other important areas can exist as islands of neutrality in a divided world is unreal, given the Kremlin design for world domination.

B. THE SECOND COURSE—ISOLATION

Continuation of present trends, it has been shown above, will lead progressively to the withdrawal of the United States from most of its present commitments in Europe and Asia and to our isolation in the Western Hemisphere and its approaches. This would result not from a conscious decision but from a failure to take the actions necessary to bring our capabilities into line with our commitments and thus to a withdrawal under pressure. This pressure might come from our present Allies, who will tend to seek other "solutions" unless they have confidence in our determination to accelerate our efforts to build a successfully functioning political and economic system in the free world.

There are some who advocate a deliberate decision to isolate ourselves. Superficially, this has some attractiveness as a course of action, for it appears to bring our commitments and capabilities into harmony by reducing the former and by concentrating our present, or perhaps even reduced, military expenditures on the defense of the United States.

This argument overlooks the relativity of capabilities. With the United States in an isolated position, we would have to face the probability that the Soviet Union would quickly dominate most of Eurasia, probably without meeting armed resistance. It would thus acquire a potential far superior to our own, and would promptly proceed to develop this potential with the purpose of eliminating our power, which would, even in isolation, remain as a challenge to it, and as an obstacle to the imposition of its kind of order in the world. There is no way to make ourselves inoffensive to the Kremlin except by complete submission to its will. Therefore isolation would in the end condemn us to capitulate or to fight alone and on the defensive, with drastically limited offensive and retaliatory capabilities in comparison with the Soviet Union. (These are the only possibilities, unless we are prepared to risk the future on the hazard that the Soviet Empire, because of over-extension or other reasons, will spontaneously destroy itself from within.)

The argument also overlooks the imponderable, but nevertheless drastic, effects on our belief in ourselves and in our way of life of a deliberate decision to isolate ourselves. As the Soviet Union came to dominate free countries, it is clear that many Americans would feel a deep sense of responsibility and guilt for having abandoned their former friends and allies. As the Soviet Union mobilized the resources of Eurasia, increased its relative military capabilities, and heightened its threat to our security, some would be tempted to accept "peace" on its terms, while many would seek to defend the United States by creating a regimented system which would permit the assignment of a tremendous part of our resources to defense. Under such a state of affairs our national morale would be corrupted and the integrity and vitality of our system subverted.

Under this course of action, there would be no negotiation, unless on the Kremlin's terms, for we would have given up everything of importance.

It is possible that at some point in the course of isolation, many Americans would come to favor a surprise attack on the Soviet Union, and the area under its control, in a desperate attempt to alter decisively the balance of power by an overwhelming blow with modem weapons of mass destruction. It appears unlikely that the Soviet Union would wait for such an attack before launching one of its own. But even if it did and even if our attack were successful, it is clear that the United States would face appalling tasks in establishing a tolerable state of order among nations after such a war and after Soviet occupation of all or most of Eurasia for some years. These tasks appear so enormous and success so unlikely that reason dictates an attempt to achieve our objectives by other means.

C. THE THIRD COURSE—WAR

Some Americans favor a deliberate decision to go to war against the Soviet Union in the near future. It goes without saying that the idea of "preventive" war—in the sense of a military attack not provoked by a military attack upon us or our allies—is generally unacceptable to Americans. Its supporters argue that since the Soviet Union is in fact at war with the free world now and that since the failure of the Soviet Union to use all-out military force is explainable on grounds of expediency, we are at war and should conduct ourselves accordingly. Some further argue that the free world is probably unable, except under the crisis of war, to mobilize and direct its resources to the checking and rolling back of the Kremlin's drive for world dominion. This is a powerful argument in the light of history, but the considerations against war are so compelling that the free world must demonstrate that this argument is wrong. The case for war is premised on the assumption that the United States could launch and sustain an attack of sufficient impact to gain a decisive advantage for the free world in a long war and perhaps to win an early decision.

The ability of the United States to launch effective offensive operations is now limited to attack with atomic weapons. A powerful blow could be delivered upon the Soviet Union, but it is estimated that these operations alone would not force or induce the Kremlin to capitulate and that the Kremlin would still be able to use the forces under its control to dominate most or all of Eurasia. This would probably mean a long and difficult struggle during which the free institutions of Western Europe and many freedom-loving people would be destroyed and the regenerative capacity of Western Europe dealt a crippling blow.

Apart from this, however, a surprise attack upon the Soviet Union, despite the provocativeness of recent Soviet behavior, would be repugnant to many Americans. Although the American people would probably rally in support of the war effort, the shock of responsibility for a surprise attack would be morally corrosive. Many would doubt that it was a "just war" and that all reasonable possibilities for a peaceful settlement had been explored in good faith. Many more, proportionately, would hold such views in other countries, particularly in Western Europe and particularly after Soviet occupation, if only because the Soviet Union would liquidate articulate opponents. It would, therefore, be difficult after such a war to create a satisfactory international order among nations. Victory in such a war would have brought us little if at all closer to victory in the fundamental ideological conflict.

These considerations are no less weighty because they are imponderable, and they rule out an attack unless it is demonstrably in the nature of a counter-attack to a blow which is on its way or about to be delivered. (The military advantages of landing the first blow become increasingly important with modem weapons, and this is a fact which requires us to be on the alert in order to strike with our full weight as soon as we are attacked, and, if possible, before the Soviet blow is actually delivered.)

If the argument of Chapter IV is accepted, it follows that there is no "easy" solution and that the only sure victory lies in the frustration of the Kremlin design by the steady development of the moral and material strength of the free world and its projection into the Soviet world in such a way as to bring about an internal change in the Soviet system.

D. THE REMAINING COURSE OF ACTION—A RAPID BUILD-UP OF POLITICAL, ECONOMIC, AND MILITARY STRENGTH IN THE FREE WORLD

A more rapid build-up of political, economic, and military strength and thereby of confidence in the free world than is now contemplated is the only course which is consistent with progress toward achieving our fundamental purpose. The frustration of the Kremlin design requires the free world to develop a successfully functioning political and economic system and a vigorous political offensive against the Soviet Union. These, in turn, require an adequate military shield under which they can develop. It is necessary to have the military power to deter, if possible, Soviet expansion, and to defeat, if necessary, aggressive Soviet or Soviet-directed actions of a limited or total character. The potential strength of the free world is great; its ability to develop these military capabilities and its will to resist Soviet expansion will be determined by the wisdom and will with which it undertakes to meet its political and economic problems.

1. *Military aspects.* It has been indicated in Chapter VI that U.S. military capabilities are strategically more defensive in nature than offensive and are more potential than actual. It is evident, from an analysis of the past and of the trend of weapon development, that there is now and will be in the future no absolute defense. The history of war also indicates that a favorable decision can only be achieved through offensive action. Even a defensive strategy, if it is to be successful, calls not only for defensive forces to hold vital positions while mobilizing and preparing for the offensive, but also for offensive forces to attack the enemy and keep him off balance.

   The two fundamental requirements which must be met by forces in being or readily available are support of foreign policy and protection against disaster. To meet the second requirement, the forces in being or readily available must be able, at a minimum, to perform certain basic tasks:

   a. To defend the Western Hemisphere and essential allied areas in order that their war-making capabilities can be developed;

204 DOCUMENTS

b. To provide and protect a mobilization base while the offensive forces required for victory are being built up;

c. To conduct offensive operations to destroy vital elements of the Soviet war-making capacity, and to keep the enemy off balance until the full offensive strength of the United States and its allies can be brought to bear;

d. To defend and maintain the lines of communication and base areas necessary to the execution of the above tasks; and

e. To provide such aid to allies as is essential to the execution of their role in the above tasks.

In the broadest terms, the ability to perform these tasks requires a build-up of military strength by the United States and its allies to a point at which the combined strength will be superior for at least these tasks, both initially and throughout a war, to the forces that can be brought to bear by the Soviet Union and its satellites. In specific terms, it is not essential to match item for item with the Soviet Union, but to provide an adequate defense against air attack on the United States and Canada and an adequate defense against air and surface attack on the United Kingdom and Western Europe, Alaska, the Western Pacific, Africa, and the Near and Middle East, and on the long lines of communication to these areas. Furthermore, it is mandatory that in building up our strength, we enlarge upon our technical superiority by an accelerated exploitation of the scientific potential of the United States and our allies.

Forces of this size and character are necessary not only for protection against disaster but also to support our foreign policy. In fact, it can be argued that larger forces in being and readily available are necessary to inhibit a would-be aggressor than to provide the nucleus of strength and the mobilization base on which the tremendous forces required for victory can be built. For example, in both World Wars I and II the ultimate victors had the strength, in the end, to win though they had not had the strength in being or readily available to prevent the outbreak of war. In part, at least, this was because they had not had the military strength on which to base a strong foreign policy. At any rate, it is clear that a substantial and rapid building up of strength in the free world is necessary to support a firm policy intended to check and to roll back the Kremlin's drive for world domination.

Moreover, the United States and the other free countries do not now have the forces in being and readily available to defeat local Soviet moves with local action, but must accept reverses or make these local moves the occasion for war—for which we are not prepared.

This situation makes for great uneasiness among our allies, particularly in Western Europe, for whom total war means, initially, Soviet occupation. Thus, unless our combined strength is rapidly increased, our allies will tend to become increasingly reluctant to support a firm foreign policy on our part and increasingly anxious to seek other solutions, even though they are aware that appeasement means defeat. An important advantage in adopting the fourth course of action lies in its psychological impact—the revival of confidence and hope in the future. It is recognized, of course, that any announcement of the recommended course of action could be exploited by the Soviet Union in its peace campaign and would have adverse psychological effects in certain parts of the free world until the necessary increase in strength has been achieved. Therefore, in any announcement of policy and in the character of the measures adopted, emphasis should be given to the essentially defensive character and care should be taken to minimize, so far as possible, unfavorable domestic and foreign reactions.

2. *Political and economic aspects.* The immediate objectives—to the achievement of which such a build-up of strength is a necessary though not a sufficient condition—are a renewed initiative in the cold war and a situation to which the Kremlin would find it expedient to accommodate itself, first by relaxing tensions and pressures and then by gradual withdrawal. The United States cannot alone provide the resources required for such a build-up of strength. The other free countries must carry their part of the burden, but their ability and determination to do it will depend on the action the United States takes to develop its own strength and on the adequacy of its foreign political and economic policies. Improvement in political and economic conditions in the free world, as has been emphasized above, is necessary as a basis for building up the will and the means to resist and for dynamically affirming the integrity and vitality of our free and democratic way of life on which our ultimate victory depends.

At the same time, we should take dynamic steps to reduce the power and influence of the Kremlin inside the Soviet Union and other areas under its control. The objective would be the establishment of friendly regimes not under Kremlin domination. Such action is essential to engage the Kremlin's attention, keep it off balance, and force an increased expenditure of Soviet resources in counteraction. In other words, it would be the current Soviet cold war technique used against the Soviet Union.

A program for rapidly building up strength and improving political and economic conditions will place heavy demands on our courage and intelligence; it will be costly; it will be dangerous. But half-measures will be more costly and more dangerous, for they will be inadequate to prevent and may actually invite war. Budgetary considerations will need to be subordinated to the stark fact that our very independence as a nation may be at stake.

A comprehensive and decisive program to win the peace and frustrate the Kremlin design should be so designed that it can be sustained for as long as necessary to achieve our national objectives. It would probably involve:

1. The development of an adequate political and economic framework for the achievement of our long-range objectives.
2. A substantial increase in expenditures for military purposes adequate to meet the requirements for the tasks listed in Section D-1.
3. A substantial increase in military assistance programs, designed to foster cooperative efforts, which will adequately and efficiently meet the requirements of our allies for the tasks referred to in Section D-1-e.
4. Some increase in economic assistance programs and recognition of the need to continue these programs until their purposes have been accomplished.
5. A concerted attack on the problem of the United States balance of payments, along the lines already approved by the President.
6. Development of programs designed to build and maintain confidence among other peoples in our strength and resolution, and to wage overt psychological warfare calculated to encourage mass defections from Soviet allegiance and to frustrate the Kremlin design in other ways.
7. Intensification of affirmative and timely measures and operations by covert means in the fields of economic warfare and political and psychological warfare with a view to fomenting and supporting unrest and revolt in selected strategic satellite countries.
8. Development of internal security and civilian defense programs.
9. Improvement and intensification of intelligence activities.
10. Reduction of Federal expenditures for purposes other than defense and foreign assistance, if necessary by the deferment of certain desirable programs.
11. Increased taxes.

Essential as prerequisites to the success of this program would be (a) consultations with Congressional leaders designed to make the program the object of non-partisan legislative support, and (b) a presentation to the public of a full explanation of the facts and implications of present international trends.

The program will be costly, but it is relevant to recall the disproportion between the potential capabilities of the Soviet and non-Soviet worlds

DOCUMENTS 207

(cf. Chapters V and VI). The Soviet Union is currently devoting about 40 percent of available resources (gross national product plus reparations, equal in 1949 to about $65 billion) to military expenditures (14 percent) and to investment (26 percent), much of which is in war-supporting industries. In an emergency the Soviet Union could increase the allocation of resources to these purposes to about 50 percent, or by one-fourth.

The United States is currently devoting about 22 percent of its gross national product ($255 billion in 1949) to military expenditures (6 percent), foreign assistance (2 percent), and investment (14 percent), little of which is in war-supporting industries. (As was pointed out in Chapter V, the "fighting value" obtained per dollar of expenditure by the Soviet Union considerably exceeds that obtained by the United States, primarily because of the extremely low military and civilian living standards in the Soviet Union.) In an emergency the United States could devote upward of 50 percent of its gross national product to these purposes (as it did during the last war), an increase of several times present expenditures for direct and indirect military purposes and foreign assistance.

From the point of view of the economy as a whole, the program might not result in a real decrease in the standard of living, for the economic effects of the program might be to increase the gross national product by more than the amount being absorbed for additional military and foreign assistance purposes. One of the most significant lessons of our World War II experience was that the American economy, when it operates at a level approaching full efficiency, can provide enormous resources for purposes other than civilian consumption while simultaneously providing a high standard of living. After allowing for price changes, personal consumption expenditures rose by about one-fifth between 1939 and 1944, even though the economy had in the meantime increased the amount of resources going into Government use by $60 $65 billion (in 1939 prices).

This comparison between the potentials of the Soviet Union and the United States also holds true for the Soviet world and the free world and is of fundamental importance in considering the courses of action open to the United States.

The comparison gives renewed emphasis to the fact that the problems faced by the free countries in their efforts to build a successfully functioning system lie not so much in the field of economics as in the field of politics. The building of such a system may require more rapid progress toward the closer association of the free countries in harmony with the concept of the United Nations. It is clear that our long-range objectives require a strengthened United Nations, or a successor organization, to which the world can look for the maintenance of peace and order in a system based on freedom and justice. It also seems clear that a unifying ideal of this kind might awaken and arouse the latent spiritual energies of free men everywhere and obtain their enthusiastic support for a positive program for peace going far beyond the frustration of the Kremlin design and opening vistas to the future that would outweigh short-run sacrifices.

The threat to the free world involved in the development of the Soviet Union's atomic and other capabilities will rise steadily and rather rapidly. For the time being, the United States possesses a marked atomic superiority over the Soviet Union which, together with the potential capabilities of the United States and other free countries in other forces and weapons, inhibits aggressive Soviet action. This provides an opportunity for the United States, in cooperation with other free countries, to launch a build-up of strength which will support a firm policy directed to the frustration of the Kremlin design. The immediate goal of our efforts to build a successfully functioning political and economic system in the free world backed by adequate military strength is to postpone and avert the disastrous situation which, in light of the Soviet Union's probable fission bomb capability and possible thermonuclear bomb capability, might arise in 1954 on a continuation of our present programs. By acting promptly and vigorously in such a way that this date is, so to speak, pushed into the future, we would permit time for the process of accommodation, with-drawal and frustration to produce the necessary changes in the Soviet system. Time is short, however, and the risks of war attendant upon a decision to build up strength will steadily increase the longer we defer it.

CONCLUSIONS AND RECOMMENDATIONS

Conclusions

The foregoing analysis indicates that the probable fission bomb capability and possible thermonuclear bomb capability of the Soviet Union have greatly intensified the Soviet threat to the security of the United States. This threat is of the same character as that described in NSC 20/4 (approved by the President on November 24, 1948) but is more immediate than had previously been estimated. In particular, the United States now faces the contingency that within the next four or five years the Soviet Union will possess the military capability of delivering a surprise atomic attack of such weight that the United States must have substantially increased general air, ground, and sea strength, atomic capabilities, and air and civilian defenses to deter war and to provide reasonable assurance, in the event of war, that it could survive the initial blow and go on to the eventual attainment of its objectives. In return, this contingency requires the intensification of our efforts in the fields of intelligence and research and development.

Allowing for the immediacy of the danger, the following statement of Soviet threats, contained in NSC 20/4, remains valid:

14. The gravest threat to the security of the United States within the foreseeable future stems from the hostile designs and formidable power of the USSR, and from the nature of the Soviet system.
15. The political, economic, and psychological warfare which the USSR is now waging has dangerous potentialities for weakening the relative world position of the United States and disrupting its traditional institutions by means short of war, unless sufficient resistance is encountered in the policies of this and other non-communist countries.
16. The risk of war with the USSR is sufficient to warrant, in common prudence, timely and adequate preparation by the United States.
    a. Even though present estimates indicate that the Soviet leaders probably do not intend deliberate armed action involving the United States at this time, the possibility of such deliberate resort to war cannot be ruled out.
    b. Now and for the foreseeable future there is a continuing danger that war will arise either through Soviet miscalculation of the determination of the United States to use all the means at its command to safeguard its security, through Soviet misinterpretation of our intentions, or through U.S. miscalculation of Soviet reactions to measures which we might take.
17. Soviet domination of the potential power of Eurasia, whether achieved by armed aggression or by political and subversive means, would be strategically and politically unacceptable to the United States.
18. The capability of the United States either in peace or in the event of war to cope with threats to its security or to gain its objectives would be severely weakened by internal development, important among which are:
    a. Serious espionage, subversion and sabotage, particularly by concerted and well-directed communist activity.
    b. Prolonged or exaggerated economic instability.
    c. Internal political and social disunity.
    d. Inadequate or excessive armament or foreign aid expenditures.
    e. An excessive or wasteful usage of our resources in time of peace.
    f. Lessening of U.S. prestige and influence through vacillation of appeasement or lack of skill and imagination in the conduct of its foreign policy or by shirking world responsibilities.
    g. Development of a false sense of security through a deceptive change in Soviet tactics.

Although such developments as those indicated in paragraph 18 above would severely weaken the capability of the United States and its allies to cope with the Soviet threat to their security, considerable progress has been made since 1948 in laying the foundation upon which adequate strength can now be rapidly built.

The analysis also confirms that our objectives with respect to the Soviet Union, in time of peace as well as in time of war, as stated in NSC 20/4 (para. 19), are still valid, as are the aims and measures stated therein (paras. 20 and 21). Our current security programs and strategic plans are based upon these objectives, aims, and measures:

19.

    a.   To reduce the power and influence of the USSR to limits which no longer constitute a threat to the peace, national independence, and stability of the world family of nations.

    b.   To bring about a basic change in the conduct of international relations by the government in power in Russia, to conform with the purposes and principles set forth in the UN Charter.

In pursuing these objectives, due care must be taken to avoid permanently impairing our economy and the fundamental values and institutions inherent in our way of life.

20. We should endeavor to achieve our general objectives by methods short of war through the pursuit of the following aims:

    a.   To encourage and promote the gradual retraction of undue Russian power and influence from the present perimeter areas around traditional Russian boundaries and the emergence of the satellite countries as entities independent of the USSR.

    b.   To encourage the development among the Russian peoples of attitudes which may help to modify current Soviet behavior and permit a revival of the national life of groups evidencing the ability and determination to achieve and maintain national independence.

    c.   To eradicate the myth by which people remote from Soviet military influence are held in a position of subservience to Moscow and to cause the world at large to see and understand the true nature of the USSR and the Soviet-directed world communist party, and to adopt a logical and realistic attitude toward them.

    d.   To create situations which will compel the Soviet Government to recognize the practical undesirability of acting on the basis of its present concepts and the necessity of behaving in accordance with precepts of international conduct, as set forth in the purposes and principles of the UN Charter.

DOCUMENTS 211

21. Attainment of these aims requires that the United States:

    a. Develop a level of military readiness which can be maintained as long as necessary as a deterrent to Soviet aggression, as indispensable support to our political attitude toward the USSR, as a source of encouragement to nations resisting Soviet political aggression, and as an adequate basis for immediate military commitments and for rapid mobilization should war prove unavoidable.

    b. Assure the internal security of the United States against dangers of sabotage, subversion, and espionage.

    c. Maximize our economic potential, including the strengthening of our peacetime economy and the establishment of essential reserves readily available in the event of war.

    d. Strengthen the orientation toward the United States of the non-Soviet nations; and help such of those nations as are able and willing to make an important contribution to U.S. security, to increase their economic and political stability and their military capability.

    e. Place the maximum strain on the Soviet structure of power and particularly on the relationships between Moscow and the satellite countries.

    f. Keep the U.S. public fully informed and cognizant of the threats to our national security so that it will be prepared to support the measures which we must accordingly adopt.

In the light of present and prospective Soviet atomic capabilities, the action which can be taken under present programs and plans, however, becomes dangerously inadequate, in both timing and scope, to accomplish the rapid progress toward the attainment of the United States political, economic, and military objectives which is now imperative.

A continuation of present trends would result in a serious decline in the strength of the free world relative to the Soviet Union and its satellites. This unfavorable trend arises from the inadequacy of current programs and plans rather than from any error in our objectives and aims. These trends lead in the direction of isolation, not by deliberate decision but by lack of the necessary basis for a vigorous initiative in the conflict with the Soviet Union.

Our position as the center of power in the free world places a heavy responsibility upon the United States for leadership. We must organize and enlist the energies and resources of the free world in a positive program for peace which will frustrate the Kremlin design for world domination by creating a situation in the free world to which the Kremlin will be compelled to adjust. Without such a cooperative effort, led by the United

States, we will have to make gradual withdrawals under pressure until we discover one day that we have sacrificed positions of vital interest.

It is imperative that this trend be reversed by a much more rapid and concerted build-up of the actual strength of both the United States and the other nations of the free world. The analysis shows that this will be costly and will involve significant domestic financial and economic adjustments.

The execution of such a build-up, however, requires that the United States have an affirmative program beyond the solely defensive one of countering the threat posed by the Soviet Union. This program must light the path to peace and order among nations in a system based on freedom and justice, as contemplated in the Charter of the United Nations. Further, it must envisage the political and economic measures with which and the military shield behind which the free world can work to frustrate the Kremlin design by the strategy of the cold war; for every consideration of devotion to our fundamental values and to our national security demands that we achieve our objectives by the strategy of the cold war, building up our military strength in order that it may not have to be used. The only sure victory lies in the frustration of the Kremlin design by the steady development of the moral and material strength of the free world and its projection into the Soviet world in such a way as to bring about an internal change in the Soviet system. Such a positive program—harmonious with our fundamental national purpose and our objectives—is necessary if we are to regain and retain the initiative and to win and hold the necessary popular support and cooperation in the United States and the rest of the free world.

This program should include a plan for negotiation with the Soviet Union, developed and agreed with our allies and which is consonant with our objectives. The United States and its allies, particularly the United Kingdom and France, should always be ready to negotiate with the Soviet Union on terms consistent with our objectives. The present world situation, however, is one which militates against successful negotiations with the Kremlin—for the terms of agreements on important pending issues would reflect present realities and would therefore be unacceptable, if not disastrous, to the United States and the rest of the free world. After a decision and a start on building up the strength of the free world has been made, it might then be desirable for the United States to take an initiative in seeking negotiations in the hope that it might facilitate the process of accommodation by the Kremlin to the new situation. Failing that, the unwillingness of the Kremlin to accept equitable terms or its bad faith in observing them would assist in consolidating popular opinion in the free world in support of the measures necessary to sustain the build-up.

In summary, we must, by means of a rapid and sustained build-up of the political, economic, and military strength of the free world, and by

DOCUMENTS 213

means of an affirmative program intended to wrest the initiative from the Soviet Union, confront it with convincing evidence of the determination and ability of the free world to frustrate the Kremlin design of a world dominated by its will. Such evidence is the only means short of war which eventually may force the Kremlin to abandon its present course of action and to negotiate acceptable agreements on issues of major importance.

The whole success of the proposed program hangs ultimately on recognition by this Government, the American people, and all free peoples, that the cold war is in fact a real war in which the survival of the free world is at stake. Essential prerequisites to success are consultations with Congressional leaders designed to make the program the object of non-partisan legislative support, and a presentation to the public of a full explanation of the facts and implications of the present international situation. The prosecution of the program will require of us all the ingenuity, sacrifice, and unity demanded by the vital importance of the issue and the tenacity to persevere until our national objectives have been attained.

Recommendations

That the President:

a. Approve the foregoing Conclusions.
b. Direct the National Security Council, under the continuing direction of the President, and with the participation of other Departments and Agencies as appropriate, to coordinate and insure the implementation of the Conclusions herein on an urgent and continuing basis for as long as necessary to achieve our objectives. For this purpose, representatives of the member Departments and Agencies, the Joint Chiefs of Staff or their deputies, and other Departments and Agencies as required should be constituted as a revised and strengthened staff organization under the National Security Council to develop coordinated programs for consideration by the National Security Council.

Source: U.S. Department of State. Foreign Relations of the United States, 1950, Volume 1: National Security Affairs; Foreign Economic Policy (Washington, D.C.: U.S. Government Printing Office, 1977).

DOCUMENT 6

George Kennan's "Opposition Memorandum"

Although Kennan still believed in his original doctrine of containment, by early 1950 he had become worried that the Truman administration was applying it incorrectly. Kennan thought containment would work against the Soviet Union in Europe, but not necessarily against all communists everywhere. While he still saw the Soviets as more dangerous than Wallace did, Kennan did not want American money, lives, and attention wasted in areas outside of Europe that mattered much less, or not at all, for American security. Kennan therefore began to reflect, in some ways, the alternative foreign policy path Wallace had envisioned, which, if followed, may have produced fewer costs for the United States, and other nations where America intervened, during the Cold War.

DRAFT MEMORANDUM BY THE COUNSELOR (KENNAN) TO THE SECRETARY OF STATE

Top Secret [WASHINGTON,] February 17, 1950.

Mr. Secretary: In the light of the current demands in the Congress and the press for some sort of a review of our foreign policy in its entirety, I think that as your senior advisor on policy formulation I should, before leaving for South America, let you have the following resume of my own views on this subject.

I.

There is little justification for the impression that the "cold war," by virtue of events outside of our control, has suddenly taken some drastic turn to our disadvantage.

Recent events in the Far East have been the culmination of processes which have long been apparent. The implications of these processes were correctly analyzed, and their results reasonably accurately predicted, long ago by our advisors in this field. The likelihood of these recent developments was known at the time when our present policies toward the Soviet Union were evolved. This prospect was not considered valid justification either for failing to do things in Europe which promised to be useful, or for doing certain things in the Far East which promised to be useless. Mao's protracted stay in Moscow is good evidence that our own experts were right not only in their analysis of the weakness of the National Government but also in their conviction that the Russians would have difficulty establishing the same sort of relationship with a successful Chinese Communist movement that they have established with some of their eastern European satellites. Events have borne out of their view that the projection of Moscow's political power over further parts of Asia would encounter impediments, resident in the nature of the area, which would be not only *not* of our making but would actually be apt to be weakened by any attempts on our part to intervene directly. These impediments are now obviously operating—to date more rapidly than we had dared to hope. Elsewhere in the Far East—in Indonesia and Indochina in particular —things are also no worse today than we would have thought likely 2 years ago.

Thus the overall situation in that area, while serious, is neither unexpected nor necessarily catastrophic.

The demonstration of an "atomic capability" on the part of the USSR likewise adds no new fundamental element to the picture. While certain features of our original position were influenced by the fact of our temporary monopoly, the assertions that the present U.N. majority proposals were predicted on such a monopoly are simply nonsense. The probability of the eventual development of the weapon by others as not only one of the basic postulates of the original U.S. position abut actually its entire motivation. Had this postulate not existed, security could easily have been achieved by our simply hugging our secret to ourselves. The whole rationale of an international control system lay in the assumption that the alternative was dangerous atomic rivalry. The fact that this state of affairs became a reality a year or 2 before it was generally expected is of no fundamental significance.

The H-bomb is admittedly a severe complication of the difficult and dangerous situation which has prevailed ever since the recent war. It gives new intensity, and a heightened grimness, to our existing problems. But it is we ourselves who have started the discussion about this weapon and announced the intention to develop it. The Russians have remained generally silent of the subject. They have said nothing about developing the weapon or using it against others, just as they have been scrupulously careful in general to deplore the very idea of utilization of the mass destruction weapons in warfare. The idea of their threatening people with the H-bomb and bidding them "sign on the dotted line or else" is thus far solely of our own manufacture. And there are no grounds for concluding that Russians, who do not require the mass destruction weapons for the establishment of an adequate military posture, are necessarily insincere in their stated desire not to see them effectively proscribed from the conduct of warfare.

This is not to say that our international situation is secure, or is one that could justify complacency. As stated above, it is both difficult and dangerous. But its basic elements are ones which were established largely by the final outcome of hostilities in 1945. Nothing that recently occurred has altered these essential elements; and in so far as we feel ourselves in any heightened trouble at the present moment, that feeling is largely of our own making.

II.

This being the case, the question remains as to the adequacy of our present policy approach in the face of this situation.

This approach, as I understand it, could be described as follows:

We recognize that the outcome of the recent war left military ascendancy on the Eurasian land-mass in the hands of a single power, irrevocably hostile to that part of the international community which does not recognize its authority, and committed to its eventual subjugation or destruction. It also placed this power in direct military control of roughly half of Europe.

It has been clear since the termination of hostilities that if this power broke out militarily and attacked the remainder of its former allies in Europe the result, whatever its chance for permanency, would obviously be in the immediate sense a major catastrophe, comparable to that which would have occurred had the Nazis won their war in Europe and forced England's surrender. This had to be avoided, if possible. But equally dangerous would have been a similar further extension of Soviet power by political means; i.e., by intimidation, deceit, infiltration, and subversion. This also had to be countered to the extent of our ability.

There was a good possibility that the Russians themselves, recognizing that this had serious disadvantages and dangers from their own standpoint, had no intention of launching a military attack on the rest of Europe at this juncture, and that they were planning to base their action on means short of war. Our best hope of avoiding catastrophe lay in exploiting this possibility and in concentrating on the strengthening of the resistance of other countries to Soviet political aggression.

Why was this?

First, because if the Russians, contrary to expectations, *did* attack militarily, there was really little that we or anyone else could do about it. We had decided to demobilize. Strength adequate for real military containment in Europe and Asia could not conceivably be built up without reviving the military power of Germany and Japan, which we were not prepared to do. We might do some things to make such an attack less likely; but we were not the Russians' keepers—we had no real control over their motives or their conduct—and if they grasped for the sword, there was no way we could really prevent the results from being a new sort of shambles for European civilization.

Second, because there *was* a chance that with our encouragement sufficient forces of resistance could be mobilized in the noncommunist world to prevent communist political pressure from having successes of catastrophic dimensions at this juncture. As for the more distant future, no one was wise enough to tell. But if 5 or 10 years of peace could be gained, there was always a possibility that by that time something would have happened to diminish the intensity of the communist threat and that the world might then somehow work its way through, without catastrophe, to an international order of greater stability and security.

This, at any rate, was the best chance. War was no acceptable alternative. Nor was the idea of some overall agreement with the Soviet leaders. A patient and wary policy of reinforcing resistance to Soviet political pressures, wherever there was anything to reinforce, and by whatever means we had of doing this, was dictated by the limits of the possible. It was not guaranteed to work. But it was the only thing that held out any real possibility of working.

The implications of such a policy, from the standpoint of the actual conduct of our affairs, were profound and varied. To understand the logical interrelationships of the various phases of diplomatic action which it demanded called for the considerable subtlety and breadth of understanding. Not all the elements of our public opinion, or even of our government personnel, possessed these qualities. Because the Russian attack, ideologically speaking, was a global one, challenging the ultimate validity of the entire noncommunist outlook on life, predicting its failure, and playing on the force of that prediction as a main device in the conduct of the cold war, it could be countered only by a movement on our part equally comprehensive, designed to prove the validity of our liberal institutions, to confound the predictions of their failure, to prove that a society not beholden to Russian communism could still "work." In this way, the task of combatting communism became as broad as the whole great range of our responsibilities as a world power, and came to embrace all those things which would have had to be done anyway—even in the absence of a communist threat—to assure the perseveration and advance of civilization. That Moscow might be refuted, it was necessary that something else should succeed. Thus Moscow's threat gave great urgency to the solution of all those bitter problems of adjustment which in any event would have plagued and tested the countries of the noncommunist world in the wake of these two tremendous and destructive world conflicts. And it was not enough, in the face of this fact, to treat the communist attack as purely an outside on, to be dealt with only by direct counter-action. Such an approach was sometimes necessary; but primarily communism had to be viewed as a crisis of our own civilization, and the principal antidote lay in overcoming the weaknesses of our own institutions.

The *principal* antidote, I repeat, not the *only* one. Since military intimidation was another of the cold war weapons used by the Kremlin, direct action had to be taken to combat this, too. Hence our own armed establishment, the Atlantic Pact and the Arms Program. These measures threw many people off. They were not part of a policy of *military* containment; but they looked like it. They served their purpose in Europe; but they misled many people there and here into false concept of what it was we were doing: into a tendency to view the Russian threat as just a military problem rather than as a part of a broad political offensive. (This error has had a great part in producing the present restlessness without policy; for through these distorted lenses the atomic energy problems, and many other things, take on quite misleading aspects).

III.

There is no reason, to date, to doubt the validity of this approach. In fact, any serious deviation from it could easily lead to most appalling conse- quences. But if it be asked whether our present policies represent the most and the best we can do to implement it, I must say that in my opinion they do not. The main deficiencies appear to me to be these:

1. In the military sphere, we should act at once to get rid of our present dependence, in our war plans, on the atomic weapon. This is necessary, first of all, in order that we may have a straightforward stance toward the problems of international control. The H-bomb discussion and

DOCUMENTS   219

other events having created such intensity of interest in this subject, a confused and hesitant position on our part becomes a dangerous matter, both domestically and internationally. Second, it is necessary because the atomic weapons are already an infirm and questionable element in our military posture, and likely to become more so as time passes. This is true both psychologically and in the literal military sense. Finally, as the power of the mass destruction weapons grows, public opinion will ill support the prospect of a war conducted with such agencies and will tend to lose its sense of perspective and to entertain wild schemes for the settlement of political conflict. The removal of our dependence on the weapon will not alone alleviate this unhealthy preoccupation; but it is a first step toward it. As long as we are determined to use the weapons willy-nilly, the conduct of warfare on that basis is inevitable. Only if we ourselves would be prepared, as a starter, to refrain from their use on a basis of mutuality, could there even be any chance of avoiding atomic warfare in the event of hostilities.

Now it is admittedly a tremendous undertaking on our part to dispense with this dependence on the atomic weapon. I should think it entirely possible that this would require a state of semimobilization, involving some form of compulsory military service and drastic measures to reduce the exorbitant cost of national defense. In particular, we must abandon the idea that the armed establishment can and should compete with the civilian economy in pay scales and amenities: that it should operate, in other words, as a function of the civilian economy. That concept rests on a great delusion, and spells impotence.

2. We must face up at once to the dollar gap problem, particularly with relation to the financial situation in the U.K. and sterling area, but also with an eye to our problems with respect to Canada and to Germany and Japan. The British situation is urgent, and will probably be back in our laps in an aggravated form within a year, even if the Congress accedes in full to executive recommendation for ERP aid. A British bankruptcy will have extremely dangerous consequences throughout the entire noncommunist world.

We cannot do everything ourselves; but the removal of our tariffs and subsidies would relieve at least a portion of the dollar shortage, and—more important still—would create a sort of clarity which nothing else could create as to the real measure of foreign responsibility for the dollar gap problem.

The situation demands, therefore, a courageous, and unhesitating attack on this problem by the executive branch of government, making plain the facts and outlining the course of action to be followed. We should aim at a program of gradual adjustment, perhaps

220   DOCUMENTS

over a period of years, and with the Federal Government stepping in to mitigate hardships and injustices to private interests. The end of this period of adjustment should be a complete absence of tariffs and subsidies, except where genuine security considerations intervene; and even in these cases we should treat other members of the Atlantic Pact group as allies rather than potential enemies, and try to spare them from being the victims of security considerations.

3. With respect to the problem of our relations to underdeveloped areas, generally thought of in connection with Point IV, I would say the following.

I think we should fight the assumption that these relations cannot be normal and satisfactory ones unless we are extending some sort of unrequited assistance to the respective peoples.

I think we must also beware of the assumption that it is invariably helpful and desirable that such people should be assisted to a higher stage of technological development. Technology is not a good in itself. Living standards are a deceiving measure either of satisfactions people derive from life or of their political stability. In particular, we should beware of the favored stereotype to the effect that low standards of living produce communism and high standards of living do not. This is an unproven thesis and probably unsound.

Finally, in the areas where we do find it desirable and useful that technological assistance should be extended, I think we will find that many modifications, and perhaps fundamental ones, must be made in the present Point IV concept before it can become fully effective. I fear that as it stands today it imputes to private enterprise an altruism which cannot fairly be demanded of it, and to government a capacity for organization which government does not and cannot possess. It also does not meet entirely the requirement that technological assistance, if it is to be really creditable and effective, must be extended in a balanced context of social and economic development, and not in isolated driblets, related only to fragments of a country's basic needs. To be effective, in other words, it would have to embrace the TVA principle that life must be looked at in all its aspects if living patterns are to be approved.

I think that we must come eventually to the creation of a central corporation for foreign developmental work involving any sort of special assistance; that this corporation must be near enough to government to be amenable to governmental policy direction and yet far enough from it to avoid the paralyzing effects of governmental restrictions on the employment and utilization of personnel And it should serve as a point at which government, private enterprise, and charity can come together in the projection of our technological capacity beyond our borders in ways which will serve rational political ends.

4. I think it quite essential that we find anew and much more effective to the problem of making our policies understood within this Government and among our own people. This relates particularly to those interrelationships of policy which are of a relatively subtle nature and for the understanding of which some knowledge of the theory of foreign relations is essential. Up to this time, it seems to me, we have been quite unsuccessful in this. You still have the most distinguished and influential of our columnists and diplomatic observers making statements which reflect an almost incredible ignorance of basic elements of our foreign policy, to say nothing of the state of mind of Congressional circles.

The first prerequisite for people who are to concern themselves with explaining policy to others is that they themselves should understand it. It is not uncharitable to point out that this qualification is not generally obtained without considerable experience and intellectual discipline. We have gone thus far on the principle that the teachers themselves require no teaching; that they imbibe what they need to know by their mere presence and activity within the institution of the Department of State. This is our first mistake.

Our second is the belief that we can achieve our purposes in this field without real ideological discipline. I think that we must not fear the principle of indoctrination within the government service. A Secretary of State is charged personally by the President with the conduct of foreign affairs, and there is no reason why he should not insist that his views and interpretations be those of the entire official establishment. There is no reason why every responsible officer of the Department and Foreign Service should not be schooled in the handling of the sort of questions concerning our foreign policy which are raised morning after morning by Lippmann and Krock and others. What we need here is a section of the Department charged not only with the briefing, but with the training and drilling, of our official personnel on political matters. And this operation should extend beyond the walls of this Department and into other departments closely concerned with foreign policy, particularly the armed services and the Treasury.

The elaboration of a body of policy thought and rationale which can be taught in this manner will do more than anything I can think of not only to improve the quality of political work within the department but also to improve our general impact on press and

Congress and public. Without this type of discipline and singleness of purpose, I do not think the problem can be mastered. And unless it is mastered, there seems to me to be serious and urgent danger that our present policy toward the Soviet Union will founder on the lack of popular support.

Source: U.S. Department of State. Foreign Relations of the United States, 1950, Volume 1: National Security Affairs; Foreign Economic Policy (Washington, D.C.: U.S. Government Printing Office, 1977).

Bibliography

Primary Sources

Blum, John M. ed. *The Price of Vision: The Diary of Henry A. Wallace*. Boston, MA: Houghton Mifflin Company, 1973.

Byrnes, James F. *Speaking Frankly*. New York: Harper & Brothers, 1947.

"Churchill's Iron Curtain Speech." Westminster College, 2014. http://westminster-mo.edu/explore/history-traditions/IronCurtainSpeech.html (accessed March 30, 2017).

Kennan, George F. *American Diplomacy, 1900–1950*. Chicago, IL: The University of Chicago Press, 1951.

Stalin, Joseph. *Speeches Delivered at Meetings of Voters of the Stalin Electoral District, Moscow: December 11, 1937 and February 9, 1946*. Moscow: Foreign Languages Publishing House, 1954. http://collections.mun.ca/PDFs/radical/JStalinSpeeches DeliveredAtMeetingsOfVoters.pdf (accessed March 30, 2017).

Truman, Harry S. "Address on Foreign Policy at the Navy Day Celebration in New York City: October 27, 1945." Gerhard Peters and John T. Woolley—The American Presidency Project, 1999–2017. http://presidency.ucsb.edu/ws/?pid= 12304 (accessed March 30, 2017).

——. "Typed Note of Harry S. Truman, September 16, 1946. Truman Papers— President's Secretary's Files." Harry S. Truman Library and Museum. https:// trumanlibrary.org/whistlestop/study_collections/trumanpapers/psf/longhand/ index.php?documentVersion=original&documentid=hst-psf_naid735240-02& pagenumber=1. (accessed March 30, 2017).

——. *Memoirs: Years of Trial and Hope, 1946–1952*. Garden City, NY: Doubleday & Company, 1956.

——. "Truman Doctrine." Lillian Goldman Law Library, 2008. http://avalon.law. yale.edu/20th_century/trudoc.asp (accessed March 30, 2017).

U.S. Department of State. *Foreign Relations of the United States, 1947*, Volume III: *The British Commonwealth; Europe*. Washington, D.C.: U.S. Government Printing Office, 1972.

224   BIBLIOGRAPHY

——. *Foreign Relations of the United States: The Conferences at Cairo and Tehran, 1943.* Washington, D.C.: U.S. Government Printing Office, 1961.

——. *Foreign Relations of the United States: The Conference of Berlin (The Potsdam Conference) 1945 (In Two Volumes),* Volume II. Washington D.C.: United States Government Printing Office, 1960.

——. *Foreign Relations of the United States, 1946, Volume VI: Eastern Europe: The Soviet Union.* Washington, D.C.: U.S. Government Printing Office, 1969.

——. *Foreign Relations of the United States, 1947,* Volume III: *The British Commonwealth; Europe.* Washington, D.C., U.S. Government Printing Office, 1972.

——. *Foreign Relations of the United States, 1950,* Volume I1: *National Security Affairs; Foreign Economic Policy.* Washington, D.C.: U.S. Government Printing Office, 1977.

Vandenberg, Arthur H. "American Foreign Policy: January 10, 1945." United States Senate. http://senate.gov/artandhistory/history/resources/pdf/Vandenberg Speech.pdf (accessed March 30, 2017).

Wallace, Henry A. "Speech on the Truman Doctrine: March 27, 1947." Ashland University: Ashbrook Center, 2006–2017. http://teachingamericanhistory.org/library/document/speech-on-the-truman-doctrine/ (accessed March 30, 2017).

Secondary Sources

Alperovitz, Gar. *The Decision to Use the Atomic Bomb and the Architecture of an American Myth.* New York: Alfred A. Knopf, 1995.

Borstelmann, Thomas. *The Cold War and the Color Line: American Race Relations in the Global Arena.* Cambridge, MA: Harvard University Press, 2001.

——. *The 1970s: A New Global History from Civil Rights to Economic Inequality.* Princeton, NJ: Princeton University Press, 2012.

Brands, H.W., ed. *The Foreign Policies of Lyndon Johnson: Beyond Vietnam.* College Station, TX: Texas A&M University Press, 1999.

Cardwell, Curt. *NSC 68 and the Political Economy of the Early Cold War.* New York: Cambridge University Press, 2011.

Collins, Robert M. *Transforming America: Politics and Culture During the Reagan Years.* New York: Columbia University Press, 2009.

Costello, Mattew J. *Secret Identity Crisis: Comic Books and the Unmasking of Cold War America.* New York: The Continuum International Publishing Group, Inc., 2009.

Costigliola, Frank. *Roosevelt's Lost Alliances: How Personal Politics Helped Start the Cold War.* Princeton, NJ: Princeton University Press, 2012.

Costigliola, Frank and Michael J. Hogan, eds. *America in the World: The Historiography of American Foreign Relations since 1941,* 2nd edn. New York: Cambridge University Press, 2013.

——. *Explaining the History of American Foreign Relations,* 3rd edn. New York: Cambridge University Press, 2016.

Craig, Campbell and Fredrik Logevall. *America's Cold War: The Politics of Insecurity.* Cambridge, MA: The Belknap Press of Harvard University Press, 2009.

BIBLIOGRAPHY 225

Cullather, Nicholas J. *The Cold War and the United States Information Agency: American Propaganda and Public Diplomacy, 1945–1989*. New York: Cambridge University Press, 2009.

———. *The Hungry World: America's Cold War Battle Against Poverty in Asia*. Cambridge, MA: Harvard University Press, 2010.

Dudziak, Mary L. *Cold War Civil Rights: Race and the Image of American Democracy*. Princeton, NJ: Princeton University Press, 2000.

FitzGerald, Frances. *Way Out There in the Blue: Reagan, Star Wars and the End of the Cold War*. New York: Simon & Schuster, 2000.

Fletcher, Luke, "The Collapse of the Western World: Acheson, Nitze, and the NSC 68/Rearmament Decision." *Diplomatic History 40*, no. 4 (September 2016): 750–776.

Friedberg, Aaron L. *In the Shadow of the Garrison State: America's Anti-Statism and Its Cold War Grand Strategy*. Princeton, NJ: Princeton University Press, 2000.

Friedman, Jeremy. *Shadow Cold War: The Sino-Soviet Competition for the Third World*. Chapel Hill, NC: The University of North Carolina Press, 2015.

Fursenko, Aleksandr and Timothy Naftali. *One Hell of a Gamble: Khrushchev, Castro, and Kennedy, 1958–1964: The Secret History of the Cuban Missile Crisis*. New York: W.W. Norton & Company, 1997.

———. *Khrushchev's Cold War: The Inside Story of an American Adversary*. New York: W.W. Norton & Company, 2006.

Gaddis, John Lewis. *The United States and the Origins of the Cold War, 1941–1947*. New York: Columbia University Press, 1972.

———. *The Long Peace: Inquiries into the History of the Cold War*. New York: Oxford University Press, 1987.

———. *We Now Know: Rethinking Cold War History*. New York: Oxford University Press, 1997.

———. *George F. Kennan: An American Life*. New York: Penguin, 2011.

Gavin, Francis J. and Mark Atwood Lawrence. *Beyond the Cold War: Lyndon Johnson and the New Global Challenges of the 1960s*. New York: Oxford University Press, 2014.

Giglio, James N. *The Presidency of John F. Kennedy*, 2nd edn. Rev. Lawrence, KS: University Press of Kansas, 2006.

Greene, John Robert. *The Presidency of Gerald R. Ford*. Lawrence, KS: University Press of Kansas, 1994.

Hahn, Peter L. *The United States, Great Britain, and Egypt, 1945–1956: Strategy and Diplomacy in the Early Cold War*. Chapel Hill, NC: The University of North Carolina Press, 1991.

———. *Crisis and Crossfire: The United States and the Middle East Since 1945*. Washington, D.C.: Potomac Books, 2005.

Hahn, Peter and Mary Ann Heiss, eds. *Empire and Revolution: The United States and the Third World Since 1945*. Columbus, OH: Ohio State University Press, 2001.

Hamby, Alonzo L. *Man of the People: A Life of Harry S. Truman*. New York: Oxford University Press, 1995.

226 BIBLIOGRAPHY

Herring, George C. *America's Longest War: The United States and Vietnam, 1950–1975*, 4th edn. New York: McGraw-Hill, 2001.

——. *From Colony to Superpower: U.S. Foreign Relations Since 1776*. New York: Oxford University Press, 2008.

Hess, Gary R. *Vietnam and the United States: Origins and Legacy of War*. New York: Twayne Publishers, 1998.

Hoffman, Elizabeth Cobbs. *All You Need is Love: The Peace Corps and the Spirit of the 1960s*. Cambridge, MA: Harvard University Press, 2000.

Hogan, Michael J. A. ed. *America in the World: The Historiography of American Foreign Relations Since 1941*. New York: Cambridge University Press, 1995.

——, *Cross of Iron: Harry S. Truman and the Origins of the National Security State, 1945–1954*. New York: Cambridge University Press, 1998.

Hunt, Michael H. *Ideology and U.S. Foreign Policy*. New Haven, CT: Yale University Press, 1987.

Inboden, William C. *Religion and American Foreign Policy, 1945–1960: The Soul of Containment*. New York: Cambridge University Press, 2010.

Jian, Chen. *China's Road to the Korean War: The Making of the Sino-American Confrontation*, Rev. Edn. New York: Columbia University Press, 1996.

——. *Mao's China and the Cold War*. Chapel Hill, NC: The University of North Carolina press, 2001.

Johns, Andrew L. and Kathryn C. Statler, eds. *The Eisenhower Administration, the Third World, and the Globalization of the Cold War*. New York: Rowman & Littlefield Publishers, 2006.

Kaufman, Burton I. and Scott Kaufman. *The Presidency of James Earl Carter*, 2nd edn., Rev. Lawrence, KS: University Press of Kansas, 2006.

Kolko, Gabriel. *Anatomy of a War: Vietnam, the United States, and the Modern Historical Experience*. New York: Pantheon Books, 1985.

Kunz, Diane B., ed. *The Diplomacy of the Crucial Decade: American Foreign Relations During the 1960s*. New York: Columbia University Press, 1994.

LaFeber, Walter. *America, Russia, and the Cold War, 1945–2002*, 9th edn. New York: The McGraw-Hill Companies, 2002.

Leffler, Melvyn P. *For the Soul of Mankind: The United States, the Soviet Union, and The Cold War*. New York: Hill and Wang, 2007.

Leffler, Melvyn P. and Odd Arne Westad. *The Cambridge History of the Cold War, Vol. I (Origins), Vol. II (Crises and Détente), Vol. III (Endings)*. New York: Cambridge University Press, 2010.

Levy, David W. *The Debate over Vietnam*, 2nd edn. Baltimore, MD: The Johns Hopkins University Press, 1995.

Logevall, Fredrik. *Embers of War: The Fall of an Empire and the Making of America's Vietnam*. New York: Random House, 2012.

Logevall, Fredrik and Andrew Preston, eds. *Nixon in the World: American Foreign Relations, 1969–1977*. New York: Oxford University Press, 2008.

Macmillan, Margaret. *Nixon and Mao: The Week That Changed the World*. New York. Random House, 2007.

BIBLIOGRAPHY 227

Mansfield, Harvey C. and Delba Winthrop, eds. *Alexis de Tocqueville: Democracy in America*. Chicago, IL: The University of Chicago Press, 2000.

Mastny, Vojtech. *The Cold War and Soviet Insecurity: The Stalin Years*. New York: Oxford University Press, 1998.

McMahon, Robert J. *Cold War on the Periphery: The United States, India, and Pakistan*. New York: Columbia University Press, 1996.

——, *The Cold War: A Very Short Introduction*. New York: Oxford University Press, 2003.

——. *Dean Acheson and the Creation of an American World Order*. Washington, D.C.: Potomac Books, 2009.

——. ed. *The Cold War in the Third World*. New York: Oxford University Press, 2013.

McPherson, Alan. *Intimate Ties, Bitter Struggles: The United States and Latin America Since 1945*. Washington, D.C.: Potomac Books, Inc., 2006.

Muehlenbeck, Philip E. ed. *Religion and the Cold War: A Global Perspective*. Nashville, TN: Vanderbilt University Press, 2012

——, ed. *Race, Ethnicity, and the Cold War: A Global Perspective*. Nashville, TN: Vanderbilt University Press, 2012.

——, *Betting on the Africans: John F. Kennedy's Courting of African Nationalist Leaders*. New York: Oxford University Press, 2014.

Pach, Jr., Chester J. and Elmo Richardson. *The Presidency of Dwight D. Eisenhower*, Rev. Ed. Lawrence, KS: University Press of Kansas, 1991.

Parker, Jason C. Hearts, Minds. *Voices: US Cold War Public Diplomacy and the Formation of the Third World*. New York: Oxford University Press, 2016.

Pleshakov, Constantine and Vladislav Zubok. *Inside the Kremlin's Cold War: From Stalin to Khrushchev*. Cambridge, MA: Harvard University Press, 1997.

Rabe, Stephen G. *U.S. Intervention in British Guiana: A Cold War Story*. Chapel Hill, NC: The University of North Carolina Press, 2005.

Rotter, Andrew J. *Comrades at Odds: The United States and India, 1947–1964*. Ithaca, NY: Cornell University Press, 2000.

Sargent, Daniel J. *A Superpower Transformed: The Remaking of American Foreign Relations in the 1970s*. New York: Oxford University Press, 2015.

Saunders, Frances Stonor. *The Cultural Cold War: The CIA and the World of Arts and Letters*. New York: The New Press, 1999.

Schmitz, David F. *Thank God They're On Our Side: The United States and Right-Wing Dictatorships, 1921–1965*. Chapel Hill, NC: The University of North Carolina Press, 1999.

——. *The United States and Right-Wing Dictatorships, 1965–1989*. New York: Cambridge University Press, 2006.

——. *Richard Nixon and the Vietnam War: The End of the American Century*. Lanham, MD: Rowman & Littlefield, 2014.

Selverstone, Marc J. *Constructing the Monolith: The United States, Great Britain, and International Communism, 1945–1950*. Cambridge, MA: Harvard University Press, 2009.

228 BIBLIOGRAPHY

Small, Melvin. *The Presidency of Richard Nixon.* Lawrence, KS: University Press of Kansas, 1999.

Smith, Tony. *America's Mission: The United States and the Worldwide Struggle for Democracy*, Expanded Edition. Princeton, NJ: Princeton University Press, 2012.

Snyder, Sara B. *Human Rights Activism and the End of the Cold War: A Transnational History of the Helsinki Network.* New York: Cambridge University Press, 2013.

Stueck, William. *Rethinking the Korean War: A New Diplomatic and Strategic History.* Princeton, NJ: Princeton University Press, 2004.

Suri, Jeremi. *Power and Protest: Global Revolution and the Rise of Détente.* Cambridge, MA: Harvard University Press, 2003.

Trachtenberg, Marc. *A Constructed Peace: The Making of the European Settlement, 1945–1963.* Princeton, NJ: Princeton University Press, 1999.

Westad, Odd Arne. *The Global Cold War: Third World Interventions and the Making of Our Times.* New York: Cambridge University Press, 2007.

Williams, William Appleman. *The Tragedy of American Diplomacy.* New York: W.W. Norton & Company, 1972.

Wilson, James Graham. *The Triumph of Improvisation: Gorbachev's Adaptability, Reagan's Engagement, and the End of the Cold War.* Ithaca, NY: Cornell University Press, 2015.

Yaqub, Salim. *Containing Arab Nationalism: The Eisenhower Doctrine and the Middle East.* Chapel Hill, NC: The University of North Carolina Press, 2004.

Yergin, Daniel. *Shattered Peace: The Origins of the Cold War and the National Security State.* Boston, MA: Houghton Mifflin Company, 1978.

Young, Marilyn B. *The Vietnam Wars: 1945–1990.* New York: HarperCollins Publishers, 1991.

Zubok, Vladislov M. *A Failed Empire: The Soviet Union in the Cold War from Stalin to Gorbachev.* Chapel Hill, NC: The University of North Carolina Press, 2007.

Sources for Main Primary Documents

Kennan's 1946 Long Telegram:
U.S. Department of State. *Foreign Relations of the United States, 1946, Volume VI: Eastern Europe: The Soviet Union.* Washington, D.C.: U.S. Government Printing Office, 1969.

Henry Wallace's 1946 Letter to Truman:
Blum, John M. ed. *The Price of Vision: The Diary of Henry A. Wallace.* Boston, MA: Houghton Mifflin Company, 1973.

The Truman Doctrine—1947:
Truman, Harry S. "Truman Doctrine." Lillian Goldman Law Library, 2008. http://avalon.law.yale.edu/20th_century/trudoc.asp (accessed March 30, 2017).

BIBLIOGRAPHY   229

Wallace's 1947 Anti-Truman Doctrine Speech:

Wallace, Henry A. "Speech on the Truman Doctrine: March 27, 1947." Ashland University: Ashbrook Center, 2006–2017. http://teachingamericanhistory.org/library/document/speech-on-the-truman-doctrine/(accessed March 30, 2017).

NSC-68—1950:

U.S. Department of State. *Foreign Relations of the United States, 1950,* Volume I1: *National Security Affairs; Foreign Economic Policy.* Washington, D.C.: U.S. Government Printing Office, 1977.

Kennan's 1950 Opposition Memorandum:

U.S. Department of State. *Foreign Relations of the United States, 1950,* Volume 1: *National Security Affairs; Foreign Economic Policy.* Washington, D.C.: U.S. Government Printing Office, 1977.

Index

Acheson, Dean 1, 75
Afghanistan 3, 34, 99, 103, 106
Allende, Salvador 101
Alliance for Progress 96
Angola 90, 102–103, 106
Armas, Castillo 93
Atlantic Charter 13, 18
atomic weapons 39, 51, 106–107, 110; Truman at Yalta 15; U.S. attack on Japan 7; U.S. tests (1946) 71
Austria 60, 105
Azerbaijan 35

Balaguer, Joaquin 96
Batista, Fulgencio 94
Berlin 45, 95; 1948–1949 Blockade/Airlift 64–65, 69
Bohlen, Charles 14, 83
Bosch, Juan 96
Brazil 96
Bretton Woods (World Bank, IMF) 21–22
Brezhnev, Leonid 99
Britain 52, 94, 101; and China 73; and Germany 36; and Greece 50; and Iran 34–35, 92–93; London Conference (1945) 17; London Conference (1948) 63; Moscow Conference (1945) 17; and NATO 64–65; postwar loan 21, 40, 50
Bulgaria 14–17, 36, 105
Burnham, Forbes 101
Bush, George H.W. 104
Byrnes, James F. 9, 16, 35, 42; Moscow Conference (1945) 17; Potsdam 16; views on foreign policy 16, 19, 36–37

Cambodia 98
Carter, Jimmy 33, 99, 102–103
Castro, Fidel 94–95
Central Intelligence Agency 58–59, 101, 103–104
Chile 90, 101
China: American China Lobby 75–76; Chiang Kai-shek/Nationalists 71–76, 92; communist victory 69, 86; and détente 99–100; London Conference (1945) 17; Mao Zedong/communists 71–76, 84, 91; Sino-Soviet Treaty/Split 75–76, 84; Taiwan 72, 74, 76, 109; Qing Dynasty 71, 73
Churchill, Winston S.: Iron Curtain Speech 36; Potsdam Conference 14; spheres of influence 8, 11, 13; Tehran Conference 11–12; Yalta Conference 12–13
Cold War scholarship: Aaron Friedberg 59–60, 109–110; Campell Craig and Frederik Logevall 59–60, 90–91, 107–110; costs of Cold War 107–111; détente 100–101; end of Cold War 105–107; Gar Alperovitz 7; John Lewis Gaddis 9–10, 109–110; Melvyn Leffler 10; Odd Arne Westad 108–109; traditional 5; post–revisionism 9–10; revisionism 5–9; Vietnam War 98–99; William Appleman Williams 5–7
COMECON 62
Cominform 8, 56
Comintern 8

232 INDEX

Congo (Belgian/Democratic Republic of)
  93–94
Congress 13, 19–20, 51–53, 55, 57, 62, 65,
  70, 75, 85–86, 99, 102–103
Council of Foreign Ministers: creation at
  Potsdam 15; London Conference
  (1945) 17–18; London/Moscow
  Conferences (1947) 63; Moscow
  Conference (1945) 17–18; Paris Peace
  Conference/Paris Peace Treaties
  36–37
Cuba 90, 94–95, 101–103, 106
Cuban Missile Crisis 45, 95, 99, 110
Czechoslovakia: coup (1948) 48, 62, 70;
  elections (1946) 8; Prague 100, 105

Declaration of Liberated Europe 13
détente 33, 74, 99–101, 107
Diem, Ngo Dinh 97
Dien Bien Phu 97
Dominican Republic 96
domino theory 50, 54–55
Dulles, John Foster 17–18

Eisenhower, Dwight D. 18, 59, 77, 91–95,
  97, 108
El Salvador 103–104
Ethiopia 102

Ford, Gerald 99, 102
Forrestal, James V. 19
France 51–52, 100; elections (1947) 60;
  and Germany 36; London Conference
  (1945) 17; London Conference (1948)
  63; and NATO 64–65; and Vietnam
  97

Germany 4, 51–52, 60; East Germany 37,
  63–65, 69, 105; and Greece 50; and
  Iran 34; and NATO 64–65;
  reparations from 13, 15, 36–37;
  postwar borders 15; Potsdam
  Conference 15; superpower tension
  over 36–37, 62–65, 95; West
  Germany 37, 63–66, 100
Gorbachev, Mikhail 106–107
Goulart, João 96
Greece 14, 50–56, 60
Grenada 104
Guatemala 92–94
Guiana (British) 101
Guinea 94, 96
Guzmán, Jacobo Arbenz 92–93

Haiti 104
Harriman, W. Averell 19
Herter, Christian 94
House Un-American Activities Committee
  76–77
Hungary: elections (1945) 8; end of
  communism 105; peace treaty on 36;
  Soviet control of 15–16, 105

Italy 36, 50–51, 60, 66
Iran 34–35, 37–38, 42, 65, 89–90, 92–93,
  103

Jagan, Cheddi 101
Japan 17, 54, 71–73
Johnson, Lyndon 94, 96, 97–98, 101

Kennan, George: letter to Truman
  (February 1950) 83–85; Policy
  Planning Staff 1, 56–57; views on
  foreign policy 1–3, 5, 28, 33, 41–42,
  44, 56–57, 66, 69–70, 79–80, 82–86,
  89, 105, 107, 111
Kennedy, John 94–101
Khrushchev, Nikita 95, 99
Korea 3, 17, 69, 76, 85–86, 90–91, 109–110

Laos 98
Leahy, William D. 19
Lend Lease 20, 34
Long Telegram 1–2, 26, 28–33, 38, 45, 57,
  78, 80, 83
Lumumba, Patrice 94

McCarthy, Joseph 69, 76–77
Marshall, George 61, 74–76
Marshall Plan 48, 51, 53, 55, 60–63, 66,
  69–70, 86
Minh, Ho Chi 97
Molotov, V.M. 6, 8, 14, 16, 62
Mossadegh, Mohammad 92–93

National Security Act 48, 58–59
National Security Council 58–59, 78,
  82–83, 103
National Security Document-68 1–2, 38;
  analysis 78–82; influence 86, 91–92,
  95, 97–101; reception 82–86
NATO 48, 51, 55, 64–66, 69, 85–86
Nicaragua 103–104
Nitze, Paul 78, 100–101.
Nixon, Richard 72, 94, 98–101
Noriega, Manuel 104

INDEX   233

Pahlavi, Shah Mohammad Reza 92–93, 103
Panama 104
Peace Corps 96
Pinochet, Augusto 101
Poland: opposition/end of Communism 105–106; Potsdam Conference 15; Soviet control of 16; Yalta Conference 13
Potsdam Conference 7, 13–16, 37

Reagan, Ronald 33, 90, 103–104, 106–107
Romania 14–17, 36, 105
Roosevelt, Franklin D. 20, 36; death 13–15, 39; spheres of influence 8, 11–13, 17

Sandino, Augusto/Sandinistas 103
Schaub, William 83
Second Red Scare 76–78
Selassie, Haile 102
Sese Seko, Mobutu 94
Solidarity 12, 105–105
Somalia 102
Somoza, Anastosio 103
South Africa 94, 102
Southern Rhodesia/Zimbabwe 102
Stalin, Joseph 6, 91, 95; and atomic weapons 7; Bolshoi Theater Speech 27–28; historians' views of 5, 9–10, 41, 109; personality 10, 14–15, 20, 41; views on Germany 11, 13, 36–37, 42, 62–65; views on Western nations 12, 13, 22, 27–28, 30–32

Taft, Robert 52–53
Tehran Conference 11–12
Tito, Josip Broz 56
Truman Doctrine 1–2, 5, 38, 48, 51–57, 60, 65, 78, 82

Truman, Harry S.: becoming president 13; and China 72–75; foreign policy views 2, 5, 10, 13–14, 19–20, 33, 35–38, 42, 44, 50–58, 60–61, 66, 69–70, 79, 90, 111; and McCarthyism 76–78; and NSC-68 78, 82, 85–86, 95; personality 10, 14, 44; and Truman Doctrine 1, 5; views on Stalin/Soviet Union 12, 15–17, 20
Turkey 12, 37–38, 42, 52–55, 60, 65

USSR: activity in the Third World 102, 106, 108; communism's collapse 105–107; and détente 99–101; and Eastern Europe 4, 5, 16, 19, 26, 40–42, 48, 54, 62, 71, 79, 89–90, 105–108; financial issues 4, 20–21, 40; nuclear weapons 69–72, 76, 81, 84, 86, 95, 106–107, 110; rebuilding/ security 6–7, 10, 16–17, 20, 26, 35, 38, 40, 45, 71, 90; reparations 4, 36–37

Vandenberg, Arthur 17–18
Vietnam 3, 45, 51, 55, 90, 97–99, 110

Walesa, Lech 12, 105–106
Wallace, Henry: firing by Truman 42, 44; letter to Truman (July 1946) 38–42, 57; opposition to Truman Doctrine 57–58; views on foreign policy 2, 3, 19, 26, 44–45, 48, 57–58, 66, 111
Wilson, Woodrow 51–52, 55

Yalta Conference 12–13
Yugoslavia 56

Zimbabwe 102

Taylor & Francis eBooks

Helping you to choose the right eBooks for your Library

Add Routledge titles to your library's digital collection today. Taylor and Francis ebooks contains over 50,000 titles in the Humanities, Social Sciences, Behavioural Sciences, Built Environment and Law.

Choose from a range of subject packages or create your own!

Benefits for you
- Free MARC records
- COUNTER-compliant usage statistics
- Flexible purchase and pricing options
- All titles DRM-free.

Benefits for your user
- Off-site, anytime access via Athens or referring URL
- Print or copy pages or chapters
- Full content search
- Bookmark, highlight and annotate text
- Access to thousands of pages of quality research at the click of a button.

REQUEST YOUR FREE INSTITUTIONAL TRIAL TODAY — Free Trials Available
We offer free trials to qualifying academic, corporate and government customers.

eCollections – Choose from over 30 subject eCollections, including:

Archaeology	Language Learning
Architecture	Law
Asian Studies	Literature
Business & Management	Media & Communication
Classical Studies	Middle East Studies
Construction	Music
Creative & Media Arts	Philosophy
Criminology & Criminal Justice	Planning
Economics	Politics
Education	Psychology & Mental Health
Energy	Religion
Engineering	Security
English Language & Linguistics	Social Work
Environment & Sustainability	Sociology
Geography	Sport
Health Studies	Theatre & Performance
History	Tourism, Hospitality & Events

For more information, pricing enquiries or to order a free trial, please contact your local sales team:
www.tandfebooks.com/page/sales

 | The home of Routledge books | **www.tandfebooks.com**